THE

LIMITS

OF

WHITENESS

NEDA MAGHBOULEH

THE

LIMITS

OF

WHITENESS

IRANIAN AMERICANS AND THE

EVERYDAY POLITICS OF RACE

STANFORD UNIVERSITY PRESS • STANFORD, CALIFORNIA

Stanford University Press
Stanford, California

Printed in the United States of America on acid-free, archival-quality paper

Library of Congress Cataloging-in-Publication Data

Names: Maghbouleh, Neda, author.
Title: The limits of whiteness : Iranian Americans and the everyday politics
    of race / Neda Maghbouleh.
Description: Stanford, California : Stanford University Press, 2017. |
    Includes bibliographical references and index.
Identifiers: LCCN 2017014961 (print) | LCCN 2017017045 (ebook) |
    ISBN 9781503603431 (e-book) | ISBN 9780804792585 (cloth : alk. paper) |
    ISBN 9781503603370 (pbk. : alk. paper)
Subjects: LCSH: Iranian Americans--Race identity. | Iranian Americans--Ethnic
    identity. | Iranian Americans--Social conditions. | Racism--United States.
    | United States--Race relations.
Classification: LCC E184.I5 (ebook) | LCC E184.I5 M335 2017 (print) |
    DDC 305.891/55073--dc23
LC record available at https://lccn.loc.gov/2017014961

Cover design: Anne Jordan
Typeset by Bruce Lundquist in 10/15 Baskerville

For Neelu, tiny but mighty,
and Clayton, "who we love the most"

CONTENTS

ILLUSTRATIONS

THE

LIMITS

OF

WHITENESS

CHAPTER 1

BEING WHITE

FOR ANY AMERICAN HIGH SCHOOL STUDENT with aims of going to a four-year university, there exists a window of repeated ethnic and racial self-identification. For Iranian American youth like Roya, from her first standardized college admissions test through her final campus housing questionnaire, she is profiled, guided, sorted, and coded into the following ethno-racial definition: "White/Caucasian: a person having origins in any of the original peoples of Europe, the Middle East, or North Africa." The politics around checking the right box are vexing to Roya:

> White teachers and counselors have tried to correct me when I claim an "other" racial identity. They say, "If you're Iranian, then you're white." And it's like, okay, can you pronounce my last name correctly, please? Tell me what other "white" countries are sanctioned, exploited, and vilified the way Iran is right now? And am I "white" like you when I'm at the airport? No. I'm not white.

.   .   .

If you drive west for thirty minutes from Houston, Texas, you'll arrive at Nonmacher's Bar-B-Que, an eight hundred–square-foot restaurant open since 1978. The walls are lined with mementos collected over time by owner John Nonmacher. There are faded rodeo ribbons, smoke-singed trucker hats, studio portraits of John Wayne, and a framed pencil drawing of Nonmacher himself. There is also an eleven- by seventeen-inch, sepia-toned poster of nineteen rifle-wielding men in ten-gallon hats mugging for the camera. Behind them are three objects hanging off an old oak tree: the flag of the United States, the state flag of Texas, and a bearded, turbaned man with a noose around his neck. His mouth is slack, and his arms hang heavy. Under the staged photograph, a caption in Old Western typeface cheerfully suggests to Nonmacher's patrons, "Let's Play Cowboys and IRANIANS!"

Nonmacher first pinned the poster to his restaurant wall in 1979, and it hangs there still today. Before his death in 2013 at age sixty-eight, Nonmacher was asked if the poster was racist. "I laughed and I'm still laughing," he said, referring to a locally organized protest of the restaurant in 2011. "I won't take it down."[1] And why would he? Business at Nonmacher's had been good, and thanks to the attention drawn by his poster and the protest over it, getting better. An enthusiastic counterprotest had packed the house with paying customers from open to close, as patient would-be eaters brandishing American flags stretched out into a line past the parking lot and down the block. Nonmacher marveled at how long customers were willing to wait for a table: "Yesterday was one of the best days we've ever had. . . . I mean, I knew we had fans and friends, but this is just golly God!"[2] One of the organizers of the 2011 protest of Nonmacher's poster, a second-generation Iranian American from Houston, remarked, "A poster like that doesn't unite people. There's no reason why there should be racism around."[3] But, if anything, the poster had seemed to unite people—in defense of racism, or something like it.

.   .   .

It is not particularly remarkable that Roya would describe frustration over her assigned demographic box or that Nonmacher would express pleasure at the controversy over his poster. What is remarkable, however, is that these everyday stories involving Iranian Americans are rarely understood as matters of race. Scholars, policy makers, and even Iranian Americans themselves typically reconcile such problems as expressions of "anything but race": ethnic and cultural difference, religious intolerance, or anti-immigrant nativism. These explanations are powerful, up to a point, but they ignore the everyday politics that provoke racial claims to an "other" identity among legally white Iranian Americans like

Roya. And in the case of Nonmacher's restaurant, they neutralize, or risk misunderstanding, the symbolic racial fantasy of how exactly American cowboys could "play" with the Iranians in their midst and why they might do so decades before today's anxieties around "nuclear Iran," Islam, and the War on Terror.

If Nonmacher's poster and the snaking line of eager customers it attracted were not inspired by race and racism, it doesn't show from the actual image captured on the poster itself. To derace Nonmacher's poster is to ignore its central reference to white vigilantism and the lynching of African Americans. To derace Nonmacher's poster is also to omit the poster's caption, which appropriates the cowboys-and-Indians trope to amalgamate indigeneity and Iranianness in the service of shorthand for a racial battle between the "civilized" and the "barbaric."[4] To explain a poster of a fantasized American lynching as ethnic bigotry, religious intolerance, or nativist hatred is to tell twenty-eight-year-old Husein Hadi, the Iranian American organizer who said, "There's no reason why there should be racism around," that at Nonmacher's Bar-B-Que there is in fact no racism around.

Likewise, it is hard to reconcile an anything-but-race explanation for teachers and guidance counselors advising seventeen-year-old Roya to check a box declaring her racial whiteness or her frustrated response as she resists. In fact, it might surprise Nonmacher and his customers to hear from one of Roya's guidance counselors that the limp, lifeless Iranian at the center of the poster is, according to US federal classification, as white as the cowboys surrounding him. And it might surprise Roya's guidance counselor to know that there is a controversial "Aryan myth" of cultural and racial superiority that circulates within Roya's own multigenerational Iranian American family and community. Yet these sorts of "rank-and-file" discrepancies over the racial classifications and self-understandings of Iranian Americans should not be confused for an absence of race—they are evidence of the prevailing presence of race.[5]

Caught in the chasm between formal ethno-racial invisibility and informal hypervisibility, Iranian Americans work, love, and live through a core social paradox: Their everyday experiences of racialization coexist with their legal, and in some cases, internal "whitewashing."[6] This paradox helps explain the frustration in Roya's voice as she is folded into a unifying white racial category beside the same white counterparts from whom she, and other minorities in the United States, most often face social exclusion and prejudice. At the time, however, Roya did not actually press the point with the authority figures at her massive California public high school. Although she disagreed with them, she understood that they were probably just following the rules of official categorization. Some of Roya's high school classmates, on the other hand, understood the rules of race in America differently, or perhaps they played by different rules altogether:

> [They] were like, "You're brown, little *chola* girl; come sit with us."[7] And you know, because my last name was different, I'm hairy, I'm Persian, my neighborhood, I was almost ashamed of my identity. But Mexican people accepted me. They saved me from hating me.

To understand Iranian American lives only through the lens of ethnicity, religion, or nationality risks mistaking or ignoring what Roya says when she describes exactly who it was that saved her and how and why they saved her. To treat Roya's experiences as being indicative of anything but race is to reify and naturalize Iranian whiteness and to ignore the many everyday moments in which Iranian Americans are imagined—and imagine themselves—outside its limits.

Racial Hinges, Racial Loopholes

The terms "white" and "non-white" are used in this book when describing the racial status of Iranian Americans across different contexts and situations. It draws on the political, moral, and epistemological meaning of the terms as described by Charles Mills in *The Racial Contract*.[8] According to Mills, the ongoing and shifting classification of people as "white"/"non-white" rests on in-group/out-group dynamics with massive social, political, and economic consequences, reproduced through cognitive, moral, and cultural frames. His political-philosophical definition of race as marked by full versus subordinate personhood is central to this book's presentation and interpretation of data about Iranian Americans. Therefore, the goal of this book is not to make prescriptive claims about how Iranian Americans should be correctly racially classified. Instead, the goal is to interrogate how Iranian Americans came to be categorized as white de jure, to explore if they are socially incorporated as white de facto, and to assess what this case tells us about how whiteness operates on the ground today.[9]

To date, studies of American whiteness have centered on European or Anglo contexts and diasporas and consistently tell a unidirectional story of how groups *become* white.[10] Thus, sociologists and historians have shown, for example, how the Irish were paid in "wages of whiteness," how Italians were made "white on arrival," and how "Jews became white folks."[11] Barring a few exceptions, there has been little orientation toward examining two areas: whiteness and its related logics of exclusion for non-Western groups, and how whiteness can be intermittently granted and revoked, or mismatched in the law and on the ground.[12]

In light of how the Iranian American case complicates our understandings of race and whiteness, I offer two new concepts. The first, "racial hinges," captures how the geographic, political, and pseudoscientific specter of a racially liminal group, like Iranians, can be marshaled by a variety of legal and extralegal actors into a symbolic hinge that opens or closes the door to whiteness as necessary. The second, "racial loopholes," describes the everyday contradictions and conflicts that emerge when a group's legal racial categorization is inconsistent with its on-the-ground experience of racialization or deracialization. In addition to complicating our understanding of whiteness by focusing on its flexibility at the outermost limits, the case of Iranian Americans also deepens our understanding of the interplay between top-down and bottom-up racialization processes, as well as troubling long-standing assumptions about assimilation by immigrant groups into mainstream American society.

Iranian American Racialization or Assimilation?

There has been a recent call in mainstream sociology to expand research on "racialization."[13] Of the major sociological approaches that draw on racialization, including Eduardo Bonilla-Silva's racialized social system and color-blind racism and Joe Feagin's systemic racism, research on Middle Eastern Americans tends to draw on racial formation theory as articulated by Michael Omi and Howard Winant.[14] Racial formation theory argues that race is inextricably connected to the state and in constant and dynamic tension with hegemonic practice from above and political struggle from below. Scholars have elaborated on the top-down half of racial formation theory with great zeal. For example, an interdisciplinary body of scholarship, critical race studies, offers major insight into the legal logic and illogic of racial categories, most often at the macro- and meso-levels.[15] Racialization research does not treat race as an unchanging reflection of biology and culture or a reflection of amalgamations of differently situated indicators like socioeconomic status and intermarriage; rather, race is a master status tied to group oppression and domination.

This book is part of an emerging movement to more completely integrate the study of immigration with the study of race and, by extension, assimilation and racialization. Research in this stream recognizes immigration as a site of racial struggle and accounts for US nativism as a battleground where "in-between" groups are browned.[16] In so doing, work that integrates the sociology of immigration with the sociology of race has pushed back against the Black/white binary that continues to motivate theoretical concerns in studies of assimilation and racialization and reengages both the top-down and bottom-up processes described by racial formation theory.

An analysis of Iranian American life demonstrates the broader conceptual and explanatory purchase of an integrated approach to the study of race and immigration through racial formation. For example, from a racial formation perspective, Roya's guidance counselor was not mistaken when she told Roya to check the "white" box. According to the top-down half of racial formation theory, and through the lens of legal and social policy around race and immigration, Iranian Americans are indeed white by law. Yet, at the same time, political constructions of Iran as a deviant, illogical, or criminal state are suffused with non-white racialization observable across each level of American society. In this way, everyday objects like the lynching poster at Nonmacher's are forms of bottom-up racial knowledge that "rearticulate" Iranianness as racially marked and incompatible with whiteness.[17] The interplay between top-down and bottom-up processes, and particularly the points of friction at which they meet, tell us not only about Iranian Americans but more generally about how white racism continually reorganizes itself to exclude those whom the legal category "white" nominally includes.

Nonetheless, when it comes to research on the immigrant second generation, racialization frameworks are secondary to theories of assimilation, which remain the default framework through which the incorporation and well-being of ethnic and racial minorities is assessed.[18] Segmented assimilation rests fundamentally on the notion that upward trends in education, income, and wealth lead to political and social incorporation into an American mainstream that is implicitly and sometimes explicitly described as white.[19] Rates of intermarriage and spatial integration, which are often used as proxies for political and social incorporation, are then extended into conclusions about the "whitening" of some immigrants or the "honorary white" status of others.[20] This literature would predict the easy positioning of Iranian Americans, perhaps more than any other recent immigrant group, into whiteness.

First, since their earliest mass arrival as university students in the 1950s, Iranians have disproportionately entered with training and experience in specialty occupations like engineering and medicine and possess higher rates of educational attainment and income than other legally white Americans. Given this socioeconomic profile, earlier research on Iranian Americans has drawn on theories of assimilation and ethnic incorporation to make sense of middle- and upper-class Iranian American lives. This literature notes a weakening of ethnic language, customs, and identities among the second generation, particularly via intermarriage and spatial integration.[21] Research in this stream on youth like American-born Roya—who are, as a cohort, now entering higher education and the workforce en masse—draws from segmented assimilation theory to make sense of data showing that high levels of spatial integration and educational attainment observed in the first generation have held steady thus far for their children.[22] Second, by the time of their next wave of mass migration to the United States starting in 1979, Iranian Americans and others from the Middle East were legally classified as white by all levels of government. Third, Iranians bring to the United States a wide range of secular and religious cultural practices, including a deeply held belief among some that Iranians are no less than the world's *original* white people.

In short, a highly educated, high-income population of legally white immigrants who arrive already believing in their own racial whiteness should predict a relatively straightforward, easy path into whiteness, according to theories of assimilation. For these reasons, a focus on Iranians within the larger pan-geographic "Middle Eastern" category makes a particularly good test case. But as the poster at Nonmacher's makes clear, a group's high socio-economic status, legal whiteness, and belief in its own whiteness do not always make it white enough to escape browning. In fact, for youth like Roya, physical and socioeconomic proximity to hegemonic whiteness in the United States exacerbates social ostracization and exclusion.[23] Knowledge about a group's socioeconomic status, intermarriage rates, or official legal classification, which are foundational pieces of the assimilation puzzle, offer only partial insights into its members' day-to-day *racial* experiences.[24]

By taking up the sociological challenge to connect formal top-down and everyday bottom-up processes of racial group making, this book uncovers the historical and legal presence of Iranians in the United States far earlier than research that precedes it.[25] By harnessing a variety of ethnographic, legal, and historical data, I show that Iranians have been pitched across a white/non-white American color line for over a century. I do so at an urgent moment when Iranians and others from the region are the highly visible targets of a 2017 Executive Order banning their immigration and travel to the United States and when Iranian Americans are on the cusp of potential federal reclassification into a "MENA" (Middle Eastern and North African) racial category separate from "white."[26] Whether by choice or by force, these individual and categorical racial crossings have been and continue to be possible because of Iranians' position at the limits of whiteness.

Overview of the Book

By probing a different ordinary social setting in each chapter, in this book I make the case that Iranian Americans (1) sit, categorically, at the outer limits of whiteness and, more important, (2) possess social experiences that reflect the outer boundaries and limitations of what "official" whiteness can achieve or mobilize. That is, an examination of where Iranians fit into an American racial hierarchy opens new sight lines into what protection, shelter, or cover "legal" whiteness does or does not offer immigrants and their children in the twenty-first century. By recognizing Iranian Americans at the limits of whiteness, we are better able to name and identify what the limits of whiteness actually are.

Rather than take up a strictly academic or legal consideration of racial classification or assume that Iranian American racial identity is wholly constituted as white upon arrival, I take stock of the racial ideologies that ordinary Iranians encounter, engage, and redefine. Using a case-based logic to sample a range of more than eighty young second-generation Iranian Americans, the book travels with them across multiple racialized sites: their home lives; their experiences in white-majority schools and neighborhoods; their securitized, transnational journeys to and from an idealized homeland; and a summer camp by and for the second generation. Iranian American racial identities are anything but stable across these spheres. Tracking the paradox of their shifting white/non-white statuses allows us to better understand the outer limits of who counts as white and under what conditions.

The following chapters chart and analyze this paradox. Chapter 2 offers a chronological account of Iranian racial construction in the United States, dating back to the turn of the twentieth century. Long before their physical presence in America, Iranians had become racial hinges in the margins of racial prerequisite cases through which different populations' claims for naturalization were predicated on an applicant's ability to successfully prove his or her whiteness. Middle Easterners such as Syrians and Armenians sometimes successfully argued in court that their similarity to Europeans and dissimilarity from dark, "fire-worshipping," and inassimilable Iranians was proof of Arab and Armenian whiteness.[27]

At the same time, South Asian claimants who identified as Parsi offered their ancestral roots in Iran as proof of South Asian whiteness.[28] These racial prerequisite cases and their subsequent "clash of civilization" court rulings, although internally contradictory, are important trace evidence of what George Lipsitz calls the "white spatial imaginary."[29] The specter of Iran was a racial hinge between white Europe and non-white Asia: a face, a body, a culture, and a concept that could open or close the door to whiteness as needed. Excavating Iranians out of the margins of these cases reveals how they have been rhetorically positioned both inside and outside white citizenship in the United States for over a century.

The second half of Chapter 2 is anchored by two turning points: (1) the 1978 US federal legal classification of all persons from Europe, the Middle East, and North Africa as categorically white; and (2) mere months later, the Iranian Revolution, which launched an unprecedented migration of Iranians into the United States and similarly unprecedented hours of television coverage about the revolution and ensuing hostage crisis. Across news and popular media in the 1980s and 1990s, Iranians and Iranian Americans were cast as "forever foreigners."[30] Their relatively high levels of income, occupational status, educational attainment, residential integration, and other conventional markers of assimilation offered limited social and racial inoculation from racist portrayal. I then bring the racial account of Iranian America into the twenty-first century in an examination of hate crimes and post-9/11 legal rulings concerning Iranian Americans. Like other Middle Easterners in the United States, Iranian Americans today find themselves caught in racial loopholes in which they are not white enough to escape racially motivated discrimination and hate crimes, but are too white to reliably secure race-based protection and legal redress for the violent and discriminatory acts committed against them.[31] To close the chapter, I scale down from federal and state-level legal cases to address racialized anti-Iranian sentiments within local municipalities. In particular, I discuss how Iranian American home-making practices are elliptically marked for obstruction and censure as racially "impure" through anti-Persian architectural housing codes in western Los Angeles.

The chapters that follow draw on data collected in qualitative fieldwork with second-generation Iranian American youth. Chapter 3 explores the racial experiences of youth at home, revealing an "Aryan" racial ideology that many first-generation parents carry over from Iran into new American contexts. Given that most first-generation parents were socialized into an Aryan and anti-Arab national history, "Caucasian" geographic location, and concomitant white racial identity as children in Iran, unexpected family situations arise in diaspora once second-generation children complain of race-based bullying in "hegemonic white" American spaces.[32] Parents sometimes encourage their second-generation children to simply return to school and assert that they and all other Iranians are white. In fact, some parents suggest, "We're whiter than Europeans!" This tactic offers little relief to second-generation youth who assert that they would be ridiculed further should they claim a belief that stands in direct contradiction to the racialized basis of the bullying itself.

Chapter 4 moves from the diasporic home into the American classroom. It analyzes second-generation experiences in elementary, junior, and high schools as well as student life and learning in university spaces. The chapter delves more deeply into the second generation's pervasive encounters with identity-based harassment at school while also making connections between large-scale, geopolitical events and the bullying of Iranian American children and adolescents. These incidents most often revolve around physical markers of an Iranian American youth's difference from a locally perceived norm image of whiteness and also sometimes occur in full view of, or with assistance from, white adult authority figures. These cases indicate that the semantics around ethnicity, nationality, and religion are insufficient to explain the totality of bias incidents and discrimination navigated by Iranians and other liminal whites. The chapter ends with the story of a successful student-driven campaign to create a new "non-white" racial category for Iranians and other Southwest Asian and North Africans in the University of California System.

Chapter 5 argues that oft-overlooked in-between places are especially constitutive of racial identity, particularly for people of in-between races. The chapter focuses on the visceral experience of traveling through space—through international airports, in particular—which is required of Iranian American youth to visit their ancestral homelands. Once in Iran, youth testify to the peculiar experience of corporeal scrutiny by their native Iranian counterparts. Common concerns about not being "Iranian" enough for one's parents and extended family in Iran are counterpoised against the lived experiences of being "too Iranian" with customs agents and security personnel. These experiences are highly gendered, with young men and women working to pass as differently raced at varied times and places in their international travels. Upon their return, a collective consciousness about the transformative process of international travel becomes part of Iranian American youth culture, as boys and girls share stories of excitement and disappointment after coming face-to-face with their shifting racialization and inherited nostalgia for the home country. These transnational crossings and direct encounters form the raw material for a specific second-generation consciousness that celebrates Iranian heritage, while also forging nonbiological kin networks across diaspora and with other liminal non-white groups.

Chapter 6 follows this thread by observing youth as they imagine and create a world beyond the limits of whiteness at an Iranian American summer camp. Camp Ayandeh (Future) is a provocative space that reveals novel forms of kinship and celebratory race making put into practice. Campers, counselors, and staff—all second-generation Iranian Americans, including the camp's founders—embrace their ethno-racial identities through games and activities that celebrate Iranianness and, more specifically, a strategically inclusive Iranian Americanness. At camp, experiences of identity-based alienation in white-majority schools and neighborhoods are validated. Old ghosts of Iranian and white ethnocentrism fade as campers are reassured that it is not only okay but also vital to align with other liminal and highly racialized groups, including Arab Americans. Cultivating these non-white identifications does not involve a rejection of the campers' immediate families' cultures, customs, languages, and values, however. It is instead an almost-utopian project, one that advances an antiracist Iranian American political identity, while widening campers' sense of self and belonging into a new racial family.

Chapter 7 concludes that we cannot sociologically account for these snapshots of Iranian American life—from Roya's "saving" to the bonds that kids forge at summer camp—without availing ourselves of an analytic that incorporates race. *The Limits of Whiteness* not only details the paradoxical case of Iranian Americans but also ends by arguing that logics of whiteness do not coherently describe Middle Eastern experiences in a time of military occupation and widespread racist backlash. The contemporary use of "Islamophobia" as a catchall term for discrimination against Iranians and other Middle Easterners in the United States efficiently but erroneously flattens the extent of genuine diversity within these groups and, more important, critically obscures the consistent racial valence of such harassment. Alongside South Asian Americans and other communities of color in the United States, Iranians and populations from the broad Middle East practice a variety of religions, hail from many separate nationalities, and attach importance to a wide range of ethnic identities. Nonetheless, together they are profiled, classed, and treated in everyday life as a "group" or "type" that is different from whites.[33] This is, of course, the language of race and always has been.

In this book I reveal how race and racism organize Iranian American lives and show that for liminal racial groups, whiteness is fickle and volatile—and, more often than not, revoked in the mundane and ordinary interactions that make up the everyday politics of race. In contradiction to their official federal classification and the expectations of sociologists that in the second generation identities should melt away, Iranian American youth regularly feel skepticism and dissatisfaction with assimilation as a desirable—or even possible—cultural and psycho-social process and whiteness as a meaningful and reflective category that describes their lives. In this way, second-generation Iranian Americans understand their status across a wide range of localities as more closely resembling that of other liminally racialized non-white groups.[34] Whether their preferred racial identity is "brown" or "West Asian" or "Middle Eastern" or "other," in a world of cowboys and Iranians, Iranian American youth are experts at navigating life at the limits of whiteness.

CHAPTER 2

IN THE PAST

WHEN I MET KAMBIZ AND NORA, he was an impeccably dressed, handsome, and tanned septuagenarian; she was equally stylish and vivacious. They had been married for over a half century. In the late 1950s Kambiz had come from Iran to study in the United States. It was as an undergraduate at Utah State where he was first exposed to the white/ Black racial binary in the United States and where he, as an Iranian, seemed to fit into it:

> You see, gym, P.E. [physical education] was a college requirement back then. They made me join the basketball team, but I wasn't any good. I hadn't played it before. One day, in the locker room, some guys cornered me; they say, "Hey! We thought you people were good at basketball," and I said, "What people?" and they say, "Blacks!'"

As Kambiz told the story, both he and Nora laughed; it seemed like one they had reminisced about before. Nora, with eyes sparkling, then said conspiratorially:

> Kambiz, your story is good, but my story is better. When we were dating, girls would say to me, "But Nora, you're so pretty and with such a nice figure! You don't need to be going out with one of *them!*"

As she said this, Nora squeezed Kambiz's shoulder with affection. Nora is incontrovertibly American and incontrovertibly white; she was born in Michigan to European American parents. According to legal US racial classification Nora and Kambiz's marriage is not, however, an interracial one. Yet across six decades their fellow Americans classified them differently. "You people," "them," and "black" are everyday racial referents used by white acquaintances, friends, and strangers in reference to Kambiz. In ordinary interaction, these descriptors racially distinguished him from Nora; his whiteness was revoked at the same time that hers was affirmed. Kambiz, an elderly Iranian American man with a faint Persian accent who self-identifies as white, understood that he is not perceived as white in day-to-day life.

At the same time that Kambiz and Nora shared their stories with me, American-born Leyla was an eleventh-grade student at one of the most prestigious private schools in the nation. Whereas Kambiz felt white but was perceived as non-white, for Leyla it was the reverse. She described first growing up in the midwestern United States before moving to the Southeast:

> I didn't really feel Iranian a lot. Which is a kind of a weird thing to say. But I mean the fact that I lived in Kansas City from four months old 'til eight years old . . . like the only Iranian kids were me and my sister in the entire place. Also I really don't look Iranian. The fact [is] that I have much paler skin than I guess most Iranians, I'd say, have. My eyes, they're not brown. I have always loved brown or black eyes. I have lighter skin and lighter eyes, and my hair is really curly. And so I don't look like a typical Iranian. Americans imagine the typical Iranian walking down the street in Iran, and that's not me. This seems like a superficial thing, but even when I ask other Iranian people, they're like, "Yeah, you don't look Iranian." On a spiritual level, and on a cultural level, I internalized it and accepted it for how it was.

I asked Leyla if she felt her physical appearance, which she described as white, shaped the way people interacted with her in Kansas City. Rather than answer the question as I posed it, she shifted it in a much more interesting direction: "Basically, as I became older, I began to put it together that if Americans say I look white and if *Iranians* say I look white, what just happened? So did we all just agree that Iranians aren't white?" The racial misrecognition described by Leyla, Nora, and Kambiz is tied up with the ambiguous, largely unwritten racial history of Iranians in the United States. How can Kambiz, an Iranian American senior citizen who identifies as white, be socially cast as non-white at the same time that Leyla, an Iranian American teenager who identifies as non-white, be socially cast as white? This seeming paradox is not new: over the last one hundred years, Iranians, as individuals and as a group, have traveled back and forth across the American color line.

In this chapter, I draw on foundational historical and legal research by scholars like Sarah Gualtieri and John Tehranian to sketch out the earliest presence of Iranians at the turn of the twentieth-century in American racial prerequisite cases.[1] Before Iranians were even physically present in the United States as immigrants, they were in the margins of cases featuring Arab, Armenian, and South Asian claimants. Arab and Armenian claimants presented evidence of their *dissimilarity* from Iranians as proof of their whiteness, while at the same time claimants from the region known today as South Asia presented evidence of their *similarity* to Iranians as proof of their whiteness. In either scenario, Iranians were "racial hinges" on which claims to whiteness swung.

Following this, I describe how a first wave of Iranians, like Kambiz, arrived in the United States on student visas in the 1950s, still straddling the limits of whiteness. By the time of the next large wave in the wake of the 1979 revolution, all Iranians in America were legally classified as white. I then describe how in reaction to the Iranian hostage crisis they were swiftly, and perhaps irrevocably, socially browned. Although still white by law, the browning of Iranians has continued after September 11, 2001, and I present recent legal and social evidence showing how Iranian Americans must navigate "racial loopholes" at the boundaries of whiteness in which they face racial discrimination that cannot be fully understood or redressed due to their white de jure racial status. The chapter closes with an extended case of cultural or color-blind racism in which wealthy and spatially integrated Iranian Americans are formally censured at the local level in Beverly Hills, California, for their perceived aesthetic and cultural departures from those of normative whiteness. All told, rather than a recent phenomenon in the United States, the transposition of Iranian Americans back and forth across the border of whiteness has been persistent in the United States for more than a century and began decades before their arrival.

The Recurring Whiteness and Non-whiteness of Iranians: Racial Prerequisite Cases in the Early Twentieth Century

Although most scholarly analyses of Iranian American immigration begin in the period following Iranians' first mass arrival in 1979–80, an Iranian presence actually appears much earlier in the American historical record.[2] From the Naturalization Act of 1790 through 1952 American citizenship for immigrants was predicated on whiteness.[3] As a result, in what are referred to as "racial prerequisite" cases, in order to obtain citizenship, liminally raced claimants could and did argue to local naturalization and federal courts that they were on the white side of the racial borderline. While there exists documentation of only a select few Iranian individuals present in the United States at any time from the nation's founding through the first half of the twentieth century, the specter of Iranian whiteness and non-whiteness was often evoked in others' claims for their whiteness.[4] Were claimants white because they were unlike Iranians, or white because they were like Iranians? In the first half of the twentieth century both claims were leveraged in US courts, and both claims were sometimes successful and sometimes unsuccessful. As a result, even long before their arrival on US shores Iranians had at once been cast and recast on opposite sides of the color line (see Table 1).[5]

In a process Nina Farnia calls "peripheral racialization," legal reference to Iran and Iranians in the arguments submitted by early claimants of Middle Eastern origin such as Syrians and Armenians have only recently been uncovered.[6] The whiteness of Syrian and Armenian claimants was made legible by being unlike "clearly non-white" Iranians. Yet the whiteness of "Parsee" Indian claimants around the same time was made legible by being like "clearly white" Iranians.[7]

TABLE 1
In-absentia racial classifications of Iranians in US racial prerequisite cases

Year	Case	Claimant	Iranians
1790	Naturalization Act	—	Unclear
1909	*In re Najour*	Syrian	White
1909	*In re Halladjian*	Armenian	Non-white
1909	*In re Balsara*	"Parsee" Indian	White
1914	*Ex parte Dow*	Syrian	Non-white
1914	*In re Dow*	Syrian	Non-white
1915	*Dow v. United States*	Syrian	White
1923	*United States v. Thind*	"Aryan" Indian	Non-white
1939	*Wadia v. United States*	"Parsee" Indian	White

The Specter of Iran in
Middle Eastern Claims to Whiteness

The first detectable presence of Iranians in the American legal record can be traced to a passing mention of "Irania" in *In re Najour* (1909), a case to determine the racial status of a Christian Syrian from a region near Beirut. In evidence submitted to the court from ethnologist A. H. Keane's *The World's Peoples* (1908), using a linguistic theory of race, Iranians were classified alongside North African, European, Indian, Western Asian, and Polynesian people under an umbrella category of "Caucasians (white and also dark)." Rejecting the government's argument that Najour was not white because as a Syrian subject of the Ottoman Empire he was not truly "free" (and was therefore "Asiatic" and not "white"), the courts, relying on Keane's definition, ruled in favor of Najour's whiteness, making him the first "liminal" Middle Eastern claimant in US history to win whiteness in federal court.[8]

According to *In re Najour*, Iranians, had they been present to file claims, would have reasonably been considered white. However, in the same year, under *In re Halladjian* (1909), which concerned the racial status of an Armenian claimant, Iranians would have been non-white. In the historical narrative conjured by Halladjian's attorney, the Middle East served as perpetual battleground between Europe and Asia and between West and

East. To make sense of Armenians as white, Iranians, or "Persians," were characterized in racial prerequisite cases as blasphemous foreign invaders against whom Armenians defended themselves "strenuously": "In the warfare which has raged since the beginning of history about the eastern Mediterranean between Europeans and Asiatics, the Armenians have generally, though not always, been found on the European side. . . . By reason of their Christianity, they generally ranged themselves against the Persian fire worshippers."[9] The *Halladjian* court, rather than look to prevailing racial or ethno-linguistic science for answers, looked to social "ideals, standards, and aspirations" to define the boundaries of the white racial category. Finding Armenians to be well positioned for American assimilation thanks to their shared Christian allegiance to "the European side," the *Halladjian* court ruled in favor of Armenian whiteness, as juxtaposed to the non-whiteness of "fire worshipping" Iranians and other Ottoman-ruled Muslims.

In three subsequent cases involving George Dow, a "Syrian Arab" in South Carolina (*Ex parte Dow* [1914], *In re Dow* [1914], and *Dow v. United States* [1915]), Dow's claim to whiteness was twice rejected before the decisions were reversed and Arabs were consecrated as white and thus eligible for citizenship. Again, Iranian whiteness pinged back and forth as arguments to legitimize Dow's whiteness or non-whiteness were made. In the first trial, *Ex parte Dow*, linguistic arguments that had the racial consequence of knitting non-white Asia to white Europe especially vexed the court. Through a core branch of the so-called Indo-European linguistic tree, how could Farsi (Persian) they asked, which was spoken by "dark colored inhabitants of the Persian Gulf or Persian Coast," be placed alongside Romance and Germanic languages, spoken by incontrovertibly white Europeans?[10] Further, how could a number of unquestionably white groups in the United States, such as Scandinavians, *not* speak languages found in the Indo-European linguistic tree?[11] Vexed by these measures of social closeness and distance, the court ultimately relied on cartographic and continental borders for racial guidance: only Europeans could be white. Therefore, the first *Dow* ruling excluded Syrians from citizenship rights based on a "commonsense" racialized geography that differentiated a white Europe from a non-white everywhere else. Iran was specifically noted as falling on the non-white side of the geographic division, as the specter of its existence was enlisted as a proxy for the non-whiteness of the Arabic-speaking, darker-hued Dow.

The second *Dow* case, *In re Dow*, was a rehearing of the original case, in which the court again considered the quagmire of ethno-racial and linguistic "scientific" evidence that risked casting such a wide white net that it would include non-Europeans like Dow. The judge reiterated that when Congress passed its first, foundational immigration law in 1790, it could not possibly have called on knowledge of the Indo-European language tree that connects the preponderance of European languages to Asia via Persian and Sanskrit:[12]

> It is safe to assume that no member of the congress that passed the act of 1790 knew either Sanscrit [*sic*] or ancient Persian, or had the remotest idea of the connection between the Aryan or Indo-European languages. He would certainly have repudiated the idea that a black Ceylonese or a dark South Persian was in the language of the enthusiastic supporters of the theory that speakers of Aryan languages are of one race, an "Aryan brother."[13]

By juxtaposing Europe against present-day Sri Lanka ("black Ceylonese") and Iran ("dark South Persian")—both regions where the Indo-European linguistic tree was firmly planted—the second *Dow* case relied again on a commonsense definition of race that grouped Syria together with the rest of the broad Middle East and Asia, including Iran. What makes *Dow v. United States* a landmark case in the history of race in the United States is what happened during a third trial: Syrians became white. The judge, Charles Albert Woods, made the limits of whiteness clear when noting that it would affect only "the inhabitants *of a portion* of Asia, including Syria, [who are] to be classed as white persons."[14] Woods, relying on the Page Act of 1875, limited whiteness beyond the reaches of other Asian claimants from China and Japan, clarifying in the final paragraph of his ruling that "include[d] within the term 'white persons' [are] Syrians, Armenians, and *Parsees*."[15] Whereas Iranians, like

Armenians, were non-white in the first two *Dow* rulings, they seemed to be white in the third, as Parsees (and the contemporary term "Parsi") is derived from the word "Persians." Judge Woods did not evoke the idea of Parsees out of thin air; they too were in the United States making their own claims to whiteness.

The Specter of Iran in Parsee/Parsi Claims to Whiteness

Given that racial prerequisite evidence hinged on a wide range of social, cultural, and physical characteristics, cases involving the specter of Iran were not only limited to regional neighbors to the north (Armenia) and west (Syria). Present-day Iran also shares a border on its eastern side with Pakistan and Afghanistan (then Hindustan). Unlike Arab and Armenian petitioners who sometimes juxtaposed their inalienable Christian whiteness against the "dark Persians" who engaged in "fire worship," some Indian petitioners claimed their whiteness in the court by asserting Parsi identities that began in "Aryan" Iran.

Parsis are an ethno-religious minority group contemporarily tied to India. As migrants from Persia in the eighth century following the defeat of the Sassanid Empire, Parsis settled chiefly in Bombay, Karachi (present-day Pakistan), and Bangalore. There are intricacies of caste, education, wealth, status, and race embedded within the technically ethno-religious Parsi identity category. Historically and contemporarily, the literacy rate among Parsis in India is exceptionally high.[16] Well educated and relatively wealthy, Parsis were known as active philanthropists who built up some of India's most prominent cultural institutions and charities. Popular racist rhetoric in some quarters of contemporary Indian life attributed these successes to an intrinsic quality found within the educated, light-skinned Parsis, and evidence suggests their elevated social status was consolidated during British colonialism, with its brutal emphases on colorism and forced assimilation.[17] The claim of Parsi identity, particularly at the time of the early 1900s prerequisite cases, reflected the community's relative proximity and access to British culture, its favorable position within a rigid racial hierarchy that privileged fair physical characteristics, and "scientific" claims to a mythological Aryan heritage.

In racial prerequisite cases spanning from 1909 to 1939, nearly every applicant for naturalization from Hindustan identified himself as Parsee, Caucasian, or Aryan and proffered Iran as both the historic cradle of white civilization and indigenous point of origin for his ancestral migration. In the *Dow* case regarding Syrian Americans, the 1915 court discussed Parsees as a relevant reference group for Syrians, drawing from *In re Balsara* (1909), in which a Zoroastrian Parsi "gentleman of high character and exceptional intelligence" successfully argued for inclusion as white.[18] In the *Balsara* case, the claimant's country of origin was India, a mark against him, yet in the racial prerequisite hearing, the court accepted his whiteness based on his stated Parsi ethno-religious identity. Ultimately, the judge ruled that the emigration of Parsi people from Iran to India was the movement of a white people to a brown place and that Parsis successfully maintained whiteness despite their millennium of residence in a non-white locale. In the *Balsara* ruling, the court went as far as to specifically equate Parsi migration to the British colonial presence in South Asia, suggesting that the contemporary presence of the unquestionably white British in the subcontinent in 1909 was simply a modern version of a much earlier white Persian presence in India.

The *Balsara* ruling was challenged, however, by the foundational 1923 case *United States v. Thind* that drew on the same Aryan myth logic that is part and parcel of the Iranian self-claim to whiteness (discussed in Chapter 3).[19] Thind's petition for naturalization included the argument that Northern India was home to "Aryan" people from "some part of Central Asia, probably from Persia" who had traveled east to conquer indigenous South Asians.[20] Combining the Aryan myth from Iran with the logic of the caste system in India, Thind built the case that high-caste Indians—ranking at the top of their particular social hierarchy—were a pure racial group unto themselves within India who maintained strict intermarriage boundaries to ensure that they, as pure, dislocated whites from Persia, never mixed with "the dark races of India."[21] Thind even argued that his Aryan roots in Persia rendered him *more white* than the European American white judges adjudicating his case in the United States—a daring claim, as it was ultimately up to these judges to consecrate him as white or not. The court, unsurprisingly, quashed Thind's Aryan argument with little restraint:

> It may be true that the blond Scandinavian and the brown Hindu have a common ancestor in the dim reaches of antiquity, but the average man knows perfectly well that there are unmistakable and profound differences between them today; and it is not impossible, if the common ancestor could be materialized in the flesh, we should discover that he was himself sufficiently differentiated from both of his descendants to preclude his racial classification with either.[22]

Thus, while Thind's lawyers drew from the history of Parsi migration from Iran to India to legitimate his claim for whiteness, the court labeled Thind with a master racial category of "brown Hindu." The court went on to narrate a racial historiography in which Europeans (white) and South Asians (brown) evolved apart from any possible common ancestor into dialectical racial extremes.

Though Thind's naturalization claim was rejected, it was not until a later decision in *Wadia v. United States* (1939) that Parsee individuals were expressly excluded from whiteness in the US context. In his petition, Wadia and his parents identified themselves as members of the "Parsee race" and followers of Zoroaster. Based on the outcome of *Balsara*, Wadia believed his stated lineage from Persia served as sufficient evidence. But the court, just as in *Thind*, deferred to a "common man's understanding" of whiteness and imagined a racial definition of "white" wholly incompatible with Wadia's nationality as Indian: "Whatever might have been the case with a Parsee, if his stock had been directly derived from Persia, one whose ancestors have resided in India for 1,200 years cannot be regarded as of a race, the members of which are commonly thought of as 'white persons.'"[23] Here, the court argued that even if Wadia's Parsee ancestors were originally from Persia, their presence in India meant they could not still be considered white. Thus, en route to identifying whiteness as mutually exclusive from Indianness, the court concluded that Persia was within the white world, implying that if Wadia's ancestors had stayed in Persia, his contemporary claim to whiteness would have gone unquestioned. According to the court, it was the Parsi community's migration and long-term settlement in India that permanently browned Wadia.

The contradictory rulings by the *Balsara* and *Wadia* courts offer insight into the liminal racial position of Iran and Iranians. Although neither court directly assigned a racial category to Persians or Iranians as "white" or "non-white," both Balsara and Wadia, as plaintiffs, used Parsi identity as a historical claim to a white racial identity with origins in Persia. In this way, Parsee/Parsi operated as racial shorthand. For the *Balsara* court, the continued existence of a coherently differentiated Parsi community in India was evidence of the community's whiteness, and by extension, Iranian whiteness. In *Wadia*, it was exactly this same continued presence of Parsis in the Indian subcontinent that served as evidence of their ineligibility for whiteness. Unintentionally consecrated in the course of these two radically different rulings was the legitimacy of a geographically Iranian or Persian-based heritage and attendant claim to white racial identity.

Whether adjudicating Middle Eastern or South Asian claims, the early twentieth-century courts and claimants themselves habitually positioned Iran as a borderland for whiteness. Syrians and Armenians juxtaposed themselves against the non-whiteness of dark-skinned Muslim and Zoroastrian Persians through which they made claims to whiteness, while in the same era, Parsi claimants used their light skin, Zoroastrian faith, and Aryan roots from Iran to prove their whiteness, notwithstanding a millennium in India. Though Iranians were cast on different sides of the color line dependent on the background of the claimant, across these court rulings Iranians fell into a consistently inconsistent pattern: they were sometimes white and sometimes not white. Throughout their evocation in early twentieth-century US racial prerequisite cases, Iranians were right at the limits of whiteness.

The Mid- and Late Twentieth Century: White by Law, Brown by Popular Opinion

By the mid-twentieth century, the "free white person" requirement that predicated the need for racial adjudication in the early twentieth century had been eradicated, although immigration by liminal and non-whites was still thwarted through country-of-origin quotas (as established by the 1924 Johnson-Reed Act) and, more covertly, an emphasis on family reunification skills and immigration policy (as stated in the 1965 Hart-Celler Act). The first significant wave of Iranians to come to the United States were not migrants per se, nor were they particularly aided or hindered by US migration policies. Rather, it was US foreign policy that had the latent effect of pushing Iranians to the United States.

In 1953, an American CIA- and British-backed military coup deposed Iranian prime minister Mohammad Mossadegh, who had abolished serfdom, improved wages, and nationalized natural resources.[24] The coup recentered power in the hands of the American-supported Pahlavi monarchy and ceded control over the allocation of profitable government contracts and natural resources to foreign interests. The dictatorship of Reza Shah and son Mohammad Reza Shah Pahlavi also imposed a series of unpopular "modernization" reforms, including cultural secularization; it further institutionalized the Aryan Iranian history being taught in classrooms.[25] In a climate in which real inequality within Iran was rising while Western powers gained control over the country's reserves of oil, the state encouraged and sponsored newly middle-class families to enroll their sons in universities abroad.[26]

Thus, in Iran's quest to modernize, its post-1953 relationship with the United States would facilitate the country's first large-scale "brain drain," with the largest proportion of Iranian students who were studying abroad doing so in American universities.[27] The students were teenagers and young adult men, like Kambiz, the "black" basketball player at Utah State who had never played basketball and whose story opened the chapter.[28] By the mid-1970s, in fact, there were more foreign students from Iran in American universities than any other national group.[29]

Despite a pronounced midcentury wave of Iranian men, and to a lesser extent, women studying abroad in the United States, the Iranian presence on American soil was not especially visible until the late 1970s and early 1980s. Within twelve months two of the most important events in the racial history of Iranian America happened. First, in 1978, the US federal government standardized racial categories for the first time, and

Iranians and others with origins in the Middle East and North Africa were definitively classified as white by law. Less than a year later, the Iranian Revolution would transform Iranian migration to the United States by catalyzing the largest migration wave yet.

Ironically, it was the 1979 revolution that produced the migration of between one hundred thousand and two hundred thousand newly official "white/Caucasian" Iranians to the United States and at the same time engendered and fomented new levels of racialized hostility, discrimination, and bias faced by Iranians upon arrival. Less than twelve months after being officially and legally whitened in the United States, a critical mass of Iranian migrants were swiftly and sometimes violently excluded from the white body politic.[30] Some scholars have even argued that "discrimination against Iranians in 1979, the beginning of the Hostage Crisis, is sometimes seen as the first example of anti-Arab [sic] bias in the U.S."[31] Nonetheless, social scientific research on the post-1979 wave of Iranian American migrants has detailed their cultural production,[32] identity negotiation,[33] demographic and sociological profiles,[34] psychological concerns,[35] and political organizing.[36] Whether arriving as refugees, exiles, or international students, the first major wave of migration from Iran remained characterized by a sense of temporariness.

Regardless of whether these new Iranian migrants felt or hoped their time in the United States would be temporary, public backlash and media panic made it clear what other Americans thought about their presence. The hostage crisis in Iran lasted 444 days and was the subject of a nightly prime-time network television show, *The Iran Crisis: America Held Hostage*, which was eventually renamed *Nightline* and is still broadcast on ABC. For well over a year the nightly program curated images of American flags on fire in the streets of Tehran and footage of protesters chanting "Death to America, Death to [President Jimmy] Carter." Back in the United States local constituencies organized a series of anti-Iranian demonstrations and rallies across the country. There was considerable newspaper and television coverage of the spectacle, particularly in Los Angeles. Drawing an overwhelmingly white European American crowd, around five thousand people at one anti-Iran rally coordinated wearing Uncle Sam, American flag, and Statue of Liberty costumes and paraphernalia while holding signs displaying the catchphrases, "US hostages free!" and "The Ayatollah dead!"[37] Two particularly popular slogans on T-shirts and collectible coins read "Fuck Iran" and "Piss on Iran" (see Image 1).

As evidenced in the most famous photograph to come from these demonstrations, American animosity toward Iranians was not only limited to those revolutionaries involved in the hostage crisis. It was also aimed at ordinary Iranians living in the United States, with what became an all-too-common sentiment: "Deport all Iranians, get the hell out of my country" (see Image 2).

Given that the number of Iranian students (fifty thousand) already registered at American universities at the time of the revolution was at its peak, it is useful to turn to their experiences to understand the racialization of Iranians at the time. The US government demanded that all

IMAGE 1. Anti-Iran rally at the Los Angeles Coliseum (1979). Source: Anne Knudsen/Los Angeles Public Library. Reprinted with permission.

IMAGE 2. Iranian hostage crisis student demonstration (1979). Source: Marion Trikosko/Library of Congress. Reprinted with permission.

Iranian students studying at American universities undergo additional screening and documentation, resulting in several thousand students being deported to Iran.[38] Campus by campus, university administrators drafted new regulations to rescind the admission of students of Iranian nationality. Onerous new tuition structures were created. One structure raised fees charged to Iranian students by more than 250 percent in Mississippi. Another limited the advancement of Iranian students in their degree programs as conditional on the release of the American hostages for campus "safety" reasons at New Mexico State.[39] More broadly, economic and political sanctions against Iran were passed by the US Congress twice, both immediately after the revolution and again in 1996. The sanctions were designed to close off trade and banking contacts and to end diplomatic relations between the two countries. For Iranian American families, returning home or sending money to relatives became a complex process involving multiple governments, financial institutions, middlemen, and mandatory airport layovers. Ten years after the revolution, a Gallup Poll determined that the percentage of Americans who had an unfavorable opinion toward Iran increased from 60 percent in 1980 to 91 percent by 1989. Before the revolution, unfavorable opinion was at 37 percent. Summarizing the implication of such a dramatic increase in anti-Iranian sentiment, sociologist Mohsen Mobasher writes:

> No other immigrant group . . . from an "enemy state" has been so politicized, publicly despised, stigmatized, and traumatized by the U.S. government as have Iranians. . . . No other immigrant group from a former ally country of the United States has lost its positive social image so quickly and has been so misrepresented, stereotyped, misunderstood, and made to feel unwelcome despite its overall high socioeconomic status and record of accomplishment in a short period as Iranians have.[40]

In the years to follow, popular anti-Iranian sentiment continued. In 1991, the Hollywood feature film *Not Without My Daughter* promised the "true story" of "an American woman trapped in Islamic Iran by her brutish husband [who] must find a way to escape with her daughter."[41] Critics like Roger Ebert recommended the film (3 out of 4 stars) despite pointing out, "If a movie of such a vitriolic and spiteful nature were to be made in America about any other ethnic group, it would be denounced as racist and prejudiced."[42] It was an odd turn of phrase, and perhaps Ebert knew that in the United States Iranians had been racially classified as white for many years yet were not exactly socially white. Rather than merely a subject of disagreement or confusion between the courts or the American population at large, by the twenty-first century, the in-between raciality of Iranian Americans came with additional legal consequence.

Racial Loopholes in Post-9/11 America

The revolution and hostage crisis that churned behind the large-scale migration of Iranians to the United States is a necessary historical backdrop to the lives of Iranian Americans in the twenty-first century. While the developments following September 11, 2001, are sometimes imagined to be the turning point in the racialization of some liminal groups, the mass public browning of Iranian Americans in the late 1970s and early 1980s anticipated the further stigmatization of Muslim, South Asian, and Middle Eastern Americans after 9/11.

This is not meant to diminish the significance of racial politics post-9/11 but to suggest that for Iranian Americans it was far from the first bout of informal or formal racialization they had experienced in the United States. Nonetheless, and in spite of their white legal designation, Iranians and other groups from the Middle East experienced widespread disapproval and discrimination after 9/11. For example, a recent survey of registered voters found that immigrants from the Middle East are believed to be "least likely" to assimilate into American culture and that US Muslims are "anti-American."[43] Although no Iranian nationals were involved in the planning or execution of the September 11 terrorist attacks, from 2002 through 2011 a special migrant National Security Entry Exit Registration System (NSEERS) required all Iranian and Iranian American men to present themselves for registration with the Department of Homeland Security. [44] Additionally, these informal and formal injunctions underscore the entanglement of race, ethnicity, and religion. These categories have never been as distinct as scholars may have intended or assumed. As argued by Steve Garner and Saher Selod with regard to Muslims, and as evidenced by the history of racial prerequisite cases, for well over a century religious categories have at times both legally and socially functioned as racial or racialized categories for liminal immigrants to the United States.[45]

In the post-9/11 context, racial complications befall Iranian Americans who seek to name or redress incidents of identity-based discrimination they face.[46] Due to their white legal designation, they have been, and continue in some cases to be, left in a legal limbo: They are targets of (seemingly, and sometimes clearly) racist actions by individuals and institutions at the same time that they lack consistent access to race-based recourse. They find themselves in racial loopholes in which they are not white enough to avoid racial discrimination but too white to have it legally redressed. Such was the case for Ahmmad Pourghoraishi, an Iranian American commercial truck driver and victim of an unclassifiable hate crime—because "white-on-white" racially motivated hate crimes cannot technically exist.

The lawsuit *Pourghoraishi v. Flying J, Inc.* (2006) precisely encapsulates the awkward predicament of Iranian "race" and US law as it stands today.

In the case, Pourghoraishi stopped to fill up his truck and use the restroom at a Flying J truck stop in Gary, Indiana. The manager of the Flying J, Steve Lindgren, allegedly prohibited Pourghoraishi from entering the restroom, unlike two other men there at the time. He initially stated that Pourghoraishi had provided "false information" to the fuel desk but later testified that he could not recall what false information had been provided. Lindgren demanded that Pourghoraishi leave the premises, and Pourghoraishi objected, stating that he had still not paid for his fuel. Larry Williams, an officer with the Gary Police Department who was working off duty as a security guard, then placed Pourghoraishi under arrest, allegedly referring to him as a "motherfucker" while telling him to "go back to your country."[47] Pourghoraishi was detained and questioned by the off-duty officer for several hours in the manager's office. Williams also searched Pourghoraishi's vehicle, took his keys, truck registration, and $160 from his wallet to pay for the gas before charging him with misdemeanor criminal trespass and disorderly conduct.

To establish a prima facie allegation of racial discrimination, a claimant like Pourghoraishi must prove all three of the following criteria of the "Morris test": (1) the claimant is a member of a racial minority, (2) the defendant(s) had intent to discriminate based on race, and (3) the discrimination involved, in some way, a contract between parties.[48] With regard to the first prerequisite, the court, in its summary judgment, conceded the paradoxical and confusing racial position of Iranian Americans that had existed for well over a century: "The first prong [race], although generally clear in most cases, is less so here," the judge said.[49]

On the original police report, Officer Williams had listed Pourghoraishi's race as "Persian." During his deposition, however, Iranian American Pourghoraishi took pains to self-identify to the court as white, even though he had brought a racial discrimination suit against a white police officer and white store manager. As Pourghoraishi stated, "According to the United States recognition, Iran is whites in their Arian background [sic]."[50] In the judge's possibly generous retelling, "Pourghoraishi correctly explained that, in this messy business of classifying persons by race, anthropologists do indeed classify Iranians into the perhaps antiquated category of 'Caucasians.'"[51] Thus, in order to consider Pourghoraishi's racial minority status for the purposes of the suit, the judge applied the broadest interpretation of Section 1981 of the Civil Rights Act of 1866, which prohibits racial discrimination, to include discrimination based on national ancestry. In summary judgment, the court therefore affirmed that Pourghoraishi met the first criterion of the discrimination claim based on his Iranian ancestry: though he was legally classified as white in the United States, for the purposes of his racial discrimination case, he could occupy a different category.

The second prong of the Morris test to bring a racial discrimination suit—that Flying J had intent to discriminate based on race—was more complex, given Pourghoraishi's own inconsistent testimony about Iranians' racial self-identification. From the perspective of the court, the only feature of the case germane to the second criterion was how the other people at the Flying J that day perceived Pourghoraishi's race. I quote at length from the judge's ruling to preserve the precise language and logic used by the court to navigate the illegibility of Pourghoraishi's racial categorization:

> In his brief before this court, Pourghoraishi maintains that "any reasonably aware and knowledgeable person would have identified Mr. Pourghoraishi as middle eastern, both by his appearance and speech." (Appellant's Brief at 18). To support this assertion, Pourghoraishi points to an affidavit in the record submitted by his criminal defense lawyer, Charles Graddick, who attests that upon meeting Pourghoraishi, it was apparent both because of his appearance and his speech, "that [Pourghoraishi] was not caucasian and that he was of middle eastern descent."[52] This declaration, however, directly conflicts with Pourghoraishi's own testimony at his deposition that he has no physical attributes that make him appear to be foreign born or of a minority race:
>
> Q: Was there any way of determining your racial background or ethnic background from anything you were wearing or anything on your body or any attribute that you had?
> A: No.

Q: Is there any attribute that you identify with yourself that identifies you as from a different origin than the United States?

A: No.

Q: Just from your outward appearance, is it your understanding that you look any different than anyone else?

A: I can't say that one to you, but you have to ask it from the officer how he figure out I'm not from this country.

Q: I'm asking you.

A: I don't.

Q: You don't think there's anything about you that looks—

A. No, sir.

Q: —different than anyone else?

A: I believe so.[53]

Pourghoraishi further stated at his deposition:

A: Iran is the only non-Arab country in this region. We are not—

Q: Is it Persian—

A: Persian is coming from—Persian came from Germany. According to the United States recognition, Iran is whites in their Arian background. That's the reason Iran means Arian. In the course of the history, [Iranian] is Arian generation, Arian generation.

As the judge noted, Pourghoraishi initially attested that "any reasonably aware" person would identify him as Middle Eastern, and as evidence offered his own lawyer's affidavit of him being "not Caucasian." The purpose of this testimony, and Pourghoraishi's adoption of it, was to distinguish the plaintiff from the defendant, the uncontestably white Flying J manager, for the purposes of the Morris test. Yet when the deposition interviewer asked Pourghoraishi if he "looks different than anyone else," Pourghoraishi said no. Pourghoraishi seemed comfortable stating that his Middle Eastern descent was clearly identifiable but uncomfortable stating that his descent made him look "different than anyone else," meaning in this case, any other white person. The second prong of the Morris test, and therefore, the racial discrimination case itself, hinged on Pourghoraishi's ability or willingness to take an accurate inventory of his racialized physical and social appearance to the white Flying J employees and, hypothetically, a reference group of more racially legible Americans.

Rather than do so, Pourghoraishi initially pushed back in his deposition; he answered the interviewer's question about "look[ing] different than anyone else" with a curt "no." He then put the responsibility of his own racial identification onto the defendants themselves: "I can't say that one to you, but you have to ask it from the officer." As the victim of self-evident discrimination, in his deposition Pourghoraishi seemed unwilling to offer the court what it wanted from him. This unwillingness perhaps reflected Pourghoraishi's unfamiliarity with civil lawsuits or with antidiscrimination policy. Perhaps it was an unwillingness to perjure himself about his own racial self-identification, which contradicted the racial identification imprinted on him that day at the Flying J.

When pressed further by the interviewer, who seemed to offer Pourghoraishi several chances to assert a non-white racial self-identification ("You don't think there's anything about you that looks—") Pourghoraishi acquiesced ("I believe so"). Later in the deposition, as he spoke more generally about Iranian identity, he drew on everyday racial ideologies common among some first-generation Iranian Americans: Iranians are racially distinct from Arabs, share an Aryan history with Germany, and in the United States are legally classified as white. When taken as a whole, Pourghoraishi's testimony was both contradictory and an accurate reflection of the core paradox of Iranian Americans' racial status. Pourghoraishi reproduced the same in-betweenness that has defined Iranian American history.

The judge, with hands tied, acknowledged the inconsistent racial testimony Pourghoraishi gave across his deposition and brief. In summary judgment, he especially noted:

> If we accept as true Pourghoraishi's deposition testimony, then we have no material issue of disputed fact. Both Pourghoraishi and the defendants agree that Pourghoraishi had no external features that would have allowed either Lindgren or Williams to identify him as Iranian or Middle Eastern or any other non-white race. And because according to both Pourghoraishi and the defendants, Lindgren selected Pourghoraishi for

differential treatment before Pourghoraishi spoke, Lindgren could not have heard Pourghoraishi's accent until after he made his demand and Pourghoraishi countered that he could not leave because he had to pay for fuel. By that time, however, the allegedly discriminatory deed had been done: Pourghoraishi had been singled out and asked to leave. In short, based solely on Pourghoraishi's deposition testimony, there are no material issues of fact regarding Pourghoraishi's dispute with Lindgren and *summary judgment must be granted for Lindgren and the Flying J.*[54]

Thus, while the judge upheld that Pourghoraishi, as an Iranian American, qualified as a racial minority for the purposes of the suit, the second prerequisite for racial discrimination was unmet, so the judge found in favor of the Flying J. Was it Pourghoraishi's strict adherence to the federal government's definition of white that was his undoing? Was it his uncritical recitation of a racist ideology that Iranians are Aryan? Or was it his repeated, dogged unwillingness to spell out exactly how he, and Iranians as a whole, might be visually identified as different from a hypothetical "anyone else"?

At the limits of whiteness, racial classification is not only murky but also carries serious consequences for justice as claimants find themselves having to work around, in, and between racial loopholes. Rather than an isolated incident, across the country in the twenty-first century Iranian Americans have found themselves subjected to white-on-white racial discrimination due to their position at the limits of whiteness in day-to-day life.

An Equal Employment Opportunity Commission (EEOC) suit filed by a luxury goods salesclerk, Parisima Abdullahi, fell into a similar racial loophole. In *Abdullahi v. Prada* (2007 and 2008), Abdullahi filed her charge against a hostile and racially discriminatory workplace based on her identity as an Iranian American and Muslim American woman.[55] According to Abdullahi, management and coworkers at a Prada retail store in Chicago made derogatory comments about bombs and terrorism to her following the terrorist attacks on September 11, 2001.[56] In her complaint she also alleged that management redirected Abdullahi's customers to other salesclerks and produced false customer complaints about her work performance. Three weeks after she filed the initial work-place discrimination claim, Prada management fired Abdullahi, allegedly in retaliation for pressing the issue through the courts.

When *Abdullahi v. Prada* was first heard in district court, Judge Samuel Der-Yeghiayan ruled that Abdullahi's claim, which was largely based on her stated national origin as Iranian, precluded the necessary condition of racial protection under Section 1981 of the Civil Rights Act. That is, the judge's interpretation of Section 1981 was that Abdullahi's white racial identity made it legally impossible for Prada to have racially discriminated against her.[57] Much like the racial flip-flopping that had occurred a century earlier in US racial prerequisite court cases, in March 2008, the same Seventh Circuit US Court of Appeals that ruled on *Pourghoraishi v. Flying J* revisited the issue of the perception of racial identity in the *Abdullahi v. Prada* case. Judge Richard Posner wrote a decision on behalf of the court stating that Judge Der-Yeghiayan had been "premature" and "wrong" to dismiss Abdullahi's claims: "Some Iranians, especially if they speak English with an Iranian accent, might though not dark-skinned, strike some Americans as sufficiently different looking and sounding from the average American of European ancestry to provoke the kind of hostility associated with racism."[58] Judge Posner asserted that although Iranians like Abdullahi are "generally regarded as 'white' . . . Iranians can be a 'race' for Section 1981 purposes." The judge was undoubtedly drawing from legal evidence that Middle Eastern Americans experience racial discrimination in contravention of their technically white status.[59] Some legal scholars have argued that these patterns of prejudice and their complex adjudication suggest that Arabs, Iranians, and North Africans in the United States need recognition as a minority group.[60] As the *Pourghoraishi* and *Abdullahi* cases show, rather than resolve the uncertainty of Iranian racial standing in early twentieth-century American courts, profound questions still remain.

Despite their legal classification as white, the twenty-first-century experiences of Iranians and other Middle Easterners exemplify an extension of Mia Tuan's concept of the "forever foreigner" in which no degree of citizenship, legal whiteness, occupational and education success, assimilatory efforts, or self-identification as "American" render Middle

Easterners fully white in day-to-day life.[61] Such has been the case for Iranian Americans in South Carolina, Virginia, Georgia, and California who were denied the sale of Apple products due to their Iranian heritage.[62] As stated by Sahar Sabet, a nineteen-year-old US citizen in suburban Atlanta who was denied purchase of an iPad after an Apple Store employee asked her which language she was speaking with her uncle, "It's discrimination, racial profiling. He didn't have any business asking which country I was from."[63]

Such was also true for US immigration judge Ashley Tabaddor, who in August 2014 filed suit against the Department of Justice (DOJ), charging racial discrimination and derogation of constitutional principles. Tabbador was dissatisfied that the DOJ first recommended and then ordered her to recuse herself from any immigration cases involving Iranian plaintiffs. The DOJ's recusal order was based on a concern that Judge Tabaddor could not remain impartial because of her participation in a 2012 White House forum on the Iranian American community. Eventually, in what has been deemed a stunning reversal of their firm position that Tabaddor's case was "unconvincing" and "lacked facts," the DOJ settled with Tabaddor in November 2015, lifting the recusal order and granting her two hundred thousand dollars in legal fees and damages.[64]

More broadly, new immigration and tourism policy changes are even more systematically transforming Iranian Americans into a class of "forever foreigners." For example, an unprecedented Visa Waiver Program Improvement and Terrorist Travel Prevention Act (HR 158) became law in 2015 under the Obama administration. It established increased scrutiny and blanket exclusions to visa waivers for American dual citizens of Iranian, Iraqi, Syrian, and Sudanese background. In addition, a 2016 bill under amendment by the House of Representatives (HR 5203) doubled down on HR 158 by proposing that members of these groups, including US-born or naturalized Iranian American citizens, submit to and pay for DNA testing in order to sponsor family members for immigration purposes.

In short order, immediately following the presidential inauguration of Donald Trump in January 2017, Iranians and Iranian Americans have been stigmatized and sanctioned again. In his January 27, 2017, Executive Order titled "Protecting the Nation from Foreign Terrorist Entry into the United States," Trump banned the legal entry and reentry of green card holders, visa holders, and dual nationals from all seven Muslim-majority NSSERS countries, broadly affecting an estimated 856,000 persons.[65] Among the seven banned nationalities, Iranians and Iranian Americans are the largest and, arguably, most referenced group in the media coverage and civil unrest that has followed.[66]

The formal and informal racialization of Iranian Americans has also resulted in street violence against other non-whites who are, based on visual cues, racially mistaken for being Iranian. Such was the case for a PhD candidate in economics at the University of Maryland, Miguel Sarzosa, himself of Colombian national origin, who was attacked in Washington, D.C., during a spring 2015 news cycle dominated by partisan disagreement and fear mongering over the "Iran Deal" (see Image 3).

Sarzosa's post-factum reflection that "the beard needs to go" reveals how, as a Latino man, he failed to manage his appearance to avoid being miscast as belonging to a wholly different racialized group; in his own words, Sarzosa "looked Iranian" and was therefore assaulted.[67] At around the same time, in Los Angeles, two white men purposely bumped the car of a Mexican American man they had incorrectly identified as Iranian.[68] Trailing him in their car, they then broke into his home and violently beat him in front of his wife and child while shouting hateful invectives about

IMAGE 3. "Physically attacked in metro yellow line because I 'looked Iranian'" (2015). Source: Miguel Sarzosa, Tweet.

Iranians. Most recently, a fifty-one-year-old white man yelled, "Get out of my country" and shot two younger men of Indian nationality in a Kansas bar, killing one and seriously injuring the other. A 911 call revealed that the shooter had targeted the two men for being "Iranian."[69] That these types of "racial misrecognition" cases consistently involve white Americans enacting violence against racial minorities whom they inaccurately perceive to be Iranian points to an on-the-ground cognitive racial status of Iranians as not-white, at least in the present-day white American imaginary.

Despite these clear cases of racially motivated violence, racial discrimination in the twenty-first century takes coded, covert, and color-blind cultural forms as well. Such is the case when the limits of Iranian American whiteness are exposed in what is believed by many to be the wealthy epicenter of the Iranian diaspora: the "Tehrangeles" of Beverly Hills in California.

Ugly Persian Houses and Aesthetic Racism

Beverly Hills, surrounded on all sides by the City of Los Angeles since its 1914 beginnings as a failed oil expedition, holds a special place in the American imagination. Although Iranians are marginal or absent from either iteration of the television show *Beverly Hills 90210* (1990–2000; 2008–13), Iranian American children make up 40 percent of enrolled students in the Beverly Hills public school system, a proportion unmatched by any other district. The presence of Iranian Americans in Beverly Hills, and their socioeconomic status as wealthy white people living in a wealthy white neighborhood, should be, by most sociological accounts, straightforward and predictive of assimilation into mainstream white America. Yet even in Beverly Hills everyday forms of scorn and exclusion position Iranian Americans as targets of a presumptively race-neutral aesthetic racism.[70]

In 2011, *Curbed*, a popular American real estate blog, featured a website called "UglyPersianHouses.com."[71] *Curbed* recommended the website's commentary on gauche Iranian American homes as good entertainment. UglyPersianHouses.com, with a banner featuring the tagline "Ruining the Neighborhood, One House at a Time," revealed a collection of anonymously submitted photographs of "Persian"-identified residential and commercial buildings, annotated with snarky captions and wisecracking titles. Rather than merely amounting to online snark, however, in West Los Angeles public and private legal codes have been enacted to specifically outlaw these "Persian palaces."[72] Drawing from the subtle, indirect political practices and protectionist logics that have contributed to the segregation of American neighborhoods for centuries, anti-Iranian housing codes in Los Angeles are not far removed from the legal racial prerequisite cases that first racialized Iranians as non-white. Thus, the notoriety of the Ugly Persian House in the late 2000s offers insight into the nature of subtle racial othering in a purportedly color-blind era (see Image 4).

According to architecture critic Greg Goldin, the Persian palace is "the architecture that Los Angeles loves to hate. . . . [It] is distinguished by

IMAGE 4. Untitled [entryway of an "Ugly Persian House" in Beverly Hills, California] (2011). Source: Umayyah Cable. Reprinted with permission.

its exaggerated moldings, numberless layers of cornices, elaborate grille-work, and columns galore. A Persian Palace brazenly combines motifs and wantonly disregards proportion and scale."[73] In effect, the homes are controversial for both their relative size and their "impure" hybridity of architectural style. Columns recalling the Greek classical style might sit behind an Italian-inspired front gate made of wrought iron; seen from above, however, the home may resemble a "box" that fits snugly within an apportioned plot of land.[74] What the terms "Persian palace" or "Ugly Persian Houses" eclipse, however, are some intriguing specifics about their backstories.

The architects, builders, and homeowners of Persian palaces are predominantly Jewish Iranians; many of them were return migrants to Iran in the 1950s and 1960s after completing degrees at universities in the United States. Departing Iran once again in the late 1970s and early 1980s following the revolution, a few returned with their families and purchased homes in Beverly Hills' Trousdale Estates. Trousdale was one of the earliest planned communities in the United States and consisted of 532 original lots. Within one year of Iranian Americans' first arrival to Trousdale Estates, white American neighbors formed a homeowners association and, by 1987, successfully enacted an official ordinance to limit exactly the kinds of home modifications Iranian American residents were making. According to Trousdale Estates' homeowners association, the aesthetics of these projects "started to destroy the character of the neighborhood."[75] Through their association, Trousdale Estates was at the cutting edge of the exclusionary tactics that are now mundane in homeowners associations and gated communities, as well as neoliberal public-private partnerships in nearly every public municipality in Southern California.[76]

Unlike the blatant and pervasive redlining that historically destabilized and denied African American homeownership and investment across the United States, Trousdale Estates successfully fortressed itself against a particular demographic group by identifying an unwanted associated aesthetic. The color-blind effect of such ordinances did some of the dirty work of controlling the extent and character of Iranian integration into the wealthy, majority-white neighborhood by pushing would-be Iranian American homeowners to surrounding areas that had yet to

formally restrict and sanction their tastes. Due to both the formal cen-
suring of their aesthetic preferences and rising property values, Iranian
Americans began to move out of Trousdale and into the surrounding
"flats of Beverly Hills," where now locally infamous residential contrac-
tors like Hamid Omrani remodeled and built homes for an almost exclusively Iranian American clientele. Neighbors whose white identities
went uncontested, in a creative bit of euphemistic backbiting, used the
term "Canadian" in place of "Iranian" or "Persian" to gossip about the
ostentatious and tacky neighbors now living among them.[77]

It was not, however, until the early 2000s that the more unassailably
white residents of Beverly Hills formalized their derision of "Canadian"
tastes through local governmental measures. In the spring of 2003, the
city conducted a survey of its residents as part of an official update to the
general plan. According to officials, those residents who participated in the
survey were "screaming" for some sort of design review process to address
"over the top and architecturally impure" construction that depressed
property values and erased the city's historical charm.[78] Leveraging ethno-
racially infused yet richly flexible terms like "charm," "tasteful," and "understated" to describe their own homes, these coded words were charged
to mean "unlike those of Iranians" in their Beverly Hills context.[79]

The crescendo of residents' concerns about charm rose on the 2005
purchase of a home on North Roxbury Drive once owned by George
Gershwin. The city gave builder Hamid Omrani permission to demolish
and rebuild the property for an Iranian American client. Angry letters
to the editor, testimonials at city council meetings, and gossip ensued.
Within weeks, a group called the LA Conservancy issued its first-ever
"preservation report card," rating cities across Los Angeles County based
on how well they preserved what the conservancy called the historical
"charm" of Southern California architecture. Santa Monica, West Hollywood, Pasadena, and other nearby cities were awarded "A−" grades,
and the City of Los Angeles, a "B+." Beverly Hills, however, netted a
well-publicized, intentionally humiliating "D" grade. Riding the tail-
winds of the "D" grade and public outcry over the Gershwin house, the
city quickly instituted a Design Review Commission.[80] Helmed entirely

by white residents and one Iranian American architect (Hamid Gabbay, praised widely for his anomalously "understated" approach), Beverly Hills quickly developed new design codes by spring 2004.[81]

Whereas the city's previous stance toward architectural styles had always followed an ownership-centered model, in fine detail the city's new design catalog articulated an official position on residential architecture and landscape. The catalog began by first narrating the history of "building patterns" in the city, describing the 1980s, when Iranians arrived en masse, as the era in which architectural "truth" was sacrificed. The catalog then listed five principal categories of approved architecture, inclusive of twenty-one approved architectural subsets.

In effect, the list of approved architectural styles was inclusive of every single architectural form found in West Los Angeles except one: the "hybrid-style" Persian palace. As noted by Goldin, "Of course, neither the word Persian nor the word Palace appears anywhere in the city's design grammar. The city planners didn't bother. It was immediately understood that the April 2004 ordinance was aimed at all those minimansions on the streets south of Burton Way and north of Wilshire. What other target could there be?"[82] The design catalog abounds with the discourse of racial antimiscegenation, holding forth on the distinction in architecture between "purity" and "hybridity" and stating plainly that "mixtures are discouraged." Various itemized architectural elements must be "appropriate" and "consistent." In a public interview, the chair of the committee, Arline Pepp, stated, "I'm very proud the Design Review Commission is performing its function correctly because we do *not* want overly built and highly ornamented homes. We want to maintain the charming character of our city. And our motto is less is more."[83] As was the case with Iranian Americans' move from Trousdale Estates to the flats of Beverly Hills, in the past decade Iranian American builders and residents have quietly migrated to a neighborhood known as Beverly Hills Post Office, which is technically in the City of Los Angeles and therefore not controlled by the Beverly Hills Design Review Commission.

While there are no longer any new "palaces" being built or renovated in Beverly Hills, the website UglyPersianHouses.com documents a vivid catalog of what it calls "Persian creep" across the rest of Los Angeles County. The most polite photo captions use phrases like "freakshow," "truly hideous," "garish," and "a monstrosity" to describe these homes. Less polite captions and comments express sentiments such as "I don't understand why people come to this country if they are going to act exclusionary and disregard everyone else," and "The architect should be hung by his testicles and dragged through the streets and stoned just like they do in the Middle East or *wherever* he's from!!!" To describe the aesthetics of these homes, user-generated annotations and texts on the website draw on notions of racial and ethnic difference between those who are positioned as "good neighbors" (unspoken benchmark groups like whites) and "bad neighbors" (in this case, disrespectful and culturally impure Iranians). The prevailing sentiment about Iranian American homeownership in Los Angeles is that Iranians are poor assimilators; set among the wealthiest denizens of Beverly Hills, their "monstrous" homes defy the law, the laws of nature, and the laws of decency.

Journalists and magazine writers, unlike Internet commenters, do not possess the cover of anonymity. Yet nearly all who have written about the phenomenon have deployed vaguely racial language, often also employing acutely feminized or sexual imagery. In a 2009 feature titled "The Persian Conquest," the West Coast editor of *W Magazine*, Kevin West, identified the first Persian palace built in Beverly Hills as a "pile [that] looks like a particularly frothy wedding cake propped up by a forest of fluted columns."[84] For Greg Goldin in the *Los Angeles Times* the Persian palace is "voluptuous as a derriere, [featuring] almost constant references to the human form, very nearly licentious."[85] His colleague at the *Los Angeles Times*, Karen Anderson, wrote that Persian palaces have "all the grace of a Humvee in a wedding dress" and are "the residential equivalent of a push up bra, vaguely obscene."[86] This twinning of sexual profligacy with racial difference is a rhetorical device of Orientalist logic and a well-trod pathway through which racialized groups are ascribed subordinate status against a majority.[87]

Despite legal censure that has been consistently amplified with the evocation of historically racialized tropes, commentators and Beverly Hills officials insist it's not that Iranians themselves aren't appropriate enough, or charming enough, or understated enough to live in Beverly Hills—it's just that their houses aren't. For Iranian Americans in Beverly Hills, their wealth, education, spatial integration, and legal whiteness are the preconditions to the evocation of their non-whiteness, as expressed through the discourse around their aesthetic preferences. Thus, with the traditional markers of assimilative integration unavailable to cast out Iranian Americans, it is the "impurity" of their cultural tastes that stand-in for the impurity of their whiteness.

Conclusion

Since a half century before their first wave of arrival, Iranians in the United States have sat at the limits of whiteness. In early twentieth-century prerequisite cases they served as racial hinges as claimants argued for their own whiteness, sometimes legitimating their claims by juxtaposing themselves to "clearly non-white" Iranians and sometimes by binding themselves to "clearly white" Iranians. The rulings of the courts, like the claims themselves, were, if anything, consistently inconsistent.

In 1978, after a midcentury wave of government-sponsored young Iranian men came to the United States to earn university degrees, the federal government classified Iranians as legally white. This could have finally clarified the matter of Iranians' racial status, but instead, the pendulum of Iranian American racialization quickly and violently swung back again as legally white Iranians were socially browned in nightly news reports and mass public demonstrations that rejected their presence.

In the twenty-first century, and in a social environment gripped with inchoate Islamophobia and strong anti–Middle Eastern sentiment, Iranian Americans found themselves stuck in racial loopholes. Legally white but socially brown, and on the receiving end of racialized enmity and discrimination, Iranian Americans and other Middle Eastern groups have lacked the strongest possible legal recourse because the law cannot make sense of white-on-white discrimination. Historically, Iranians functioned as racial hinges in other groups' racial prerequisite cases; a century later in racial discrimination cases today, Iranian American plaintiffs are pitched back and forth across the limits of whiteness in an inconsistent and ad hoc fashion due to racial loopholes. As discussed in the case of Beverly Hills housing codes, as socially non-white forever foreigners, and in contradiction to long-standing sociological theories about immigration and assimilation, no amount of occupational prestige, income, wealth, or residential integration can seemingly save Iranian Americans from being cast out as culturally impure, and by extension, racially non-white.

.   .   .

In the summer of 2011, I set out at dusk with my friend Umayyah, a Palestinian American scholar and photographer, to drive around Iranian Beverly Hills and see what happened to some of the homes that had been "under review" by the Design Review Commission after the adoption of the new codes. Like Iranian Americans themselves, the classification of these homes seemed still stuck in legal limbo. I was most interested in 647 Greenwood Drive; from publicly available documents, it seemed the renovation plans had been contested for three years.[88] The owners wanted to expand the square footage on the property, change the shape of some windows, and simplify the landscaping by cutting some trees and paving part of the lawn for a larger driveway. The most current information, now a couple of years old, was that the design commission told the owners and their builder/architect, the infamous Hamid Omrani, to go back to the drawing board with their plans.

When we reached the residence, it was clear to us what had happened, or rather, had not happened, to the property once it was targeted by the anti–Persian palace codes. There was no signage suggesting ongoing repairs or renovation, and bricks were crumbling off the front yard wall. The vegetation had dried up: hydrangeas, roses, palms, and an ash tree were beyond saving. A basketball hoop, rusted with a net dangling loosely from the rim, hung over the driveway. Tiptoeing around to the backyard, Umayyah and I found what had once likely been a nice children's swing set; now the wood was dried out and peeling, and the metal had oxidized (see Image 5).

As we walked around the property and back to the front door, we were careful not to step on glass shards and vinyl screens that lay unattended beneath the broken windows. The stucco on the first floor had crumbled away in places, with plywood now holding the gaps together. Approaching the front door, we saw a mailbox sit at the threshold next to a soggy phone book. A hopeful solicitor from Hacienda Plastering in Mission Hills had left a business card on top. Peeking into the house, we saw that it had been gutted, although there was a refrigerator in the middle of what looked to be a first-floor bedroom. The copper had been stripped from inside the walls. The staircase looked unsafe.

Just then, we heard loud voices coming from the street in front of the house. A young man exclaimed, "This house is fucking haunted!" to which a woman responded, "Eww, I've run around here so many times and never noticed it! Oh my god!" As they passed by us, we saw that they were teenagers in fluorescent running clothes. "Yeah, they say a little girl died here," we heard the young man say. Across the street, from inside a neighboring Persian palace, an older woman bellowed out to the passing teens: "Who do you think you are? Who the HELL do you think you are?" in a Persian accent.

IMAGE 5. Untitled [entryway of a vacant "Ugly Persian House" in Beverly Hills, California] (2011). Source: Umayyah Cable. Reprinted with permission.

Throughout our day trekking around Beverly Hills, Umayyah and I compared notes. We concluded that, almost exclusively, the homes with any signs of human life inside were the ones from which the sounds of Persian or accented English spilled out into the street or the ones from which savory and tart smells of Persian cooking wafted through open kitchen windows. Despite their architectural impurity, all those balconies, the simple landscaping, and the arched, columned doorways were in some ways aspects of an open stage on which the homeowners lived. Unlike the homes around them, they were not closed to the outside world. The openness of these lives and homes was, for the unquestionably white residents of Beverly Hills, no doubt yet another mark against Iranians' not-quite-whiteness and another part of the problem.

The aesthetic of a Persian palace does heavy work. It has to hold a life lived in two parts. It must be big enough to contain grandmothers and aunts and uncles and cousins and second cousins and in-laws; even if they do not live in the house, they will no doubt congregate there. The homes are at once subtle and unsubtle about the people who live inside, who they have been, and who they might come to be again. Little wonder, then, why Beverly Hills would change its laws to manage, control, and ultimately reject them. Thinking back to the vacant house at 647 Greenwood, I was left wondering what happens to a neighborhood once cultural aesthetics and racism are formally codified and controlled by local government. When given the option between an architecturally pure but abandoned property and an impure one in which real live Iranians cook, eat, argue, and play, affluent, majority-white neighborhoods like Beverly Hills seem to have made their preference clear.

Although their open windows might be a source of tension for the neighborhood, the homes of Iranian Americans still hold racial secrets that are likely unknown to their neighbors. The foremost of these secrets is that while the position of Iranian Americans at the outer limits of whiteness may feel obvious to their irrevocably white neighbors, when the doors are closed, the racial hierarchy within Iranian homes looks quite different from that of the world outside. This is the subject of the next chapter.

CHAPTER 3

AT HOME

ON A RECENT TRIP from where I live in Toronto to my childhood home in Portland, Oregon, I lugged my two-year-old toddler on my back and a heavy glass bottle of liquor in my suitcase. The liquor was a *soghati* (souvenir) for my dad, who had called me earlier in the week to say that during his monthly get-together with a handful of other first-generation Iranian American dads he had tried "Iranian vodka! Made in Canada! I'll send you a photo!" The photo was of a large frosted glass bottle with a black, gold, and red label. On the label was a logo featuring a winged sphinx, with the body of a lion and the head of a man. It was a two-dimensional reproduction of a real bas-relief from the ruins of Persepolis.[1] The sphinx was encircled with the words "Persian*" across the top, "Empire" down the middle, and "Canada's No. 1" across the bottom. I wasn't sure what function the asterisk served or how easy or difficult it would be to find Persian* Empire–branded vodka in Toronto, but I did know that my dad was suggesting I bring him a bottle.[2]

Like a dutiful daughter, I went to several of the government-owned liquor stores in my neighborhood and found it at the fourth one, shelved in the liqueurs section. Not actually vodka, it was *arak saggi*—literally, "dog alcohol," traditionally made in Iranian homes from raisins. I held the bottle in my left hand and posted a picture of my treasured find to Instagram. In the moment, I felt proud to have recently moved to a country where Iranian "dog alcohol" was widely available for sale, and in government-run liquor stores no less. At the same time I felt a little embarrassed to be handing my coveted bottle of Persian* Empire to the young white man at the cash register. Were Iranians the only people buying Persian* Empire dog alcohol? What did it mean to purchase alcohol that branded itself through an escapist, ethnocentric nostalgia for the good old days of Persian global domination two millennia ago? If the white salesclerk knew any of this, would he care? Likely not, I figured. My neurotic concerns about Persian* Empire alcohol were also decidedly not my father's concerns; in lieu of self-consciousness, he just seemed happy for its existence. Later that night, as I carefully wrapped the bottle in soft clothing in my suitcase, more than anything else I felt happy that I had been able to fulfill my dad's not-quite-spoken request. I also thought of an autobiographical passage I had recently read by the novelist Porochista Khakpour: "There is a reason my father and mother constantly spoke of the glories of the Persian empire, discussed ancient Persia like it was just a generation before—because when one is dealing with a loss of ethnic and cultural identity, there is no limit to how far back the narrative can take you."[3] Khakpour, a 1.5-generation Iranian American herself, knows well the dynamics of identity, nostalgia, and loss within the immigrant home.[4] The narrative of an ancient Persian Empire can function, as she describes, like a salve for Iranian American loss. The narrative also has a racial vector. It pulls some Iranians, like Khakpour's parents' generation, into a white racial identity bolstered, in no small part, by cultural mythologies of an ancient, honorable, and dominant Aryan Persian empire that ruled the world. This same narrative can also stoke intense ambivalence among the American-born second generation, whose ethnic, cultural, and racial relationship to whiteness is often very different from that of their parents.

.   .   .

Donya, age seventeen, lives with her parents in a northern suburb of Los Angeles, twenty-five miles from the Ugly Persian Houses of Beverly Hills described in the previous chapter. Perched on the edge of an office chair in her childhood bedroom, she held out to me a school photograph of herself at age ten. In it she's lanky, all elbows and braces and with a tangle of inky-black hair. "I didn't like myself," she began:

> I thought I was ugly. I go to a mostly white school. and kids would say, "Wow, you have a unibrow. You have really bushy eyebrows. You're so hairy; you're a gorilla." And I would be like, "Okay dude, I know. Thanks for the reminder." Society kept reminding me. I told my parents, "The kids in my class are making fun of me, and they're calling me gorilla, making 'ooh ooh' noises. They said Bin Laden is my dad." And my mom said such a typical Iranian parent thing. She goes, "Donya *joonam* [dear], tell them we are the original white people! We are Aryans, you know, Iran comes from the word Aryan." I knew the kids bullying me would laugh if I said, "I'm *white* you guys . . . ," so I just kept quiet after that.

Donya shared this story in response to a fairly open-ended question I had asked: "Tell me about growing up in your neighborhood." I was struck by her candor and how centrally race figured in her description of growing up. Unlike other white youth in the United States, who tend to describe their social worlds in postracial or color-blind terms, Donya was acutely aware of being on the wrong side of the color line at school. In her words, "society reminds" Iranian American youth that they are seen as gorillas and terrorists, at the outer limits of whiteness.

In their own homes Donya and other second-generation Iranian American youth experience a very different kind of racialization. Overwhelmingly they describe growing up in households where they were told—either elliptically or explicitly, and most often by their own parents—that Iranians are white. Even those who couldn't recall hearing this from their own parents remember learning that Iranians are white from fellow Iranian American peers who had, in turn, heard this from their own parents. Unlike some of their experiences in day-to-day life, from within the physical and emotional shelter of their homes, first-generation Iranian American immigrants do not typically position their families at the outer limits of whiteness, let alone entirely outside its borders. Rather, when asked by their US-born children and grandchildren, "What race are we?," first-generation Iranian Americans mostly depict Iran and its people as the central historical antecedents for ethno-racial categories like "Aryan," "Caucasian," and "Indo-European." In other words—as described and decoded by my teenage and young adult interlocutors—first-generation Iranian Americans tend to tell the second generation that they are unequivocally ethnic, cultural, and racial whites and always have been.

Contrary to what they hear from elders, however, second-generation youth are mostly skeptical and often critical of self-identifying as white. If they once believed it, their more incontrovertibly white peers have disabused them of the notion. Instead, Iranian American youth describe a profound conflict between the white identities asserted within their families and the stigmatized racialization they (and their families) actually experience in the world outside the home. In Donya's case, the outside world included majority-white classmates who belittled her through visible markers of her physical appearance to draw a racialized boundary— citizen versus terrorist, human versus animal—between themselves and her. Given her failure to fit the normative appearance of whiteness in America, Donya understood that the internal racial logic her mother offered as consolation ("Tell them we are the original white people! We are Aryans, you know") held little coherence beyond her front door.

I was moved by Donya's story of childhood bullying, and it has haunted me throughout my research with other young Iranian Americans. As a sociologist of race, what I found most remarkable was not what was said to Donya at school but what was said at home: that "Iran" comes from the word "Aryan," meant to prove that Donya was every bit as white as the European American peers bullying her. The fact that Donya did nothing with her mother's "typical Iranian parent" suggestion to assert a white or Aryan self-ID—except to "just ke[ep] quiet after that"—indicates that divergent racial self-identifications between different immigrant generations within the same immediate family, behind closed doors, are essential to understanding Iranian Americans' racial identities. Predominant American theories of race and assimilation for ethnic white immigrant groups like Iranians anticipate that each successive immigrant generation will demonstrate greater attachment to whiteness as a social identity. Instead, the Iranian case suggests the opposite: first-generation Iranian parents who, in some cases, arrive in the United States being certain of their own whiteness are raising a second generation increasingly certain that Iranians are in fact *not* white. Contrary to earlier expectations of their integration in the United States, multi-generational Iranian American families appear to socially and successively "brown" over time rather than "whiten."

In this chapter, I describe and analyze stories of race and identity that youth shared about their families. Family is the first major socializing institution in their identity formation. It is also the first site of racial learning; children are directly and indirectly taught by parents and other caregivers to embody the "right" race. For many, although not all, Americans this formative racial identity work is so seamlessly integrated with ordinary everyday life that children and parents unconsciously both learn and teach lessons about race. Importantly, my young interlocutors' Iranian American families were diverse; intermarriage across race, class, religion, ethnicity, and nationality in the last two generations of their families was fairly common. In fact, nearly one-quarter were raised in mixed households that included a non-Iranian parent or stepparent. Yet, across all families, when the "What race are we?" conversation came up, as it often did, white Iranian identities were exclusively constructed and fostered by elders. That is, in accounts by youth of everyday household talk, Iranian-ness was made synonymous with whiteness through a constellation of mutually reinforcing, deeply racial explanations offered by parents and other older adults.[5] The reasons for this are complex and draw not only from the protected and valorized status of whiteness in the United States, but also from the specific status and history of whiteness in Iran. My conversations with youth reveal that terms associated with whiteness, such as "Persian," "Aryan," "Caucasian," and "Indo-European," are regularly passed down from Iranian immigrant parents to children as answers or explanations for the question of what racial category they fit within.

Drawing on both historical and ethnographic examples, I describe how Iranian American claims to whiteness are brought with migrants from Iran and are rooted in notions of cultural and racial purity as well as exceptionality and superiority vis-à-vis neighboring groups in the broad Middle East. As a result, intergenerational conversations about racial identities within Iranian American families reveal three recurring conflicts: (1) the veracity of an insoluble, historical synonymy between Aryans and Iranians; (2) what traits might be considered unique to Iranians in the ethno-racial landscape of the broader Middle East; and (3) a deeply held belief in "Persian exceptionalism," as manifested through the figure of the incredible, exceptional Persian. These conflicts, common and seemingly banal to the youth who shared their stories, are provocative evidence of the internal making and unmaking of a specifically Iranian American shade of whiteness.

"Iran Comes from the Word Aryan"

Although it is impossible and inaccurate to suggest that all Iranian-born parents aspire to impart a white identity to their American-born children, the first generation of Iranian American immigrants were nonetheless inculcated with an Aryan account of Iranian heritage and history while growing up in Iran as children themselves. To understand the limits of whiteness for second-generation youth, it is necessary to delve into this history. The belief that "Iran comes from the word Aryan," which Donya described as a "typical Iranian parent thing," exists within a broader, dominant national ideology of Persian cultural and racial purity that dates itself back twenty-five hundred years. Persia (as Iran was known globally until 1935) was reeling from a traumatizing loss of territory and self-determination through something approximating British and Russian colonization or dispossession during the Qajar era (1789–1925).[6] In this era the Persian Empire—its borders, global influence, and self-confidence—had drastically diminished, and according to historian Reza Zia-Ebrahimi, "European ideas were hybridized by Iranian thinkers to serve their ideological needs."[7] For example, homegrown Orientalists like Hassan Pirnia exhumed the premodern word *arīya* (noble) from a sacred text of Zoroastrianism, the dominant pre-Islamic religion, and promoted it as an antecedent to the "Aryan" racial science coming out of Europe. In its ancient usage, *arīya* had been an ethnic and territorial self-designation,

without racial connotation.[8] By the time the first mass-education historical textbook of the Pahlavi state was released in 1928, however, the newly
invigorated term drew direct ties between *arīya* and "Aryan" as it was
being used by European racialists.[9] The goal of the national racial project
was to lessen Iran's subordination by crafting a national narrative that
linked Persian ancient and modern history with Eurocentric racial science
through the figure of the Aryan.[10]

Youth like Donya, despite being born and raised in America, are still
initiated into the myth's most fundamental axioms: "Iran" and "Aryan"
are ethnonyms; the categorization of Persian as an Indo-European language corroborates an essential likeness between Iranian and European
people;[11] Zoroastrianism is an ancient monotheistic antecedent for Western Christianity; European art, culture, and science trace back to the
Persian Empire; the modern notion of human rights was first established
in the 550 BC rule of Cyrus the Great; today's Europeans are actually
centuries-old migrants out of Iran; and the existence of recessive human
traits like fair skin, blue eyes, and light hair within the population is a
glimpse into what Iranians *used* to look like.

Alongside the Eurocentric, Islamophobic, anti-Arab, and white supremacist beliefs that form its basis, the Aryan myth relies on the illusion
that Iranians have remained ethnically pure and racially white across
two millennia of cultural exchange and variable borders by sidestepping
out-marriage and other reproductive encounters with non-Iranian populations. The idea that Iranians are racial Aryans remains pervasive in
Iran and its diaspora, despite a century of successive revolutions, governments, and uprisings opposed to the very regimes that concretized
the myth.[12] Perhaps most disturbing to some second-generation Iranian
Americans, the myth remains pervasive despite absolute refutation of
the racial science on which it was constructed. It strongly shaped the
conversation between Donya and her mother. It also formed the basis of
a blunt conversation between another interlocutor, Javad, and his parents
in New England.

When Javad was twelve years old, he would look in the mirror and
see "white skin, much whiter than other Iranians. Considering my nose

and everything," he told me, "my skin is weirdly white." As Javad said this, he held his arm up for me to inspect, marveling at it and feigning disbelief. We were eating breakfast at a diner in his small New England hometown, where his parents work as doctors and where he has lived since they emigrated from Iran when he was two. What Javad saw in the mirror as a pre-teen provoked a direct conversation with his parents about race. "I've asked them, 'Why do I look the way I do? Why is our family whiter than most Iranians?' They give different answers: 'Iranians are not Arabs,' 'Iranians are actually Indo-Europeans,' and 'Iranians colonized the Central Asian plateau.' They say, 'We're the Aryan race; we are the Aryan people.' But I need to know why!" Javad pushed the remainder of his French toast from one end of his plate to the other while acknowledging, "As much as I know it doesn't matter, it does to me." As a young Iranian growing up in America, Javad is not out of the ordinary for having asked his parents to help him make sense of his physical appearance. All of the teenage Iranian Americans in my sample who shared recollections of their early childhoods described candid conversations with their parents about skin tone, facial features, and other physical attributes they felt separated them from "white people" in their schools and neighborhoods. In Javad's case, he perceived a mismatch between the size and shape of his nose, which he codes as "Iranian," and the shade of his skin, described as "much whiter than other Iranians." Even five years after the conversation with his parents, he remained vexed by this observation ("I need to know why!") and vaguely dissatisfied with his parents' answer to it. He also revealed a new anxiety about the dominant color-blind ideology of his environment when he included the phrase, "as much as I know it doesn't matter." He continued to seek a conclusive explanation for the constellation of features that, in his words, make him look both white and Iranian. For second-generation youth like Javad, looking white and looking Iranian are two separate realities that cannot reasonably be conjoined.

Given the everyday distinctions Javad and other second-generation Iranian Americans made between looking white and looking Iranian, as children, they sometimes asked their parents anguished questions about their bodies and faces. The content and commonality of their questions, despite Iranian Americans' official racial categorization in the United States as white, reveals Iranians' complicated social position in the American racial hierarchy at the limits of whiteness. Iranian bodies, faces, and identities are not necessarily white in local American contexts but rather often carry a racialized stigma of being visibly foreign and "different."

The reaction of first-generation parents to their children's testimonies of race-based exclusion reveals even more complexity in the relationship of Iranian Americans to whiteness. Javad's parents, as he described, drew from no less than four different, related arguments to prove to their second-generation immigrant son that he is white.[13] The most common racial argument is that Iranians who "colonized the Central Asian plateau" are "not Arab" but "actually Indo-European" and "the Aryan race." Donya's mom echoed this view when she told her daughter, "We are Aryan" and "the original white people of the world." In these instances it is clear how the Aryan myth is imported into diaspora from its original, better-understood Iranian context. Its appearance in Iranian American life should not be particularly surprising, however: as children in Iran, first-generation immigrant elders were intensely socialized into a white Iranian national narrative, despite later possessing a variety of political affiliations and commitments toward their homeland in diaspora.

Drawing from his second-generation subjectivity, however, Javad went on to describe how "Aryan" was an ill-fitting, off-putting, and racist identity for him to claim in the United States: "[In the U.S.] 'Aryan' is used by neo-Nazis, white power groups. . . . Even if we're technically of an 'Aryan' race, that *doesn't make sense here!*" His voice dramatically shifted into a hush as he used his hands to signal air quotes around the word "Aryan," before he raised his voice to conclude that it "doesn't make sense here!" His keen awareness of the public setting in which we were talking and subsequent modulation of his voice illustrated the difficulty he and other youth describe in reconciling Aryanness with their American experiences of race and racism. For Iranian youth who were raised in the United States, claiming an Aryan racial identity for themselves is synonymous with declaring membership to a white supremacist hate group like the Ku Klux Klan. As a result the familial insistence to claim whiteness, particularly through the rhetoric of Iranians' Aryan roots, becomes a source of confusion, consternation, and shame for youth. Javad's desire to disavow the relationship between Iranian Americans and whiteness, "even if we're technically of an 'Aryan' race," demonstrates how difficult it is for second-generation Iranian Americans to wade through murky labels and racial explanations that "don't make sense here."

"Iranians Feel That They Are Hottie Patotties"

Soon after I visited Javad and a handful of youth in their New England hometowns, I headed to California for an academic conference. The university that hosted the conference is predominantly attended by Latino and Asian American students, who, together, make up about 75 percent of the undergraduate population; another 10 percent identify as either black or mixed race; and white students, including those of Middle Eastern and North African heritage, make up less than 15 percent of the student body. One of these students was eighteen-year-old Feri, whom I had met and visited in her childhood home two years earlier. She was halfway through her freshman year and living in a dorm on campus. We had been text-messaging about meeting for frozen yogurt in between conference panels (for me) and courses and intramural sports (for her). We found two hours of overlapping free time in the early afternoon on my first day there. I headed over to her dorm.

From behind the locked doors I saw Feri bounce down the stairs to meet me—bright eyes sparkling like marbles, still pulling back her thick dark brown hair with the same big headbands and bows she had worn since junior high. She showed me around the building and offered introductions to anyone we passed, while sharing observations with me: "Neda, here's the guys I was telling you about who are like the guy versions of me and my roomies; guys, this is Neda; . . . okay, so this is the common room and it's a total dead zone; we hang out in each other's rooms." We went to Feri's "triple" where she and her two roommates proudly showed me around their tiny but meticulous dorm room packed with lotions, hair dryers, photos, and pillows. On three cinder-block walls hung flags that each girl had brought to college. There was a large Mexican national flag that hung across the room, as well as a tiny national flag of the Philippines, and right above Feri's raised bed was a *Shir o Khorshid* flag from Pahlavi-era Iran (1925–79). To diasporic Iranians, Feri's flag tends to mean one specific thing: opposition to the Islamic Republic, particularly among those exiles who were formerly well-placed nobility or military in prerevolutionary Iran.[14] The flag in her room took me by surprise. I couldn't recall Feri or her parents ever displaying sympathy or nostalgia for the old regime.

Later, after Feri and I took a walk around campus, through walkways lined with bougainvillea and massive construction projects, we stretched out on warm slabs of rock in a courtyard between academic buildings. I asked her what it was like to attend a majority-minority university. Her enthusiasm was infectious: "Honestly, I love it. I mean, you saw my roommates. We're Iranian, Mexican, and Filipina. We've got commonalities. We grew up juggling, you know, being born here but treated in America like . . . I dunno, like outsiders. There's no commonalities between Iranians and white people unless they know someone who's Iranian." After Feri said this, she looked a little surprised at herself; it made me think that perhaps this had been a thought that had occurred to her in the past but that she hadn't yet said out loud to another person. I nodded my head a little to indicate that I understood what she meant and did not object to her having verbalized it. Feri continued:

> Okay, so earlier this morning, I'm walking out of my anthro[pology] midterm, and this guy walking out at the same time as me goes, "So what are you?" He's white, and I get the feeling he's trying to figure out if I am too. I say "Iranian," and he gives me this blank look, like he did *not* understand that word. So I go, "Persian?," and then he's like, "Yeah." I'm annoyed that I had to call myself Persian for him, you know. That's like . . . for people who don't wanna associate with Iran, that's not me, and just . . . that's not me.

From her annoyance with the word "Persian," I suspected that Feri's flag was perhaps not an outright rejection of the Islamic Republic or meant to signal a longing for the shah's regime—but I still hesitated asking her about it directly, asking instead about her self-identification:

> Q: So you don't usually call yourself "Persian" then?
>
> A: I used to say I was "Middle Eastern," but then every time I would do that, my parents would say, "No you're *not*, you're white." But I would never put white [on a form]. I would always put "other" and fill in "Middle Eastern." Because I never considered myself white. Yeah, we have light skin sometimes and white features or whatever. I mean, I don't know . . . I just *know* we're not white. It's something I've always felt. For my parents though . . . they associate Middle Eastern as only Arab. And as Iranians, it pisses them off if you call them Arabs because we're not. Even though we're right next to their countries, we're not Arabs because we're descendants from the Aryans. There is a hierarchy there, and Iranians feel that they are hottie patotties and better than everyone else. I don't really get it. I feel like, whatever, no, we're not.

Feri caught me off guard when she said, "Iranians feel that they are hottie patotties." The tone in her voice belied the fact that it was more than just a funny expression, said in a charming way. Her phrase also succinctly captured the chief achievement of the Aryan myth in diaspora: that some Iranian immigrants and their offspring believe themselves to be at the top of a racial hierarchy vis-à-vis other immigrant and minority groups in the United States. In addition, Feri didn't simply relate that she heard *other* Iranians feel this way, but rather she substantiated the observation from experiences within her own family. Her first-generation immigrant parents urged her to reject "Middle Eastern" or an "other" ethno-racial identity for the whiteness that, according to them, she and other Iranians were entitled to claim through the Aryan myth. Feri interpreted their strong, negative reaction to her self-identification as "Middle Eastern" to come from a long-standing Iranian fear of being identified as Arab. She understood this misidentification as threatening to her parents' and other Iranians' self-understandings as Aryan. Although Feri rejected a belief in Iranian superiority to Arabs ("I don't really get it. I feel like, whatever, no, we're not"), she did not question the Aryan myth itself. Rather, for her, the statement "we're descendants from the Aryans" was simply an accepted fact. Nevertheless, Feri forged a racial identity for herself that was different from that of her parents. In fact, three of the most deeply authoritative institutions in Feri's life—her immediate family, other Iranian American elders, and the federal government—either wanted or demanded that she accept a white self-identification. In her own words, though: "I never considered myself white. . . . I just *know* we're not white." In her alternative understanding of race, "even if some Iranians have light skin or white facial features," their social experiences have proved contradictory. To Feri, "there are no commonalities" between "white people" and Iranians. In her everyday life, she experienced more social connection and affinity with her second-generation immigrant Chicana and Filipina roommates than her white classmates. This is especially noteworthy given that she grew up in a high-income Northern California city among white neighbors, attending school with them and sharing a compulsory racial classification with them by the authority of her parents and the government. Nonetheless, for Feri, every time a white schoolmate asked her a question like "So, what are you?," her place as an Iranian at the limits of whiteness was reinforced.

Feri identified with Arab Americans and others from the broader Middle East to an even greater degree based on her subjective experiences as a second-generation Iranian American. She knew that certain distinctions, like language and religious denomination, had historically inscribed a group boundary that separated Iranians from Arabs. Further, she knew that these distinctions were deeply meaningful to her parents and Iranian Americans who had learned them during their own childhoods in Iran. From her social location in diaspora, however, Feri felt she shared a racialized similarity and affinity with the same Arabs and Middle Easterners from whom her parents explicitly told her she was different, or even superior to. Such internal hierarchies and distinctions among Middle Eastern groups that were clear-cut and meaningful to her parents were irrelevant and even offensive to Feri. Within the racial hierarchy she was most familiar with in the United States, Iranians are subject to a stigmatized racialization infused with Orientalist and

Islamophobic sentiments and actions. Therefore, she found Iranians' self-conceptions as "hottie patotties," undergirded by the Aryan myth, to be annoying and unhelpful: "I don't really get it. . . . No, we're not [better]." Most important to Feri's sense of identity while growing up in the United States was the social proximity or sameness ascribed by other Americans to Iranians and those from the broad Middle East.

How did it come to pass, then, that first-generation Iranian immigrants like Feri's parents would feel so strongly about maintaining categorical distance from Arabs? And how does this presumed distance (social, geographic, cultural) from Arabs find expression in diaspora as an Iranian American racial claim to whiteness? Put another way, why are differences of culture and ethnicity between Arabs and Iranians somewhat meaningless for US-born youth like Feri while resonant in the broader, multigenerational Iranian diaspora? I explore how one key cultural difference—linguistic—between the primary languages spoken by Iranians (Persian, or Farsi) and Arabs (Arabic) has been marked by global and Iranian anti-Semitic, antiblack racial science.

The Pseudo-scientific History of Iranian Whiteness

One of the strong claims in nineteenth- and early twentieth-century racial science was that boundaries of linguistic difference correlated with physical anthropology. The then-new European science of ethnology was built on a related theory that linguistic similarity was evidence of common heritage and, therefore, of biological similarity. Based on this, ethnologists organized humankind into groups and hierarchically ranked them as more or less morally, culturally, and intellectually developed. Western Europeans were determined to be an exclusive and supreme group unto themselves. Linguists of the era had already drawn connections between ancient Sanskrit and western European languages. They also developed an Indo-European language tree, of which Persian (Farsi) was one branch. In the same manner that Iranian nationalists claimed Aryan identity, they seized the opportunity to draw ethnological connections between Iran and Europe through the Indo-European language tree, which also established "scientific" distance from Semitic languages like Arabic and Hebrew.

Though the Persian language had long been peppered with Arabic loanwords, following the nineteenth-century ethnological turn, Iranian nationalists promoted replacing the loanwords with "pure" Persian. Approximately twenty-five hundred new Persian words were created by the end of Reza Shah's reign in 1941.[15] Eliminating any hybridity between Arabic and Persian was thought to place the latter into more secure pre-Islamic kinship with Greek and Latin, further supporting Iranian claims of similarity to Europeans. The national project to construct an exceptional Iranian through ethno-linguistic means fit neatly into the broader scientific racism disseminated and promoted in Europe and North America. In the hands of Iranian nationalists, linguistic associations between Persian and European languages offered strong, purportedly unbiased evidence to back up their racial claims of Iranian superiority to Arabs, Jews, and other Semitic groups.[16]

The assertion of Iranian cultural and racial superiority was made explicit during the imperial modernization projects of Reza Shah (1925–41) and Mohammad Reza Pahlavi (1941–79), who ruled Iran before the 1979 revolution. As described in Chapter 2, both regimes were politically repressive and propped up by American and British geopolitical and economic interests. During Reza Shah's rule, they exerted increasing control over Iran and its natural resources; with Iran's autonomy undermined, the shah promoted an internal ideology of nostalgia for the ancient Persian Empire (550–330 BC). Financially and politically backed by the state, Persian literary and intellectual elites reconceived Iran and its people as a glorious, learned, and rich civilization of Aryans that had rescued Persian language and identity from Arab invasion across all time.[17] This ideology was disseminated in schools and in both popular and high culture. The Aryan myth also offered an ideological pathway out from beneath British and American control, with foreign investment and economic ties to Nazi Germany strengthened by both countries' strategic assertion of a shared Aryan lineage.

An even more immediate hazard for the Pahlavi regime than its subordination to the British and Americans, however, was the diverse composition of Iranians themselves.[18] At the time that Reza Shah took control, the population of Iran was heterogeneous, spanning a wide range of ethnic, linguistic, and cultural practices. Through a variety of compulsory means, both shahs forced a unified national language, history and identity, underpinned by the Aryan myth, onto their subjects. Since then, across each decade and political regime up through the present day, the notion of an Aryan Iran has been reinforced by Iranian power elites as a cultural, linguistic, and nationalist descriptor with overt racial conclusions. Those who would go on to become the parents of second-generation Iranian American youth, the first generation of Iranians in the United States, brought to their new diasporic homes powerful notions of an Aryan cultural heritage, Caucasian geographic origin, Indo-European language, and concomitant white racial identity.

Henry Field and the Discovery of the "Iranian Plateau Race"

The nationalist work of racially distinguishing "Aryan" Iran from the "Semitic" Middle East was also a global project that involved Americans, although the role of the United States in consolidating the Iranian Aryan myth has not yet been analyzed. To understand the racial valence of terms like "Aryan" and "white" in the American diasporic context of the second generation, however, requires that these intersections be explored. By the mid-1930s, American physical anthropologists like Henry Field, head curator of the Chicago Field Museum of Natural History and nephew of Marshall Field, regularly collected "anthropometrics" on groups from the Middle East. This was part of a larger geopolitical project in the interwar period, formalized by President Franklin Roosevelt. One of the intentions of this project was to use anthropological science to move away from American isolationism toward US-led internationalism.[19] With the official approval of Reza Shah, Field analyzed corporeal measurements collected among a convenience sample (comprising largely male laborers, prisoners, hospital in-patients, and other vulnerable groups) from four major ethnic groups in western Iran. For the explicit purposes of "racial classification," Field offered a taxonomic schema of Iranian facial and body types, including charts, graphs, and hundreds of anthropometrical (or proto–mug shot) photographs (see Image 6).

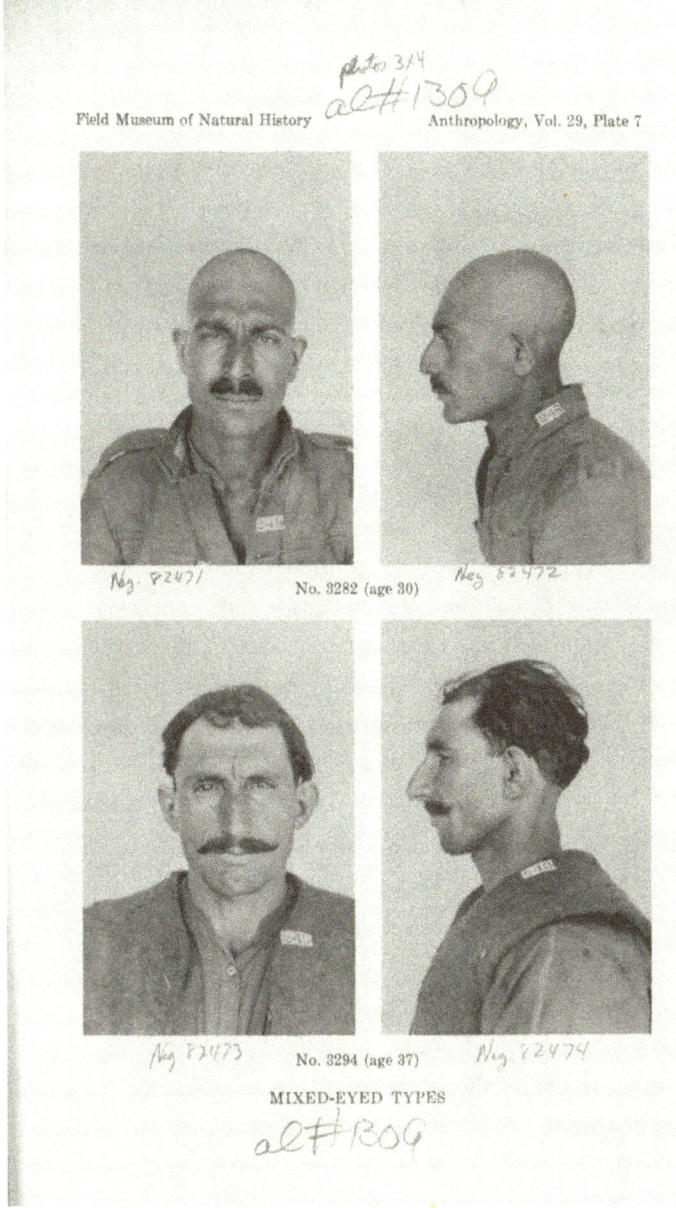

No. 3282 (age 30)

No. 3294 (age 37)

MIXED-EYED TYPES

IMAGE 6. No. 3282 and no. 3294, "Mixed-Eyed Types" (1939). Source: Richard Martin/Field Museum of Natural History. Originally published in Henry Field, The Physical Anthropology of Iran, vol. 2 (1939), photographic plate 7. Reprinted with permission.

From this research, Field, who became the official anthropologist to the US president, "distinguish[ed] a new, fundamental division of the White race," called the Iranian Plateau race.[20] As summarized in a 1941 review in *American Anthropologist*, "[The Iranian Plateau race] is distinguished mainly by a high hooked nose; its features as given are otherwise those of the classic Mediterranean, although it is definitely larger and more rugged in facial skeleton."[21] Comparing measurements from Aryan Iran against his earlier fieldwork done in Semitic Iraq, Field cited the overwhelming presence of "convex-nosed long-heads" in the Iranian population as evidence of whiteness. In strong language, Field summarized the implications of his research in Iran: "This new racial type, now for the first time, takes its place beside the Nordic, Mediterranean, and Alpine races."[22]

Field's conclusion was provocative. In a review published in *American Anthropologist*, W. W. Howells expressed skepticism based not on the "evidence" cited by Field but on its political-racial implications: "I would question putting up such a race beside the Nordic, Alpine and Mediterranean without immediately considering the implications of this. What general background of racial history is being referred to, and how, if at all, is this background affected?"[23] In effect, Howells criticized Field not on the basis of data or analysis but on the basis of having transgressed boundaries of race by professing a new race of credible whites outside Europe—that is, Iranians. Though Howells did not explicitly state the danger of grouping Iranians alongside Europeans, the publication of his concerns in the most prestigious journal in anthropology signals how disruptive Iranian whiteness could be to the accepted racial order. For the shah and other elites in Iran, however, Field's research was a valuable endorsement that used the legitimacy of American science to concretize the Aryan myth.

The Incredible, Exceptional Persian

When we met in a strip mall deep in the exurbs of northern Virginia, fifteen-year-old Yara had just gotten out of her mom's eggshell-colored minivan. The minivan had racked up many, many miles in the past half year after she convinced her parents to drive her an hour each way from their "super-white" town to attend a majority-black high school for the arts in the city. When I interviewed her a few months earlier, Yara was a newly graduated eighth-grader, excited but also anxious to start at the arts school. I was eager to hear how her ninth-grade year was going. We were in a chain sandwich shop snacking on potato chips when a peculiar expression came across Yara's face as she fished a chip out of the bag. Holding it up with a thumb and index finger, nails painted mint-green, she said in a matter-of-fact way:

> My dad told me Iranians invented potato chips. He brings it up all the time! Anything that could be in any way connected to Iran. It's like they're always trying to get me to feel proud of being Iranian, and it gets to where I'm like, "Okay, whatever, sure." Math, medicine, human rights, anything to benefit society . . . all Iranian.

When Yara told me her father attributed the invention of potato chips to an Iranian, I was surprised. I was not surprised that she had been told such a thing but that I myself hadn't heard the potato chip legend before. The other inventions Yara mentioned are well-worn bits of historical legend in Iran and its diaspora: math was discovered by al-Khwarizmi, a Persian after whom algebra is named; the physician/ philosopher Ibn Sina (Avicenna) invented what is now called medicine; in 576 BC, Cyrus II of Persia (Cyrus the Great) wrote the first code of human rights.[24] To be sure, Yara's father's potato chip claim had little factual merit; common consensus places the first potato chip, perhaps unsurprisingly, somewhere in early 1800s England. The first potato chip likely only arrived in Iran through channels of British colonialism half a century later. Yara went on: "But sometimes, I *do* think there are things we don't get credit for. This year we read Hafez and Sufi poetry in class, and I felt . . . like proud or something; it was weird. I'm not usually like 'rah-rah Iran' like my parents. And *they're* not even that bad." Yara described her own second-generation feelings of pride about Persian poetry as "weird." So, for her, the unverified claims that potato chips were invented by an Iranian were just another example of "rah rah

Iran" sentiment she had noticed among Iranian American families like her own, who were, relatively speaking, "not even that bad."

Reza, a premed student at a small liberal arts school, told me that conversations like these seemed to be a way for Iranian and Iranian American elders to connect to him: "I was always interested in science anyway, but people in the Iranian community, they would hear I'm premed and be like, 'Some ancient Persian invented this life-changing medical technique that's still applied today.' To give me pride or show more pride with that bit of knowledge." While Reza maintained measured neutrality about his encounters with prideful Iranian American rhetoric, Yara had observed that some Iranian Americans were "bad" at keeping nationalistic pride in check. I asked Yara if she had an example in mind, and she was quick to answer.

> There's like, someone my dad went to elementary school with [in Iran] who lives here; he's related to the shah or something. My dad gets really annoyed with him; they fight because that guy is *really* like a lunatic about Iran. He was freaking out that Google changed "Persian Gulf" to "Arabian Gulf" on Google Maps.[25] His daughter and son are like this too. I think it's really bad to be forcing your opinions on other people, especially when being Iranian isn't . . . like some people don't think of it as a good thing.

In the span of one minute, Yara ricocheted from offering a humorous comment about the provenance of potato chips to solemnly remarking that "being Iranian . . . some people don't think of it as a good thing." Yara's last remark helps make better sense of why a first-generation Iranian immigrant parent might offer something as mundane as a potato chip as evidence of a notable group-level achievement from the motherland. Second-generation youth like Yara perceptively contextualized the stories about potato chips and other national achievements that floated around their homes. Rather than outright accept or ignore their parents' claims, they hypothesized that their elders were trying to instill a sense of Iranian identity or pride in American-born children, who risked low self-esteem or lack of accurate knowledge because of stigmas associated with Iran.[26]

In Yara's case, provoked only by an association with potato chips, she recalled that her first-generation parents were eager to inculcate pride in their children by teaching them, as she put it, about things "we don't get credit for." Yara moved from describing her parents' ardent efforts to claim math, science, and medicine as rightfully "Iranian," to admitting that she herself felt that Iranian contributions to humankind were often unacknowledged, to then reflexively offering an example of when pride goes too far: describing her father's childhood classmate who was "related to the shah or something" and a "lunatic" about promoting Iran's place in the world. When I asked Yara to expand on her final observation, that "being Iranian . . . some people don't think of it as a good thing," she surprised me with her answer: "If there are good things happening there right now, I don't know about it, and maybe I should educate myself on it more. [It's been] eclipsed by all the negatives, and it's hard to find good examples from now, which would be better than bringing up examples from thousands of years ago." I had asked Yara to say more about her comment that some people have negative associations with being Iranian, not expecting that she would include *herself* among those who "don't think of it as a good thing." Yara admitted she found it challenging to identify good things happening in present-day Iran that might mitigate the negative stigma of being Iranian. She took herself to task, along with first-generation parents and other Iranian elders, for deferring to ancient history in search of positive representations or information about Iran. More contemporary, relevant examples would be, in her words, "better than bringing up examples from thousands of years ago." Whether she meant present-day examples would more effectively improve global, public perceptions of Iran or her own perception of being Iranian, she was nonetheless aware of the pervasive nostalgia that informed Iranians' own perceptions of themselves.

Along similarly nostalgic lines, usage of the self-descriptor "Persian" accomplished important boundary maintenance within the Iranian diaspora, about which youth had mixed feelings. In the North American diaspora, the ethno-national term "Persian" has sometimes been used as a cover for the more stigmatized, politically explosive "Iranian."[27]

Accordingly, interlocutors described a small proportion of elders in their families identifying as Persian to avoid negative attention associated with present-day Iran, but that the usage of the term also came with subtleties that might escape most other non-Iranians. Very few youth described any sort of intrinsic or affective preference for the term "Persian" themselves. Rather, they were savvy about how "Persian" was situated in the implicit and explicit ethno-racial hierarchies articulated by their families. To them, identifying as Persian was the strongest possible tool their Iranian American elders could use to distance themselves from Arabs—the group into which they seemed to feel the greatest danger of being misidentified in the United States. Sima, a high school junior, described her relationship with Persian identity this way:

> I used to always say "Iranian," and then one of our family friends told us we should say "Persian" because Iranian has an Arab influence and all this stuff and how our true roots are Persian so we should use that word. So then I started using "Persian." But then I started thinking that "Iranian" is more accurate to describe a majority of people there. It *is* our culture. Our parents *did* grow up in Iran, not Persia, and we do have Arab influence in our culture. But it's more accepted in America to say you're Persian. If I say, "Yeah, I'm Persian," people are like, "Oh, okay, cool." But if I say I'm Iranian, they're like, "*Oh,* you're from *eye*-ran." There's a suspicion there. But honestly, half the time when I say I'm Persian, I think people don't even know what that means. They're like, "Oh great, I have a Persian friend!," and they have no idea it identifies with the country of Iran.

For Sima, it wasn't her own parents but one of her parents' friends who encouraged her to identify as Persian, drawing from the same anti-Arab ideology circulated by Iranian nationalists over the last hundred years. Though she was initially swayed by the friend's argument that "Persian" was a preferable term to use, she came to understand another reason Iranians might identify as Persian: "it's more accepted in America." In fact, Sima guessed that "people don't even know what [Persian] means," obfuscating any relationship to Iran or perhaps even the Middle East. [28]

Sima was of two minds about having switched from identifying as Iranian to Persian. After thinking about it some more, she concluded that calling herself Persian was in fact less accurate or honest than calling herself Iranian. The latter was, she thought, both more accurate as a reference to the country in which her parents grew up and also more inclusive of its true ethnic diversity and cultural influences. The former not only actively disavowed the real influence of Arab culture in Iran but also reinforced an anti-Arab attitude that didn't reflect Sima's second-generation politics.

Hanna, a high school sophomore in the suburbs of Chicago, described a similar process of disidentification from the term "Persian":

> I was always all about like Persian pride, like "Persians are number one." But the more I learned about it and I was doing research on it, like Googling it, I don't use the term "Persian" just because um . . . it's very exclusive. And like . . . I think that's actually a big deal. The fact that we use the term "Persian" a lot, you're just excluding all the Baluches, all the Lurs, all the Turks, all the Kurds. You know what I mean? And of course all the Iranian Arabs. Not everyone who lives in Iran is necessarily Persian.

Hanna described engaging in the act of critical, self-directed Internet research to learn more about her ethno-racial identity. After realizing that a range of ethnic groups in Iran, including Arabs, had been forcefully consolidated or disappeared from its Persian national identity, Hanna moved from "Persian pride" to refusing to use or identify with the term from that point forward. Hossein, also a sophomore in high school, offered a more pragmatic reason for his disidentification from "Persian" when we hung out at his house one weekend.

Hossein's mother had just, in a very traditional gesture of hospitality, brought us a tray of black tea, sugar cubes, and fruit while he and I sat on the back deck of their snug ranch-style house in a commuter town outside New York City.[29] With a mischievous glimmer in his eye, Hossein thanked his mom, using what interlocutors sometimes called "Persian dad" voice, which was basically English spoken in a slowed down, exaggerated Persian accent paired with small hand waves and side-to-side head movements: "T[h]anks very much, mommy *joon* [dear]. So Persian right now." Without missing a beat, his mom quipped back in an equally over-the-top version of "Persian dad": "Vat else but the best for my *azizeh delam* [sweetheart], *pesaram* [my son], my Hossein *joonam* [my dear]." I laughed awkwardly and tried to thank his mom in formal Persian to reaffirm the boundary between me, a young outsider in her house, and her, the hospitable elder. Out of his mom's earshot, I asked Hossein if this type of teasing was common between him and his parents. He described a household full of jokes and laughter where he teased his first-generation parents for being "*so* Persian" and they in turn teased him for being "*so* American." Rather than generational differences causing a split in Hossein's family, it was the generational differences themselves through which his family bonded. I then asked Hossein if he tended to use "Persian" more than "Iranian," or vice versa, when describing his family background. He thought about it for a moment before saying,

> Look, I don't really care one way or another. I actually just want everyone to use *one* label. I want everyone to either say "Persian" or "Iranian." Because when we mix the two up, then it turns into two different . . . not for ourselves, but for those looking onto us as representatives of Iranian culture. If we use the word "Iranian," maybe they would learn that not all Iranians are like what's portrayed in the news about the government. And that we're open minded. But if we all use the word "Persian," then there needs to be a reason behind that. And so now I'm trying to use "Iranian" more.

To Hossein, "Persian" was not a strategic option to avoid the negative stigma of being Iranian. In fact, he conceded that if "we all use the word 'Persian,' then there needs to be a reason behind that" and described instead "trying to use 'Iranian' more." His most urgent concern was that debates around Iranian American self-identification come to a swift, clear-cut resolution, pointing out that the inconsistent use of "Persian" rather than "Iranian" within the community risked confusing outsiders. Most revealingly, he tied these issues of self-identification back to the stigmatization of Iran, arguing that perhaps "Iranian" should be the preferred term to combat negative images of Iran in American media and politics. Though Hossein prefaced his opinion with the caveat that he didn't "care one way or another," he actually advocated embracing "Iranian" precisely because using "Persian" as a cover term might only further the stigmatization of Iranians and Iran in the United States.

The majority of respondents, like Hossein and Feri, preferred using "Iranian" rather than "Persian" as a self-designation, and several shared with me their overt disdain for nostalgic Persian exceptionalism. One young woman in particular, Newsha, described encountering peers at her Southern California university who, like her, verbally identified as Iranian American but also adopted motifs associated with the figure of the exceptional Persian or Aryan. In our conversation, Newsha recalled the way a college classmate and friend (also an Iranian American) explained Persian/Aryan exceptionalism:

I remember it [the e-mail from my friend] because it was so funny. This was her exact quote: "The *Iroonis* [Iranians] who wear *faravahars* [ancient Zoroastrian amulets] around their necks and think their grandfathers were Zoroastrian," and I was like, that is so funny because there *are* people who think that. If someone who is Zoroastrian wears [the *fara-vahar*], that makes sense. But people who wear it as a symbol of Aryan and Persian pride, I mean, it's literally a symbol of divine authority for the king, right? I don't know if these people know that or not, but they remove it from that context, like "it's just me being Persian."

Like the novelist Porochista Khakpour, Newsha and her friend understood how ancient Zoroastrian iconography like the *faravahar* came to assume a revisionist historical purpose in diaspora. In their e-mail exchange, they were humorously critical of how the *faravahar* had become a symbol for "Aryan and Persian pride." They discerned that a minority of their Iranian American peers, by wearing the *faravahar* and asserting that "it's just me being Persian," strived to imagine themselves as only two generations removed from a glorious, exceptional pre-Islamic Aryan and Persian past. Left unsaid, however, and perhaps not even understood, is that given the demographics of the Iranian American community, most grandparents of these second-generation youth were certainly not Zoroastrian and were likely observant or secular Shia Muslim. Yet at the same time, the repurposing of the *faravahar* did not first emerge with Iranian Americans but has a longer history.

The *faravahar* itself is a holy Zoroastrian symbol originally etched on the walls of Persepolis, exactly like the bas-relief reproduced on the bottle of Persian* Empire I bought for my dad. The image is of a winged older man in profile, left hand pointing to the sky and right hand holding a ring. Rather than present-day Iranian Americans having repurposed the *faravahar* as a symbol of Persian exceptionalism entirely on their own, the Pahlavi regime in twentieth-century Iran recast the *faravahar* into a secular symbol of ancient nationhood, incorporating the holy icon into the family's coat of arms and other various emblems. As described by Newsha, the *faravahar* is often found in the tattoos and social media profile photos of Iranian Americans, or worn in diaspora as a necklace pendant. It was also newly prominent in the viral music video for "King" (2015), featuring rapper Snoop Dogg, by the Iranian American recording artist Amitis.[30]

The video, saturated in various shades of gold, intertwines global pop signifiers with broad Orientalist and Persian aesthetics. Amitis (whose name recalls Amitis Shahbanu, queen of the Persian Empire and wife of Cyrus the Great) is fashioned as a neo-Cleopatra, mouthing lyrics from a Persepolis-inspired harem while a servant (played in an uncredited cameo role by self-described "half-black and half-Iranian" comedian and reality-show celebrity Tehran Ghasri) pours red wine into a golden goblet.[31] Musician and marijuana advocate Snoop Dogg is greenscreened onto a large *faravahar*-shaped throne to literally and metaphorically puff his way through his guest verse (see Image 7).

Haphazard Zoroastrian symbols are combined with pop allusions (Snoop Dogg) and luxury consumer goods (chinchilla fur) to gesture to the ancient opulence of the Persian Empire. The use of these raced and classed identity markers, albeit likely celebratory by Amitis and the music video director, evoked sharp reactions over social media among

IMAGE 7. Screenshot of "King" music video by Amitis, featuring Snoop Dogg (2015). Source: Avang Music.

some second-generation Iranian American youth, ranging from ephemeral shudders and cringes to outright embarrassment and denunciation. Recalling Hossein's observations over chai that identifying as Persian mystified Iranians' presence in the United States and contributed to troublesome divisions within the community, young people's reactions to the video went beyond just the artistic properties of the song itself. Although it could be comforting to assume otherwise, to second-generation youth like Newsha, draping oneself in a *faravahar* and claiming a Persian identity could be politically repellent—and by no means a foolproof escape hatch for avoiding racism or violence.

For example, the "Persian" ethno-racial label was at the center of a recent case of assault in the suburbs of Chicago.[32] "Hey, Persian!" an eighth-grade boy yelled before pummeling his Iranian American classmate to the ground, breaking his collarbones and, after a long hospitalization, curtailing his achievements as a nationally ranked junior swimmer. The victim, like many of the youth in this book, possessed distinctively Persian first and last names and also a mixed background;

in this case, his mother is fair skinned and Puerto Rican, and his father a darker-skinned first-generation immigrant from Iran. The victim himself possesses medium brown skin, a broad nose, and other features that differentiate him from normative whiteness. That the attacker, in this case, a fellow student of color, preceded his physical violence with the phrase "Hey, Persian" suggests that Persianness was somehow relevant to the attack. Regardless of the complexities of Iranian Latino identity, in this interaction, Persian was the master status that overrode other ascribed and achieved identities. It functioned here as an explanation for violence based on racialized difference.

Conclusion

Throughout this chapter, second-generation youth have described childhoods shaped by a growing awareness of Iranian Americans' uncertain place in an American racial hierarchy. Additionally, they described growing up in homes and families that were steeped in lessons about Iranian culture and history. These lessons emphasized parents' common, unwavering answer to children's observations of Iranians' liminal racial status: "We are the world's original white people." Sometimes the racial lesson about Iranian whiteness was subtextual; perplexed youth sensed pressure from elders to claim white identities through nationalistic narratives of Persian exceptionalism and a glorious, ancient Aryan past. At other times, the racial lessons were more direct; parents or other Iranian American adults explicitly rebuffed young people's expressions of an alternative, non-white racial self-identification.

When youth brought these racial lessons to bear against their real-life experiences—as racial hinges—in a United States full of racial loopholes, they were largely unconvinced or frustrated by their white de jure status. Being told to assert one's Aryan identity in an American social setting felt at best clueless and at worst unequivocally xenophobic. Being told to fight back with millennia-old examples of cultural greatness when bullied for one's ascribed identity and appearance was for them equally troublesome. Yet, ultimately, second-generation youth were also perceptive about *why* racial narratives of Iranian whiteness circulated within their families. They understood that sometimes these stories were told to bolster their knowledge in and pride for their (often-stigmatized) Iranian backgrounds. It was simply the "best" resource elders felt they had to offer perplexed, and sometimes traumatized, American-born children. Though outside the boundaries of this book, it bears questioning how intensely first-generation individuals actually feel about the sacrosanctity of Iranian whiteness after extensive experience living in the United States. Yara, the fifteen-year-old who surprised herself by feeling pride over Persian poetry, put it this way:

> I think maybe also first-generation people get harassed a lot. I think if asked, my parents wouldn't want to tell, but they're doing their job to shelter me from it.

> Actually, I remember that at an old job, my mom's boss told her, "If I saw you in the street, I'd run you over for being Arab." This was her boss. It was just crazy, you know? It's like, (A) We're not Arab [laughing], and here's like, another example of how Iranians thinking they're sooooo different than Arabs is just like "hahahaha" yeah, no, and (B) that's like, really serious. That threat.

> In general, I don't know to what extent [my parents] even want to bring [being harassed] up with me. But it's like, obviously, they face it. If *I* face it, and I have no accent, but my mom and dad have really thick accents, especially my mom, it's more prominent. If most people can tell that I'm not American, then what does that mean about them? In a way, maybe I'm getting less of it. And they're not going to tell my brother or me about it.

Yara understood that despite hearing little from her parents about their encounters with harassment and threats of violence, it was likely that despite their self-identification as white they may not experience some of the ordinary protections and privileges of whiteness. From Yara's account, it was unclear whether her mother's boss described running her over with his car for *appearing to be* Arab or whether he actually believed her to *be* Arab. For Yara and other second-generation youth, the salient point was not whether their first-generation parents experience racial exclusion or discrimination; most youth assume that their parents do. Rather, it is the suspicion that their parents are selective about which of their American racial experiences they draw on to confirm a white self-identification. Within the intergenerational immigrant family, contradictions of Iranian American whiteness in a racist, Islamophobic society are complex. The contradictions create an atmosphere in which uncomfortable family secrets are held; the motivations for behavior and beliefs go unexpressed and, further, are obscured by obvious inconsistencies.

This chapter introduces a few of the underlying complexities of race and racism within Iranian American families.[33] Within the immigrant home, the uncertain racial position of Iranian Americans is seemingly resolved through three major rhetorical themes: uncovering the "Aryan" roots of Iran, identifying the exceptionality of Persians in the Middle East, and reclaiming the glories of the Persian Empire. First, from a geographic point of view, by embedding Iran into a racist genealogy defined by Aryans and Semites, the pervasive Aryan myth airlifts the country out of Asia and into Europe. By asserting equivalence between the terms "Iran" and "Aryan," twenty-five hundred years of internal complexity, shared borders, and cultural exchange with the broader Arab world are overlooked and ignored. More important, the nostalgic narrative of a pure Persian race and language that were forever compromised by the seventh- and eighth-century "invasion of Islam" remains intoxicating even in diaspora for the way it salvages Iranian territorial losses to Arabs and others from within spurious "scientific" European racial thought. The common claim that "Iran" is synonymous with or comes from an ancient word "Aryan" is actually a racial fiction born in the last 150 years of Iranian history.[34]

In an American society in which resources and privileges are extremely stratified by race, the Aryan myth finds a robust afterlife in the Iranian immigrant household. The frequency with which Iranian racial liminality is resolved through the assertion of Persian pride highlights how urgently Iranian American parents want their children to feel secure about their Iranian identities and about Iran's place in Eurocentric and

racist annals of civilization. Simultaneously, the reflexive urge to empha-
size Iranian achievement within the immigrant home is meant to help
offset the stigma of being a social outsider in America. But for second-
generation youth, narratives of Persian exceptionalism and pride do not
provide emotional protection from the racism they experience outside
the home. Their stories demonstrate that the uncomfortable paradox of
shielding oneself from racist, anti-Iranian sentiment in the United States
by employing a white supremacist narrative of the Aryan Iranian is not
only ineffective but is, itself, a source of racial distress. To better understand stories like the one shared at the beginning of this chapter, in which
Iranian American children like Donya are regularly bullied about their
identities and physical appearances, I move in the next chapter out of
the diasporic home and into the American classroom. Despite their parents' mythologies of whiteness and their legal classification as white in the
United States, the limits of Iranian whiteness come into relief as large-
scale, geopolitical events are locally staged and made ordinary through
the racialized bullying of second-generation youth in schools.

CHAPTER 4

IN SCHOOL

YASMIN IS AN IRANIAN AMERICAN college sophomore who lives in Rock Creek, a suburb of Washington, D.C. She and her brother Bijan, a college junior, attend college together. When they're not attending class, studying in the library, playing soccer, or working at starting-wage jobs, they're spending time with their family, usually in their childhood home. They, and their oldest sister, Shabnam, dote on their little sister Ensie, who at age fourteen just started ninth grade at their alma mater, Rock Creek High.

Rock Creek has not always been welcoming to outsiders, especially non-white outsiders. Until 1966 Rock Creek relied on explicit residential codes that limited the ownership of homes to "white Caucasians." This redundancy of terms would not have been lost on youth like Yasmin. Her family, like other Iranian American families, is technically white, but their local status as white seems always in question. Rock Creek is located in a county in which twenty-one of twenty-three elected representatives are Republican, under a local party platform that advocates greater police involvement in immigration enforcement and observance of Confederate History Month. Before 2008, it had been forty years since Rock Creek residents voted for a Democratic presidential candidate.

The town might not seem like an obvious destination for immigrants. Yet it is, and the demographics of Rock Creek have changed considerably in the last thirty years. The four siblings ended up at Rock Creek High by way of their family's initial move from Iran to England and then later to the United States. Although the specific origins and intermediate locales are different for other immigrant families who have ended up in Rock Creek, this type of multistop migration journey is not uncommon. Residents of Rock Creek have not always appreciated the town's demographic changes. Rock Creek has three public high schools. Rock Creek High, which Ensie attends, is the newest, most prestigious, and whitest of the three. Although Rock Creek High, built in the late 1990s, is by no means the most posh or highly rated public school in the broader region, among the three high schools, it is the only one ranked in an annual list of the nation's "Top 200." It has the lowest proportion of students receiving reduced or free lunch and boasts the highest standardized test scores in the area. The frequent redistricting of neighborhood schools has instead funneled the newer diversity of the area to the other two public high schools. These majority-minority schools do not offer their students the same benefits as Rock Creek High, such as a wide range of advanced placement and college prep courses. Redistricting, however, can go only so far. Although the Rock Creek High student population is still two-thirds white, the remaining third are Asian, Latino, and African American in equal proportion.

Like other youth her age, Yasmin documents her day-to-day life in Rock Creek and at college across multiple social media platforms. Most of Yasmin's social media posts lovingly depict her home, faith, and political commitments. Her photos include a picture of her hands, adorned with "Allah" rings and beautifully lacquered fingernails, another holding a protest sign declaring "Education is a right not a privilege," and a selfie in front of a spray-painted mural of the Palestinian flag. Others are portraits or videos of her little sister Ensie: sitting in her pajamas at home on their parents' sofa playing the "Law & Order" theme on the setar (a long-necked, stringed Persian instrument) or posing with two fingers in a peace sign alongside a black-and-white poster of Yoko Ono and John Lennon. Though most of Yasmin's photos are unaccompanied by text, on a fall afternoon in 2012 after Ensie came home from school, Yasmin posted on Twitter with uncharacteristic anger: "Some kid called my high school aged sis 'Osama' today & mentioned that 'your family prob[ably] knows a lot about explosions huh.' This is wrong."

In this chapter I trace Iranian American interlocutors' racial experiences in schools: from elementary school, to middle and high school, and then to college. I examine the paradox of Iranian racialization to understand why it is that Iranian American youth, who are counted as legal whites in the United States, report persistent identity-based bullying by white peers and even teachers. As in the example of Ensie in Rock Creek, the intimidation and harassment of Iranian youth relies heavily on rhetoric drawn from the contemporary War on Terror. This harassment also targets other sites of difference like physical appearance, familial connections to Iran and the Middle East, Persian names, and varying degrees of bilingualism. Iranian American youth respond by allying themselves with other "racialized ethnicities" and by advocating in schools for formal recognition as students of color.[1] Drawing from time spent with Iranian teenagers and young adults in their hometowns, neighborhood schools, colleges, and universities, I offer empirical examples of the everyday forms of bullying and harassment reported by them across a range of US geographic contexts (e.g., northern, southern, heartland, coastal; urban, suburban, rural). These disparate school settings share one key characteristic: in them, second-generation Iranian Americans are habitually racialized as non-white.

Elementary School: "Shut Up, Terrorist"

Farzaneh is a sixteen-year-old in the Pacific Northwest, with long, wavy, dark hair. She had lived in the same small city her entire life and attended her public neighborhood schools throughout. We met up at a "block party" fund-raiser for her old elementary school. While we sat on a sidewalk curb and watched little kids run around, Farzaneh reflected on some of her most prominent memories from early childhood:

> At school, somehow the conversation always turned to Iran and the Middle East, even in elementary school, when it's just a bunch of kids repeating what they've heard adults say. Kids made comments to me, and I'm just like . . . mind-boggled: "People in the Middle East don't believe in freedom. I can't trust you because you're Iranian and your people are doing all these things to threaten our country. You're not trustworthy. You're

in a terror cell." My first reaction was "that's what you think of the ordinary people who live in Iran?!" before it even registered like . . . "Oh yeah, what do you mean, my people? Um, I was born here like you."

Farzaneh's experience of being bullied for her Iranian identity in early elementary school is typical among the stories shared with me. As shown in the previous chapter, Iranian American youth tend to grow up in households with strong emotional and cultural ties to Iran. These ties are characterized by complicated racial self-identifications informed, on the one hand, by a pervasive Aryan myth imported to the United States by first-generation parents and, on the other hand, by contradictory experiences of identity-based discrimination. These experiences aggregate dramatically once Iranian American children enter elementary school, most often in racially homogeneous, highly class-privileged neighborhoods. Historical narratives that undergird Iranian claims to whiteness or racial superiority are lost in translation in broader American institutions like school. They are also explicitly challenged by anti–Middle Eastern and anti-Muslim sentiment in media, national politics, and adults' attitudes that trickle down to school-age children. It is in elementary school that Iranian American youth learn firsthand that neither their legal "white" designation nor the "Persian pride" instilled through family and community insulate them from the racializing specter of the War on Terror and long-standing mores that tie "real American" identities to white, European-American bodies.[2] Unlike their families, elementary schools are typically the first major social institution to provide real-time feedback to Iranian American youth about the limits of their whiteness.

To more fully understand the stories of identity-based harassment that Iranian American youth share, it is important to consider the local environments in which they have grown up. Second-generation children born to immigrant parents who themselves moved to the United States in the last thirty to forty years grow up in gateway communities different from the teeming, turn-of-the-century urban landscapes that other white immigrants like the Germans, Irish, Italians, and Polish met on their arrival. Social scientists and scholars of immigration most frequently compare white Iranian immigrants to the United States against

European groups from the nineteenth and early twentieth centuries. The neighborhoods inhabited by today's Iranian Americans, however, are very different from the cities that received white immigrants one hundred years before. Excluding those in West Los Angeles, Iranians reside largely on the outskirts of gentrifying urban cores and more frequently make their homes in suburban and exurban communities whose racial composition is diversifying. Unlike the white immigrants who populated the ethnic enclaves of major cities a century ago, the majority of second-generation Iranian American youth in this study did not grow up within entire neighborhoods of other Iranian Americans. Scattered across majority-white, non-Iranian towns, the experiences described in this chapter highlight the extent to which Iranians are marked as "racial others" in contrast to their European American white counterparts who are classmates, authority figures, and others in the community.

I met Nazanin in Northgate, her suburban New England hometown; we drank hot chocolate in a popular Northgate High School hangout, a Starbucks built to look like a shabby-chic barn. Nazanin said she was the "weirdo" among her friends from elementary school who all hailed from generations of proud New England Irish and Italian American families. She related that it took several years of exposure to her family—their food, customs, Persian language, and her parents' accents—for her friends to feel comfortable coming over to her house after school, as she would frequently do at theirs. She remembers the early teasing of her friends as good-natured and mostly based on unfamiliarity: "You know, 'eww your food smells weird,' that kind of stuff. Shallow stuff that it's like, once they ate my mom's food, they were like, 'Oh never mind, this is tasty!'" She told me that September 11, 2001, was a major breaking point in the way she was perceived by her classmates. While the good-natured teasing of her friends in past years had not bothered her, by third grade she began experiencing harassment and bullying exclusively focused on her Iranian background and the perceived connection that she had to terrorism:

> People were really racist after 9/11. Before 9/11, I was the Persian cat, the Persian princess. Not just among my friends but in my whole town.

But after 9/11, I got some of it. At my school, which is mostly Italian and Irish, bullying was especially directed to the Lebanese kids and to me. I look Middle Eastern; I look like the images they show on TV. Friends and strangers would say to me, "Shut up, terrorist." They would make comments about Muslims that were really hard to hear. They did it to like, socially intimidate me. They would make snide comments when I'd defend myself. I'd be winning, but they would just completely shut the fight down with a comment like, "Okay, go bomb somewhere." And then they walk away like it's okay and like they've won. And it's unfair because what are you supposed to say to that? You can't be like, "Oh excuse me, I'm Iranian; I'm not the Saudi Arabian bomber you think I am." To them, it's the same thing. I was shunned by some of the white people at my school after that.

Despite her rich and early friendships with Irish and Italian American friends in Northgate, Nazanin never occupied a racially neutral status among her peers either before or after September 11. Her roles as the "weirdo" or "Persian cat" and later as a "Middle Eastern bomber" had their own racial legacy and were externally ascribed labels that distinguished her from the white youth in her area. Yet in Nazanin's own words, the nature of the bullying following September 11 took on an overtly negative and hurtful tone. The formal legal categorization of Lebanese, Iranian, or Saudi Arabian as "white" failed to register in the new War on Terror context of Northgate. Nazanin described her Iranian identity as not just "being" but also phenotypically "looking" Middle Eastern. After years of liminal whiteness in which she was labeled as an "off-white Persian cat," her ascribed identity took an unequivocally non-white and racially stigmatized turn.

As Farzaneh described and Nazanin remembered, as early as elementary school, talk of geopolitical unrest between the United States and Iran found its way to the classroom and schoolyard. Easy characterizations of a Middle Eastern "them" that threatened an American "us" provided fertile ground for the othering of Iranian-heritaged youth. Even in elementary school, Iranian American teenagers described having been called on to defend, explain, or contextualize the actions of supposedly "untrustworthy" and "freedom-hating" Iranians. As Farzaneh remembered, this geopolitically infused scrutiny followed her from the playground to outside school hours and into her social life at white peers' homes:

> Going to my *sefid* [white] friends' houses, the things their parents said to me, it's shocking. "Do they really hate us?" or "Are the women slaves to men [in Iran]?" or "Aren't you glad you were born here and not there?" And they know that I have family in the Middle East and Iran, but they feel no fear or problem with saying this to me.

In her suburban, majority-white school, Farzaneh became a totem for the status of women and girls in the Middle East. She remembers not knowing how to answer questions such as "Aren't you glad you were born here and not there?" She not only had never lived "there" but at the time had visited Iran only once. Speaking with me retrospectively, she was also upset that even as an elementary school student, she had been held accountable for complex geopolitics about which she had no special knowledge. By the time she was in high school, she began to doubt how well intentioned these questions actually were. She suspected that the rhetorical white American "here" belied a savior mentality that cloaked Islamophobia and global intervention as a selfless, righteous concern for women and girls in the Middle East. Now, when Farzaneh "answer[s] back that women in Iran participate in politics and go to college more than women in America, they just say I'm lying or that I'm brainwashed. Because of who I am, they don't trust my facts in an argument." Although with age, Farzaneh began to push back when forced into these types of arguments, they remained ones that she wished she had never been provoked into having at all.

When I first met eighteen-year-old Reza, he had just graduated from high school in a small New England town not unlike Northgate, where Farzaneh grew up. Although he was born in the States, he spoke Persian with fluent ease. This was all the more surprising given that, as he humorously and hyperbolically described, he grew up "where there are like five Iranians in the whole state." Reza said that his family's relative isolation made his parents even more committed to having their children speak Persian. He expressed being thankful for that commitment. We reconnected during his second semester at college, in a small liberal arts school in a big city:

> In elementary school, I got teased. It wasn't critical in my development, I don't think. It didn't break me. It was mostly in the hallways or the cafeteria or by the lockers. Places where there were other students, but no teachers or principals. One of the things I remember is, "I heard your uncle crashed into the Twin Towers," and "Your uncle is responsible," referring to Bin Laden. Or "How's Al Qaeda these days? What's their next plan?" Like I had inside information. At the time, it totally upset me, but I wouldn't react. I just kept my head down, waiting for it to die down.

A gifted athlete, Reza spent his summers off from college working as an emergency medical technician and coaching sports. He did not seem like the type of young man who would find himself the victim of consistent bullying, much less the type to "keep his head down" in the face of it. Yet Reza described habitual encounters with peer harassment directly related to his Iranian heritage. While Reza and others quietly endured bullying beyond the purview of teachers and principals in unmonitored corners of their schools, Sima was teased and taunted in the middle of class. As described later, it was in full view of a teacher who didn't intervene.

If you drive about thirty minutes on the Washington, D.C., beltway from Yasmin and Ensie's modest home in Rock Creek, you will reach Sima's house in the exclusive suburb of Brickvale. "It's a political city, D.C., and so everything in the schools I've gone to—the sports teams, the classes you take, the teacher rec[commendation]s—it's all pretty political," she explained. In a town that caters to diplomats and wealthy expatriate families, Sima's parents enrolled her in a French-immersion public elementary school. She recalled that the first few months were difficult. She had grown up speaking only Persian at home, and the adjustment to communicating with new people in two unfamiliar languages, French and English, was difficult. As early as elementary school, Sima had the distinct feeling that "being Iranian isn't cool" in the same way that her new schoolmates proudly discussed their Irish or French family backgrounds. One of her parents' most enduring stories about Sima's childhood was her plaintive question about her looks after she started attending the school. As Sima described, "I would say to them, 'Why can't I have red hair, freckles, and green eyes like [my best friend] Margaret? Am I always going to look like this?'" Despite her parents' best attempts to help Sima view her dark features as beautiful and unique in Brickvale, she felt plagued and alienated by them. By third grade, her eyebrows had grown into a single thick line over her wide eyes, and her anxieties about having a "unibrow" were grounded in direct, memorable experiences of bullying.

One incident stuck out in particular to Sima. As she progressed through fourth and then fifth grade, her feelings of insecurity about her "uncool" Iranian heritage and physical features began to recede as she learned that she could survive the taunting. She had even won some white classmates over, befriending them and hanging out with them after school. She knew she had "made it" when her friends' reactions to hearing Sima speak to her parents in Persian went from "What are you saying? Your language is so weird" to "Wow, you speak so fast! Can you teach me some bad words?" Sima even decided to run for president of her elementary school in fifth grade, something she would have never dreamed of doing before. She worked for weeks preparing her speech and outlining a campaign agenda based on an anti-bullying platform in which older students at their school would mentor and support younger students.

She recalled being nervous on election day, trying to keep a quiver from her voice as she rose in front of her fifth-grade class and delivered a speech she had rehearsed many times in front of the mirror. As she recounted this story to me in her brightly decorated bedroom six years later as an eleventh-grader, I could still detect the sense of accomplishment the achievement represented for her. To Sima, the achievement was not in winning an election—she ultimately would not win—but in choosing to render herself visible and legible in front of her fifth-grade class. She had light brown skin, curly hair, eyebrows and all, but her sense of accomplishment came from simply running for elected office.

At this point in our conversation, Sima took a deep breath. "I'm never going to forget this," she said, before describing what happened next.

She delivered her campaign speech and reeled with adrenaline and nerves. Then a boy named Tommy stood up at his desk to ask her a question. "In front of the entire class," Sima remembered, "he said, 'So if you win, are you going to make us say the pledge of allegiance like this?'" while taking his right hand from his heart and putting his index finger across his eyebrows. "He was making fun of my unibrow," she remembered. The room became electric to her as giggles erupted out of her classmates. All eyes were on Sima to see how she would react. No friends stood to defend her, nor did the teacher interject with any sort of admonition to Tommy. Sima describes her reaction as going into "fight mode," like she was floating above the classroom and watching herself react. She recalled turning her whole body toward him and feigning a strong, enthusiastic tone of voice. "Okay, Tommy, sure if you want! You want one of these?" At this, she mimicked the unibrow salute he had made just moments before. "Like, we can do this for you if you really want!"

Sima didn't remember what happened next. All she remembered is that she didn't win the election and Tommy moved away to Australia shortly thereafter. He bullied her throughout elementary school, so she was honestly relieved to see him go. Until, that is, she encountered him again in Brickvale for their junior year at a large public high school. She was shocked when he handed her what she described as a "five-paragraph essay" detailing and apologizing for the many ways he had bullied her about her appearance. Sima accepted his apology. "I was like, 'Ha ha, Tommy, don't worry about it, it's okay!'" Years after the fact, both Sima and Tommy remembered in detail the bullying that continued to knit them together even after he had moved halfway across the world.

The nature of Tommy's bullying of Sima, by honing in on her physical appearance and doing so in a public setting in front of an audience, resonated with stories other Iranian American youth offered. Micro-level interactions like Tommy's bullying draw on the ugly but pervasive perception that people like Sima, with foreign-sounding names and physical appearances that are coded as not just non-white but un-American, cannot represent fellow Americans in elected office. Here, it is also important to identify the negligent role of teachers and authority figures in such interactions. In Sima's situation the teacher allowed the bullying to continue without disagreement with the act or its content. As Sima herself described, she had built the necessary emotional reserves to defend herself by the time the election incident happened. Her resiliency was fortunate because in the majority-white schools that the plurality of my respondents attended, teachers and administrators either turned a blind eye to identity-based bullying or were perpetrators of bullying themselves.

By middle and high school, after experiencing years of powerlessness in exchanges with school officials, some of my interlocutors described forming new friendships with the rare few peers of color in their local settings. Whether to literally push back against bullying from white peers, or to seek refuge, interracial friendships became crucial sites of Iranian American survival in school settings dominated by white authority figures.

Middle and High School: "You Can't Go to the Teacher"

Sima shared another story, with her characteristic good humor and wit. This was a more recent incident, from just a couple years ago when she was in junior high:

> I remember my gym teacher in eighth grade called me "Perusian," and I was like, "What is Perusian?," and he was like, "Perusian!," and I was like, "No, it's either Peruvian or Persian. And I'm *Persian*, Iranian; I'm not Perusian!" And then he was like, "Well, *what's* the difference?" I said, "Well, Peruvian is from Peru and Persian is Iranian, and there's no such thing as Perusian, and you just made up a word." Iran and Peru are on two completely different continents with two completely different cultures. And he was like, "Oh . . . Persian is Iranian?," and he didn't even know. He had no idea. He goes, "They're the same thing?" And he didn't even say "Iranian." He goes "*Eye-rain-ian* and Persian are the same thing?" I say, "Yeah," and he says, "I thought Perusian and Peruvian were the same thing," and I say, "No. Again, Perusian doesn't

exist." I mean . . . he's a *teacher*. Is he messing with me? Can you be hired by our school district and really think that Perusia is a place?

As Iranian American youth graduate from elementary school and move on to middle and high school, teachers and other school authority fig-ures begin to feature more prominently in experiences of intimidation and unbalanced treatment. Some youth characterized the role of their teachers as "hands off" or "unaware" amid race-based bullying among students, while others spoke of being mistreated on the basis of their Iranian heritage by majority-white school authorities themselves. Such was the case for Amir, who at eighteen years old shared stories of his own troubles getting along with white faculty and administrators as a consequence of overtly racist punishment meted out against his older brother and students of color.

Although I initially met Amir in 2009 through his volunteer work at an Iranian American youth organization, it was not until two years later that I found myself sitting across from him in a park on a quiet summer afternoon. "It's kind of weird that I've never told anyone in the organiza-tion this story, because it kind of says a lot about me," he began. Preced-ing the 1979 Iranian Revolution, Amir's parents first moved to Canada, where Amir and his brothers were born in a multiracial neighborhood in London, Ontario. Five years later, their family moved to the United States. Amir started seventh grade in Woodward, a rural midwestern town, where 96 percent of his peers in junior high were white. Back in London, Amir's dark olive skin and light eyes had gone unremarked on. But in Woodward, things were very different. It was there, through micro-interaction, that Amir first learned how profoundly "not white" his new American peers found him.

White classmates called him "nigger" a few times during his first year at Woodward Junior High and "sand nigger" with a regularity that de-pressed him. Within a month "my anger issues were really getting bad," he told me, "because I was constantly ready to throw down for a fight. Then the thing with my brother happened. . . . It was the day after Bush declared war with Iraq." At this point, Amir trailed off and rapped his knuckles against the picnic bench before describing what happened next.

Shahram, Amir's older brother, was entering his senior year of high school when the family moved to Woodward. Not knowing anybody at his new school, he felt fortunate that two students he had met in the commons area, both second-generation immigrants themselves (one Pakistani, the other Ghanaian), were amenable to letting him sit with them. Only a couple minutes after sitting down with his potential new friends, Shahram looked up from his tray to find twenty or so white varsity football players surrounding their table. First, two of the young men began yelling at Shahram: "Sand nigger! Camel jockey!" "You America-hating motherfucker! Fucking terrorist scum!" Then another knocked his books and lunch off the table. Shahram sat in stunned silence while the rest of the football players egged on their teammates by chanting, "Fight! Fight! Fight!" A school security guard intervened and dispersed the crowd before the altercation could advance any further. Here, Amir interjected his own retelling of the story with a clarification about Shahram: "You need to know that my brother, he isn't like me. He's not a knucklehead. No anger issues. He's a gentle guy, he's a really intelligent guy. He just says to the officer, 'I want to report this to the school administration. I just got harassed because of my race. This isn't supposed to happen.'" As requested, the school resource officer took Shahram to see the assistant principal, Mrs. Murphy, who was in charge of discipline at Woodward. After listening to what happened, Mrs. Murphy—and here, many years later, Amir got visibly upset while recounting these events—wrote up Shahram for detention. She cautioned him that many of his classmates were concerned for the safety of their family members and friends serving in the military, and perhaps he should be more sensitive about how his Iranian heritage could trigger strong emotions at his new school. It wasn't until several days later that Shahram realized that although he had been sent to detention, none of the football players had been or would be punished for assaulting him.

Admittedly, I was disturbed by Amir's story about what happened to his brother—even more so once I returned home from our interview and located a report on the incident in the town's newspaper. In it Mrs. Murphy confirmed Amir's account and its aftermath, explaining that she tried to "make [Shahram] aware of how emotional" President Bush's announcement of an impending war with Iraq was in their local community. Shahram's Pakistani American schoolmate was quoted in the article as well. He pointed out the irony that this all took place during Woodward's participation in National Safe Schools Week, an event meant to inspire more inclusive and less violent campus climates.

While National Safe Schools Week addresses peer-to-peer aggression, in this case, it was instead an adult authority figure that most severely sanctioned the victim. To Amir and Shahram, the message was clear: Racial slurs and threats of violence were acceptable at Woodward, and their presence as Iranians during the War on Terror was not. In fact, it was enough to provoke white peers into committing a hate crime. Amir says that what happened to Shahram was a watershed moment in his own development; it exposed for him the paradoxical racial truth of what it means to be Iranian in America. From that point forward, he understood that "my kind of 'white' isn't the same as their 'white,' you know? Teachers, vice principals, they don't look out for minority kids. It made me bitter and angry." In Amir's experience, racial slurs were easily deployed against him and his brothers by white American peers and excused by white administrators, placing Iranian Americans clearly outside the boundaries of whiteness in the institutional setting of their school.

Upon moving to Woodward, Amir had been taunted by white peers who called him "sand nigger" and "nigger." The strong majority of my interlocutors report having been called the same or similar racialized slurs in school. These slurs possess long, well-known histories tying them to slavery and colonialism, two devastating macro-level racial projects separating white from non-white. The slurs also performed racially formative work at the high schools attended by interlocutors: in an uncomplicated way, they rendered Iranian identities and bodies outside the limits of whiteness. This exclusionary and racist boundary maintenance, which typically happened in front of classmates, also sometimes happened in plain sight of teachers and principals who ignored or excused it across a range of meso-level school settings. As another respondent, fifteen-year-old Keyvan, explained: "When it's the teacher who just stands by or is bullying you, you can't go to the teacher."

Iranian American youth are not completely isolated in schools, however. Recall that Roya's Mexican American friends "saved her from hating herself" and that Shahram's Pakistani American friend in Woodward, who was a witness to the harassment, later testified to a local newspaper of its irony during National Safe Schools Week. With or without other Iranians in their local communities, by the time they are in high school Iranian American youth usually have forged friendships with other immigrant youth and peers of color who were typically "more respectful" than white peers.

Choosing Social Sides: "I Went Over to Asians"

At age seventeen when I first spoke to her, Donya had been removing the hair from her legs, upper lip, and in between her eyebrows for about five years. She recalled starting to beg her parents for a pink "ladies" drugstore razor starting at age ten:

> In fifth grade, I'm like, "What the heck, why do I have really hairy legs?" I'm ten years old, and this is now a major concern in my life because the white kids are like, "You're so hairy!" It really brought my self-esteem down, all the bullying. Genuinely, I didn't know what to do with my life. I needed to be around other people who don't look like the standard. In my school, I went over to Asians.

Although interlocutors described varying degrees of teasing and bullying about their physical appearance and Iranian identities at their schools, they were not social isolates. Instead, they formed a variety of friendships with peers whom they viewed as both similar and dissimilar to themselves. Usually, after having refused (or failed) to modify or mute their Iranianness to blend in with white peers, some students like Amir forged alliances with non-white students from their broader neighborhood schools to fight back against the bullying. Others like Donya and Javad found commonalities in cliques of racialized immigrant youth who faced similar social exclusion in majority-white schools and neighborhoods.

Maryam, on the other hand, had maintained longer friendships with her majority-white peers than most of the Iranian American youth I interviewed. She was enrolled at a flagship university in the rural South when I interviewed her on a sunny summer afternoon. She had joined the Greek system in her freshman year and, as a result, become close friends with her all-white sorority sisters. Maryam had grown up in Shelburn, a wealthy white town of about sixteen thousand on the southeastern seaboard and attended Shelburn High. It was a "Top 100" high school in the nation and third-highest-ranked high school in the state. Maryam struggled with her Iranian identity at Shelburn High, though, and carried the insecurities she described developing there with her to college. For Maryam, who had been teased about her appearance, these insecurities were mostly expressed through internalized feelings of romantic undesirability.

> It was hard because I knew that no white guy would ever date me or touch me in high school because I was teased for how I looked. Being so dark, so hairy, I didn't look like a "Katie" or a "Britney." Even though I've had white boyfriends since starting college, it's a feeling of shame I still carry with me.

In spite of Maryam's struggles with feelings of physical unattractiveness in romantic relationships, both in high school and in college she had little trouble cultivating friendships with white students. She handily dealt with what she described as occasional good-natured teasing about Iran. Had Maryam successfully assimilated into mainstream white society? Seen through one lens she had successfully traversed majority-white spaces. She joined a predominantly white sorority at a southern state university and felt at ease around white friends who, she felt, treated her as an individual. In accordance with her white racial status and her privileged upbringing in white-majority spaces, what happened to Maryam was mostly as expected: she blended in. But Maryam was still acutely aware that when it came to one specific color line—the one around heterosexual romantic or sexual relationships with white men—she hovered somewhere at the limits of whiteness.

Javad, who in the previous chapter marveled at his Iranian family's fair skin, attended South Hempstead High, a public school that sends more than 90 percent of its students to four-year colleges. After breakfast, we took a walk around the neighborhood. Though he grew up surrounded by elite prep and boarding schools, Javad was pleased to have attended public schools throughout, where "we have *at least* a little bit of diversity." He shared that, since moving from Iran to the United States at age two, he had decided that his Iranian identity made him more Asian than white. He pulled a gloved hand out of his fleece jacket and pointed down the block:

> Have you heard of the book *Battle Hymn of the Tiger Mother*? They live here. Take a left on that road, and you'll find the author's house. Her kids go to the private school here, and the older one is my age. My girlfriend is Facebook friends with her because they're both Chinese. When I read the book, I hated it. I was so frustrated by the mom and how she treated her daughters. But I also had to laugh. Like, this is my life! And when I look at my group of friends, I mean, we are mixed with some white and some Asian, but even one of my white friends, her parents are Russian immigrants. We're all bonded by the fact that we are kids with foreign parents. On a scale of one to ten, American to Asian, my parents are about a seven "Asian." I'm like them. I'm considered as an outsider in America; I've been here since I was a baby, but I'm foreign.

Javad, like other Iranian American youth, recounted stories of bullying in relation to his identity. From his position at the limits of whiteness in a wealthy white-majority town, "Asian" was a binary reference point to "white" in his local context.[3] And within this context, he gave himself a "seven Asian." Javad, Maryam, and Amir were all navigating, in different ways, their "racialized ethnicities" as Iranian Americans.[4] Of course, the key paradox is that unlike their racialized peers, Iranians and other Middle Easterners are technically classified as white. Once they leave high school and enter college and university settings, second-generation Iranians continue to find their Iranian backgrounds racialized. From the limits of whiteness in their majority-white childhood neighborhoods, Iranian Americans nonetheless enter college eager to find new communities to join and new identities to claim.

College/University: "This Isn't Fair to Us White Kids!"

Several years ago, I shared an early-morning elevator ride with Pedram, a college junior at the same institution where I was earning my PhD. Though we didn't yet know each other, I suspected that we were both headed to the same introductory Persian class in the Department of Middle East Studies. Pedram and I were among twenty Iranian Americans enrolled in the class who could be categorized as "heritage learners." Ten of our classmates were not Iranian: six were Reserves Officers' Training Corps (ROTC) students, and another four were linguistics and political science majors, all of different ethnic and racial backgrounds.

Since 9/11, there has been an expansion of university classes like these through "critical language" Title VI monies from the Departments of State and Defense. Consequently, more Iranian American university students than ever before have the opportunity to enroll in formal Persian-language classes. These courses typically draw a variety of students: (1) Iranian Americans, for whom a college Persian class is often the first opportunity to be in a classroom alongside co-ethnic peers; (2) linguistics majors interested in the Indo-European language family; (3) social science/area studies majors who need the course for academic and professional work; and (4) ROTC students who receive both college credit and military stipends for enrollment.

Heritage learners are usually semilingual; think of Spanglish, or in this case, "Pinglish." In this particular classroom, even the least fluent among us could more or less respond to the directives of our first-generation immigrant parents: "Set the table," "Say hello to your grandfather," "Be careful!"[5] In spite of our shared ability to pronounce the more guttural Persian consonants and vowels as a consequence of proximity in our childhood homes, the full range of our heritage reasons for enrollment were far less uniform. Two students told me that they were using Persian to fulfill a foreign-language requirement for their global studies and political science majors. Five others were chemistry and biology majors who admitted enrolling for the assumed GPA bump it would add to their otherwise challenging "hard science" transcripts. The other twelve Iranian (and one Afghan) heritage learners were motivated to enroll as a consequence of second-generation desire, responsibility, and/or shame over their shaky Persian-language skills. As Pedram later told me, "It just gets embarrassing when you have to interrupt yourself all the time to ask your parents for the right word." For Pedram and the other heritage learners, the Persian classroom offered a promising way out of moments when the right word seemed just out of reach.

In contrast to heritage learners, second-language learners like ROTC students and linguistics majors are characterized by their lack of previously sustained contact with the language and culture being taught in the classroom. This creates what some education researchers have termed an "intimidation gap," where second-language learners are overwhelmed or frustrated by heritage learners' previous exposure to course material.[6] Yet quite rapidly in this introductory course (the only Persian class offered during this particular academic year), a second and separate intimidation gap emerged between self-declared white ROTC students and those they deemed non-white, which included all of the civilian and heritage learners.

Much of this two-way intimidation gap was established from the first day. Some heritage learners seemed uncomfortable and initially confused about why ROTC students were enrolled in their class—a class from their perspective that had been designed to strengthen their cultural identities and heritage-language skills. In contrast, some ROTC students looked to be uncomfortable and initially confused about why a class designed for military stipend and career advancement seemed overwhelmingly populated by students who already knew Persian. This boundary was compounded by the fact that the ROTC students and non-ROTC students were easily identifiable on the first day of class, as the ROTC students all wore non-military-issued "US Army" and "Marines" branded T-shirts, sweatshirts, or hats.

Over time, an impregnable boundary formed between the civilian students and the ROTC students. This was most clearly expressed through the students' social partitioning of the small classroom space.

From the first day ROTC students sat together at one end of the large conference table, farthest from the instructor. The seats offered good sight lines to the three frequently used chalkboards. The heritage learners and linguistics majors were intermingled in equal number along the long sides of the table or behind the long sides of the table in chairs without desks. They would balance their textbooks and notebooks on their knees and, at times, crane their necks to see the chalkboards. Even when ROTC students were absent or tardy, their preferred seats were left empty and non-ROTC students avoided sitting there.

While the heritage learners in the course likely contributed to an intimidation gap because of their familiarity with Persian pronunciation and conversational language, the ROTC students benefited from an intimidation gap due to the camaraderie of having previously known each other as well as their quasi-military status. Although never openly addressed in class, heritage learners and linguistics majors expressed dissatisfaction when ROTC students were disruptive and "not taking the class seriously." Two ROTC students owned up to this in private conversation. Most upsetting to the non-ROTC students was the way the ROTC students demonstrably expressed their disinterest. One non-ROTC linguistics major recalled, "The ROTC students would write on the board [in Persian script], and you couldn't at all tell what they were trying to write, which made me think they weren't trying, or maybe they wanted it to be really obvious that they weren't trying. They would bust out laughing during the Friday language labs." Several heritage learners noted that it was particularly hurtful that the expression of disinterest was most severe when ROTC students were asked to take Persian cultural traditions and customs seriously. White people actualizing their whiteness through the assertion of the inferiority of non-white cultural heritages and customs is a key component in what has been termed "laissez-faire racism," yet the locally constructed racial fault lines that rendered Iranian Americans as non-white in such a way would not be explicitly articulated until the second semester of the course.[7]

In honor of the approaching spring equinox, all students were asked for the first time to write prose for their homework assignment: two paragraphs summarizing the major activities and traditions surrounding *Nowruz* (Persian New Year). From the far end of the table where ROTC students sat, three ROTC learners in a rare, but exceptionally clear racial tone, expressed anxiety over the assignment:

ROTC student 1: This isn't fair to us *white* kids!
ROTC student 2: Yeah!
ROTC student 3: We didn't grow up with it! So not fair!

The first student's comment, the second student's affirmation, and the third's explanation were an expression of the intimidation gap that non-heritage learners felt. They did not, in the moment, realize that the instructor simply expected all students to consult Wikipedia. But their explicit reference to racial categories was equally telling. Following this dialogue, nearly all of the Iranian American heritage learners stared downward at the table while the ROTC students' facial expressions ranged from indignant to sheepish. Most interesting was that under the newly verbalized racial logic of the classroom, one of two linguistics majors— a self-described Chicano with no special advantage in Persian, and the other, who identified as from mixed African American and white descent, also without "heritage" advantage—were cast together with the Iranian and Afghan students. Perhaps even more notable was that the ROTC student who yelled out "Yeah!" in affirmation was a light-skinned Latino, cast here as white.

The classroom's micro-interactions expose the complexity and interplay of perceived and actual racial identities: a technically white population of Iranian students were locally understood as non-white by their mostly European American military counterparts; a Chicano man and mixed-race woman were cast as having an unfair advantage in Persian cultural traditions because they were non-white; and another Latino man was cast as white due in some part to his ROTC status. This was not the first time that heritage learners noticed that their classification as "white" did not afford them a comparable social whiteness as that of the European Americans. But for a few, this was the first time the white/non-white racial distinction was articulated so clearly in a classroom. It is perhaps not surprising that the explicit racial status of Iranian students would shift to "non-white" in a critical language class, where "liminal soldiers" like ROTC students come into contact with a heritage-speaking population who can be, however explicitly or implicitly, imagined as domestic stand-ins for foreign others.

Already aware of the limits of their whiteness, Iranian American college students adopt grassroots strategies to further their claims for recognition of their on-the-ground non-white racial status. Across a wide swath of university contexts, second-generation Iranian Americans have banded together with other "invisible" Middle Eastern minorities to petition for and ultimately form Middle Eastern resource centers. In one significant case, they have secured recognition under a new, non-white racial category called "SWANA: Southwest Asian and North African."

Pan-ethnic Campus Space:
The Case of a Middle Eastern Resource Center

Azzi, age eighteen, was a freshman at a private university in Southern California when I first met her. In the consent form for this project, I had introduced myself as a researcher interested in learning more about identities of Iranian American youth, inclusive of race. I had barely turned on the tape recorder before she shared her honest opinion about race:

> Middle Eastern is considered white, which *always annoys* me. So if there's a space to write in, I would *always* write "Iranian" or "Middle Eastern," and I *always, always* if someone asks me where I'm from, I say "I'm Iranian." I was born and raised here [in the United States], but I would never say "white" or "American." That's *not* what people are looking for when they ask where I'm from, and it's not what I feel that I am. If there was some kind of box . . . there should be some kind of box.

In the last half century, colleges and universities across the United States have become sites where ethno-racial identities—political, cultural, and social—are forged and refined by young people of color. After the high point of civil rights movement activism, the formation of ethnic studies departments and co-curricular programming was the direct result of campus activism that challenged de jure and de facto racism.[8] In the years since, campuses with sizable and diverse Muslim populations have faced increased pressure to acknowledge and redistribute resources to meet these students' needs.[9] Apart from these important programs, efforts to build official departments and programs in the study of Middle Eastern diasporas and Middle Eastern Americans have been mostly unsuccessful.[10] But even on campuses where permanent faculty and long-term academic commitments have yet to be sought or secured, some Middle Eastern students and their allies have successfully established permanent spaces for social and cultural congregation.

As demonstrated previously, Iranian American college students often turned to Persian-language classrooms for curricular and social needs. Beyond these courses, funded by and at least partially meant to serve national defense agendas, Iranian-heritaged students established an intimate sense of place and ownership by successfully gaining institutional support for Iranian student organizations and Middle Eastern Resource Centers. I present views and perceptions from one such center to describe how an "inherited nostalgia" for the homeland operated as a nimble and successful tool to make legible the feelings of ethno-racial difference that Iranians and other Middle Eastern American students articulate in university settings.[11]

The Iranian Student Group at one such university holds its weekly meetings in the campus Middle Eastern Resource Center, which is affectionately referred to by students as the "MERC." It is a thirty-five- by forty-five-foot room with almost twenty-foot-high ceilings, situated between the Asian Resource Center and the Black Resource Center in a student union building. At the time of research, a large imitation Persian carpet dominated the center of the room, deep plum, beige, and gold, with a floral pattern reminiscent of the Aubusson or Louis XIV style often found in the homes of Iranians in Iran and in diaspora. Richly hued pillows and textiles were draped over most of the furniture in the room. A small stereo sat on a low desk next to two Persian music CDs: Googoosh's *Greatest Hits* (a compilation of the superstar's biggest "oldies" hits from prerevolutionary Iran) and a mix of contemporary Top 40–style pop by the Los Angeles–based duo Kamran and Hooman. On the walls were reproduction prints of Persian miniature paintings and several full-color posters of archaeological and historical sites. A calendar featuring Islamic minarets was open to the wrong month (October, "Ramadan/Shawwal"). Under the calendar rested a stack of handouts for a website called IranianSingles.com.

In the darkest corner of the room, there were two large unlocked display cases containing an assortment of historical-looking artifacts: miniature painted boxes, a copper pot, a decorative mirror, small goblets, a tablet, and a shisha pipe. Above the cases was a poster titled "Iran," a dusky photograph of three human figures, outsized and overshadowed by the prehistoric carving they examined. When I was there, two women undergraduates, from the Lebanese Club and the Iranian Student Group, took notes while studying at a large table. I asked what they were working on, and they smiled and explained an upcoming Model Arab League simulation for their global studies course.

As I sat in the center of the room, cataloging its contents for my field notes, two young men, who appeared to be white, poked their heads in: "Hey, we're from the Middle East! Let's study here!" one said, giving me a mischievous look. "No we're not!" the other hissed, awkwardly tugging his friend. The global studies students continued reading from their books and did not bother to look up.

What sense can be made of the myriad references to an original past embodied within the Iranian Student Group's meeting space at the MERC? The very old was represented by the pseudo artifacts in the glass cases and the draping of textiles and photographic images of historical sites. They sat in juxtaposition to the present day, represented by the Persian-language pop music and advertisements for an Iranian American dating website. The interplay between old and new as embodied in the physical space of the MERC possessed special meaning in its second-generation context. The Iran poster, in particular, engendered a poignant and disarming experience: staring at others who were staring at a relic from the past. These decorations, taken as a collective whole, were a nostalgic display of Iranian knowledge that transcended spatial and temporal boundaries. By channeling the weight of history and certain larger-than-life enduring symbols of Iranian history, second-generation Iranian American college students, who may not have found what they were looking for in a Title VI–funded Persian-language class, called on nostalgia and authenticity to craft a pan-ethnic home with other Middle Eastern organizations at the university.[12]

Although the MERC was open to all members of the university community, the incident in which two young men ducked in and quickly ducked out ("No, we're not [Middle Eastern]!") highlighted the symbolic boundaries of the space. Both the name of the center and the local knowledge produced there set it apart from places that are often framed as "racially neutral" in college campus environments.[13] It made sense, then, that the photographs, souvenirs, and CDs strewn about the MERC facilitated an exchange of unspoken nostalgia and longing among the second-generation youth who spent time there. When I asked eighteen-year-old freshman Taraneh what she thought of the MERC, she said, "It's so cozy. It looks like home, like the place where a lot of us grew up. I feel a kind of pride when I look around the room. And it's a place where I know there will be someone I recognize, no matter what time of the day." Taraneh, as a second-generation Iranian American, drew from her personal experience and familial history when she explained the utility of the MERC in her campus life. Behrooz, a sophomore, explained his appreciation for the MERC this way: "I can blast Persian music [here] without worrying what people will say, like in the dorms. This is a place where we can share our history and tell our history to ourselves. If we don't remember, who will?"

The MERC offered space for Middle Eastern–heritaged second-generation youth to more freely express the visual and auditory dimensions of their Iranian American identities. Iranian American students explained their dedication to consuming Persian-language music and availing themselves of nostalgic, expressive material culture from Iran and the Middle East. As Taraneh later remarked, it felt like a way to "support Iran and its place in the global system." Beyond simple nostalgia, then, these cultural formations gesture to an Iranian American subjectivity that rejected normative ethno-racial assimilation into the majority population. College was the first time in most of their lives where interlocutors felt they could exert an enhanced degree of choice in their identities and commitments away from their families and neighborhoods of origin. Nostalgia intertwined with political consciousness to produce a new and unanticipated experience of their Iranian American identities. These identities were defined by their pan-ethnic distance from mainstream whiteness and their symbolic reference to an Iran far from their everyday circumstances.

From White/Caucasian to SWANA

In recent years, Iranian American college students have banded together with other Middle Eastern American peers commonly categorized as "white/Caucasian" to advocate for an elective racial category on their university demographic forms, usually under the banner of SWANA. Institutional and national efforts to break out of the "white box" have been in play since Middle Eastern Americans were first formally placed in the "white" category in 1978 by the federal Office of Management and Budget (OMB). These national efforts found renewed energy in the lead-up to the 2010 census and are again up for significant revision for the 2020 census. Until this point, Arab, Iranian, and Middle Eastern advocacy organizations have seen their requests to add an "Arab/Middle Eastern" category to federal racial and ethnic categories rejected in every major review cycle.

Beginning in 2013 and for the first time in its 150-year history, the nation's preeminent and seventh-largest public university system, the University of California (UC), has formally recognized Iranians and other SWANA populations as students of color. Across the last decade of American intervention in the Middle East and increased domestic surveillance of Middle Eastern and Muslim-identified American residents, this is an especially rich development in the history of US higher education. During the UC application process, Iranian American students now have the option to self-identify on university demographic forms under a primary

"SWANA" ethno-racial category. Previously, Iranian and other Middle Eastern–heritaged students were funneled into any number of subcategories ("Middle Eastern," "North African," "other") that were later subsumed into a "white/Caucasian" racial group. Thus, institutional- and system-level statistics regarding Middle Eastern enrollment, achievement, and treatment at UC were never disaggregated from those of white European Americans. Consequently, due to their white racial categorization, Middle Eastern–heritage students had been unable to access educational resources, faculty and administrative hiring lines, student recruitment and retention support, and other programmatic funding reserved for diversity and equity purposes. In an interview with the *Daily Cal*, UC Berkeley's campus newspaper, an Iranian American student activist, Sahra Mirbabaee, noted that, under the old UC designation, "I have to put myself in a category where I don't fit in. I have dark skin so I don't think it's correct for [me] to be in the category of white, because it doesn't represent how I'm perceived by society."[14] The newly adopted "SWANA" category represents one possible outcome for the reconciliation of the racial paradox described throughout this book: to officially recognize Iranian and other Middle Eastern students like Sahra as racial minorities and extend applicable resources to them.[15]

How did these student advocates successfully contest their white racial classification? Across separate UC campuses, student activists formed a SWANA Campaign Committee to petition their campus governance bodies to recognize the contradictory racial status of Middle Eastern students as "legal whites" who, despite "invisible minority" status, remained nonetheless "hypervisible in the American imagination as an omnipresent threat."[16] Town hall–style meetings and brainstorming sessions with Middle Eastern student organizations across the UC system determined a list of thirty-two ethno-national subcategories to be included under the new racial category.[17] Some 140 student organizations from across the UC system were recruited, including those representing students of color, to pledge solidarity via a "statement of support." Following the grassroots determination that "'Middle Eastern' was problematic due to the colonial and Orientalist origins of the term," "SWANA" was found preferable in that it emphasized "the geographic boundaries of the region."[18] A resolution, spearheaded by two young women (an Armenian-Egyptian American student and an Iranian American student, both at UC Berkeley) was drafted and ultimately approved by the separate student government bodies at Berkeley, Davis, Irvine, Los Angeles, and San Diego. It affirmed the creation of a new ethno-racial category. Among the many justifications the activists provided within the resolution document was the following statement:

> Whereas because of the lack of representation in the United States, the Middle Eastern community has formed into an "invisible minority," or a minority group that faces issues similar to other minority groups, but does not receive recognition as such . . . and due to this status as an "invisible minority," the Middle Eastern community is often excluded from programs centered on diversity and multicultural communities on a national and institutional level.[19]

In keeping with the testimony of the youth in this book, the language and claims of the UC SWANA resolution were a direct response to contradictory and politically frustrating experiences as "legal whites" and everyday racial others. On May 2, 2013, UC president Mark Yudof confirmed that "SWANA" would be, from that point forward, adopted in the race/ethnicity portion of the systemwide UC application. SWANA youth, mostly second-generation immigrants, had successfully banded together with the help of their peer allies at UC to pull off a large-scale feat of pan-ethnic racial recategorization that their generational predecessors were not able or interested to accomplish. In the words of the student advocates themselves, "We no longer have to be an 'invisible minority' in the eyes of the UC system. We no longer have to assimilate into a group of people we truly do not feel like we identify with. We are here, and we will be counted."[20]

Conclusion

From elementary school through college, Iranian Americans are told by peers, teachers, and other authority figures in schools that neither their legal racial status nor their parents' racial origin stories translate to substantial inclusion into mainstream whiteness. Instead, as children, Iranian Americans are continuously reminded of the limits of their whiteness through teasing about their physical features, "weird" names, bilingualism, and "untrustworthy" origins. They navigate their social worlds in ways most similar to those of other non-white racialized youth.

What happens to the racial contradictions that define second-generation Iranian life in the United States when youth "return home" for visits to Iran? In Chapter 5, I track their transnational movements as in-between people moving through in-between spaces. Here, common concerns about being too Iranian for customs agents and security personnel in the most common layover stops of Amsterdam, London, and Frankfurt (where Iranians and other Middle Easterners have long been the primary racial referents in political debates around assimilation and culture) are counterposed against not being Iranian enough for one's extended family in the home country. A collective consciousness about the racializing process of international travel becomes part of the cultural currency for Iranian American youth, as they share stories of excitement and disappointment after coming face-to-face with their "inherited nostalgia" for the home country.

CHAPTER 5

TO THE HOMELAND

ASA, A SOPHOMORE at a midsize rural public university in the western United States, has been to Iran twice with her family. When they visit, they spend the entire summer and stay with relatives such as her grandmother, who lives in Tehran when not living with Asa's family in the States. Summers in Iran were far from her mind, though, as she watched TV on a Sunday morning in the living room she shares with two roommates.

Watching *Family Feud* with her roommates is part of Asa's Sunday ritual. When I asked her to explain, she said, "The living room is our destressor space. We don't do work there. We'll use On Demand to just pick a couple random episodes of *Law & Order* or *Family Feud* and destress before studying." On this particular Sunday, she was recovering from a "busy and weird" weekend helping friends campaign for student elections and driving two hundred miles home and back to see her family and a large group of younger cousins of various ages. Now curled up on the couch, settling into her destressing mode, Asa absentmindedly checked her phone while *Family Feud* host Steve Harvey posed a question to the contestants, the Mayfield and Flammia families: "Name a place where no one wants to go."

As Asa recalls, "Part of what's fun about watching the show is guessing along with the contestants. And I guessed the first few 'places no one wants to go' . . . 'hell,' 'work . . . '" Still splitting screens between the television and her phone, Asa remained vaguely aware that the Flammias earned their third strike with an incorrect answer so the Mayfield family could go for the steal. She heard the Mayfields correctly guess the fourth most popular answer, "funeral/cemetery," to steal eighty-two points from the Flammias and end the round. But with two unguessed answers still on the board, Asa's attention snapped back to the television when she heard Harvey read the first answer: "I looked up from my phone when I heard 'Iran' because it was just so weird. There aren't usually answers like that on *Family Feud*. My next thought was, 'This is messed up!' So I rewound it and watched it again. And then I paused it." From her vantage point on the couch, and still holding her phone, Asa uploaded a photograph of the frozen TV frame to Instagram and Facebook. It showed the board in full, with a caption she added: "The question was 'name a place where no one wants to go'" (see Image 8).

As a seasoned fan and longtime viewer of the show, Asa was familiar with the conventions of *Family Feud*; as it is with *Law & Order*, watching it for her is a way to relax because its structure is entirely formulaic. On *Family Feud* the "survey of one hundred Americans" draws from everyday, popular knowledge for its content, with the host interjecting with PG-rated sexual innuendo for laughs. So it was this particular episode's

IMAGE 8. "Name a place where no one wants to go" (2015). Source: Screenshot of Facebook/Instagram social media post by Asa.

inclusion of two real place-names—unconventional for the typical light-hearted jokiness of *Family Feud*—that startled Asa out of her repose on the couch. And it was the inclusion of "Iran" as one of the real place-names that, for Asa, merited posting on social media. Replayed in syndication and On Demand, and archived on Asa's Facebook and Instagram pages, "Iran" and "Siberia" exist in perpetuity alongside "jail" and "hell" as places no one—or at least no one surveyed by *Family Feud*—wants to go.

I tracked down the episode (original air date September 11, 2012) to see for myself. Siberia was perhaps on the list as shorthand, at least in everyday American English, for a place considered remote, undesirable, and punishing, harkening back to its relationship to Russia as a penal colony where political prisoners were disappeared. In colloquial talk "Siberia" (the place) tends to be deterritorialized from its geographic location and, for the most part, removed from political significance. We use "Siberia" (the idea) to refer to a place found undesirable because of how few people live there and how remote or bleak it appears. Siberia is an emblematic signifier because it can be, at once, both any place and not any particular place.

"Iran" does not work as informal shorthand in quite the same way; it is the opposite of deterritorialized. Apart from any unscientific *Family Feud* survey, today 80 percent of Americans hold a "mostly" or "very" unfavorable opinion of Iran.[1] Every presidential administration's paradigmatic stance toward Iran since Jimmy Carter means that Iran does not operate in a symbolic sphere apart from its empirical, geographic location as what policy makers call the Middle East's universal joint. Unlike Siberia, Iran is not a euphemism for something else; it is not shorthand that will stand in for *any* undesirably remote place. In fact, Iran is a "place where no one wants to go" precisely because of *where* it is and because of *who* lives there. Of course, *what* Americans say about Iran—and how Iranian American youth interpret it—is far more complicated.

Second-generation Iranian American youth are, for the most part, born into homes where Iran is romanticized while growing up in a country where, with few exceptions, Iran is stigmatized. As a result youth like Asa are socialized to think about their ancestral homeland in contradictory, confusing, and contentious ways: Iran is a place where everyone wants to go; Iran is a place where no one wants to go. Throughout this book, young people's experiences have been located materially on American soil while culture, memory, affect, and knowledge have moved between Iran and the diaspora. The analysis up to this point has thus privileged the racialized Iranian American body as a site of material and symbolic information within its American context. This chapter conceptually follows young people as they leave the United States and travel to Iran. This is an experience that a majority of research participants have had at least once in their lives.

I focus on how young Iranian Americans negotiate international travel between homes. By centering their bodily experiences, a core, intersectional tension is revealed: The class-privileged ability of Iranian American youth to experience travel to the "homeland" is also mediated by racialized and gendered concerns. To avoid or mitigate scrutiny, youth and their families craft a variety of strategies to first navigate international airports and, later, unfamiliar everyday settings in Iran. Depending on age, for example, it is sometimes easier—or riskier—to be masculine or feminine in motion. Depending on the situation, it is sometimes easier to present oneself as *just* Iranian or *just* American, depending on who is looking. It is through these embodied micro-interactional experiences that youth continue to wrestle with how to be Iranian, how to be American, how to be neither, and how to be both on a trip home.[2] Thus, for second-generation Iranian Americans, Iran is not "a place where no one wants to go" but the one place they desperately *want* to go, a place that often disappoints as much as it delights.

The travel experience to Iran begins with early and specialized preparations. In these initial stages, widely circulated, impression-based knowledge from everyday sources such as television and casual conversations within American-based social networks shape some of the expectations youth bring to their impending trips. Simultaneously, the layers of bureaucratic red tape that mediate travel between Iran and the United States necessitate that youth and their families seek coordination and assistance from a variety of diverse players; these include relatives near and far, diasporic travel agents who assemble documents and itineraries, and seemingly unrelated groups like the Embassy of Pakistan in Washington, D.C. Concerns over fulfilling *sarbazi* (mandatory military service) place restrictions on Iranian American boys and young men, impacting their ability to become the effortlessly fluent, transnational subjects that some long to be. After preparations have been made, the actual act of travel also relies on gendered and raced interpretations of risk and security, as well as the ability to fluidly oscillate between Islamic modesty and Americanized secularity. In preparing for travel, Iranian American young men, in particular, exercise caution and creativity to manage their appearances.[3] They are well aware that security agents like Transportation Security Administration (TSA) officers draw on professional training that despite any presumption of rationality, is steeped in racial and cultural stereotypes to assess who can proceed without impediment. Once in Iranian airspace, securitized scrutiny turns more acutely to girls and women, who must adjust their appearance to conform to mandatory hijab. Following touchdown, youth of both genders describe necessary shifts in identity management that cut across on-the-ground categories of class, race, gender, sex, and nationality in Iran.

Before Departure: The Hype

I first met sixteen-year-old Farhad at the end of his tenth-grade year: gregarious and sympathetic, a physical and emotional embodiment of the "gentle giant." He wore his hair cut close, face clean shaven, with kind, dark eyes contrasted against the burnt-sienna of his skin. Six years later, when he was a graduating senior in college, I asked him to reflect on the summer trips he had taken to Iran as a youngster: "I never understood what a big deal it was. Something that reminds me what a big deal it is, though, is my peers, roommates, people I live and I work with. They can't believe I've been [to Iran]. They see Iran as a violence-stricken, backward, threatening country that doesn't have its shit together." Typically, youth like Farhad who are planning to travel to Iran experience "the hype," an emotionally charged mix of excitement, anticipation, and worry. As another interlocutor described it, the hype is not just about *going* to Iran but also the complex process of *getting there*. The hype is catalyzed by a myriad of sources. One source comes from non-Iranians who draw on media images, anecdotes, and commonplace understandings of foreign policy to express surprise at their Iranian American peers' travel plans. Second-generation youth who have little firsthand experience in Iran are exposed to the same media depictions of the country as their American peers and must wade through this knowledge to make sense of their identities and their impending trips.

In contrast to the negative hype about Iran, youth also hear a considerable degree of positive hype from parents, especially about their prerevolutionary lives there. These nostalgic stories of the middle- or upper-class pleasures of growing up in Iran paint a very different and more accessible picture of the country. Their first-generation immigrant parents' stories include recollections of desire and coming of age in pluralistic cities like Tehran, Isfahan, and Shiraz and road trips on holidays to the storied *shomal*, northern Iran's shoreline on the Caspian Sea. For second-generation youth, these stories can cohere into a cosmopolitan and politically deterritorialized narrative, creating what I call a rose-colored *inherited nostalgia*.[4] As a result, parents' wistful memories create an imaginary portrait of life in Iran, without the suffering and deprivations of war or the losses of diaspora. In reality, youth know that present-day Iran is different from the Iran of their parents' stories, but the anticipation they feel about walking the same streets mentioned in their parents' celebratory stories functions as positive hype nonetheless.

This optimistic version of the hype is also buttressed by first-person testimonials from fellow co-ethnic peers about what Iran is like today. Peers who have recently visited the country report back about their adventures and triumphs: stories of hard-earned travel bona fides like drag racing down dark city streets in the backseat of a cousin's car while ironically clutching a can of Delster (a locally brewed, nonalcoholic beer), or heading out for early-morning vats of steaming *kaleh pacheh* (boiled sheep's head and hooves) at hole-in-the-wall breakfast spots, or scouring bookstores to find and photograph the most clever, or incomprehensible, examples of the Islamic Republic's editing and censorship. Within peer networks, these experiences are a form of cultural currency, and the anticipation of bringing this experiential capital back to the States also adds to the positive hype. Through their Iranian parents' and peers' stories, soon-to-travel youth are infused with optimism, excitement, and anticipation. Other recurring themes on the positive side of the hype include the promise of improved facility with the Persian language; personally meaningful pilgrimages to sites like the tomb of Hafez in Shiraz or Imam Square (Naqsh-e Jahan) in Isfahan; tearful reunions or unifications with family; and—among the most coveted and memorable—interactions with new friends, usually same-aged young Iranians at the farthest rings of one's social circles (e.g., the friends of same-aged cousins). But sometimes just the act of getting to Iran can bé enough to catalyze hype, as explained by Farhad:

> I think my biggest bragging right wasn't that I had seen anything specific but that I had even been there. Like, there was an assumption from our family friends who had wanted to go to Iran but hadn't been able to, like for paperwork reasons or personal reasons, that hadn't gone back, and they were fascinated and amazed that I had.

Gender also mediates the sense of hype that youth describe. For girls this often resulted in a tension between the promised pleasures of travel to Iran—a long-sought sense of belonging, an answer to haunting questions about one's origins—and non-Iranians' concern about women's corporeal safety. Behnaz, a seventeen-year-old girl, explained it this way: "On one shoulder were my Iranian [American] friends, other [second-generation] kids who had been [to Iran] saying, 'This is going to be the most life-changing experience you've ever had,' and then American friends saying things in a kind of joking voice like, 'Don't get lashings or stoned while you're over there.'" For girls, a tension between positive and negative hype had to do with perceptions of safety. Girls did not feel especially safe either in the United States or in Iran and were offended when their non-Iranian friends imagined otherwise. For boys, a different dueling tension between positive and negative hype had to do largely with Iran's mandatory military service and how to avoid it while moving between the two countries.

Though the specific tensions are different for boys and girls—and their strategies for managing the tensions are thus different as well—the ins and outs of travel, such as documentation and passports, impact how diasporic citizens of both genders prepare for their travels to Iran.

On a practical level, special travel sanctions levied by the United States prohibit American carriers from operating in Iran, making direct flights to Iran impossible from American airports. This prohibition thus requires American-based travelers to fly to Iran with international carriers and to book itineraries that include a layover in a place not under US diplomatic sanction. Frequent warnings from the Department of State about travel to Iran and the broader Middle East are exacerbated by decades of long-standing and uneven media coverage of American-led wars that have produced mass social instability in the broader region. Thus, diasporic travelers to Iran rely on unofficial knowledge of the bureaucratic obstacles as well as practical methods by which to avoid trouble while abroad. Preparing to navigate these complex international rules and systems adds urgency to the hype. Iranian American peers and elders who have traveled to Iran or returned more recently trade information about travel conditions and strictures. Accessing this hidden co-ethnic knowledge is important for youth, helping them balance out the warnings they hear in non-Iranian circles.

Before Departure: Paperwork

I met up with Pasha, a compact and muscular athlete who rarely strayed from his personal uniform of basketball shorts and short-sleeved T-shirts, for a conversation that was supposed to be about the experience of visiting family in Iran. Pasha's thoughts on the matter turned instead to an accounting of the specific practices that shape *how* he travels to Iran. "Going to Iran is not like, 'Oh, I'm Italian and I'm going to Italy,'" he explained. "Like, I need a separate [Iranian] passport to get there. Like, you have to be conscious of so much."

Second-generation youth who traveled to Iran typically did so using two separate passports: Iranian and American. This is a consequence of the lack of diplomatic relations between the two nations. The need for two passports also symbolized the duality of youth's identities in transit: a metaphoric and literal "crossing over" must happen to move between their homes. Acquiring both passports is a complex process that also belies an easy claim to either American or Iranian citizenship. Neither Iran nor America recognizes dual citizenship and, in practice, both governments claim the holder of their passport as theirs and theirs alone.

Second-generation youth born in the United States benefit from jus soli, automatic American citizenship based on the location of their birth and the subsequent ability to travel with relative ease on an American passport. But due to the lack of official diplomatic relations between the United States and Iran, they are unable to go to Iran with their American passports without special provisions.[5] Options include obtaining a travel visa, which is facilitated through the Pakistani embassy in Washington, D.C., a private guide, or tour group or under the authorized supervision of an Iranian family member or friend. The process can take anywhere from two weeks to months, and the Iranian tourist visa, the most commonly offered form of authorization, is good for only thirty days of travel before needing to be renewed.

Given these significant limitations, there is a work-around solution that—if one qualifies—makes the process much easier. Iranian Americans born in Iran (first- or 1.5-generation immigrants) and second-generation youth with an Iranian-born father qualify for their own Iranian passport, even in diaspora.[6] Thus, traveling with both passports is considered the preferred arrangement for Iranians living abroad and is the predominant way that the youth from my sample traveled to Iran. In this scenario, they used an American passport to exit the United States and to enter a transitionary layover airport—most typically in Amsterdam, Dubai, Frankfurt, or London. Now outside US airspace, they then used their Iranian passport to board the flight departing for Iran, which they also used at entry and exit in Iranian airports. This passport swapping while in transit was common knowledge and unremarkable to Iranian Americans who traveled to the homeland, but it was often a source of fascination and surprise for non-Iranians. As Farhad described, "Up until age fourteen I was on my dad's passport, and my sister was on my mom's. I have dual passports now. It's a bragging point for sure, like I will always use it during ice breakers in college, like Two Truths and a Lie [a party game], people always say, 'No way!' and don't believe me."

As Farhad went on to describe, the process of obtaining an Iranian passport required new passport photos that specifically conformed to the standards of the Iranian government. For these photos, Iranian American girls covered their hair more conservatively than the relatively flexible covering typically seen on urban Iranian streets. In line with the formality of the document itself, passport photos required a strict interpretation of proper hijab and an expressionless, closed mouth. For boys, in their passport photos the expectation was to project sternness. Most were not used to this. Farhad explained both of these gendered demands:

> We always had to make sure our passports were up to date, and the first sequence most recently was to get our photos done at Costco. My dad got in a fight with my sister about not showing too much hair and dressing appropriately in "muted" [quote gesture with hands] colors, and my dad telling me not to smile with my teeth, to be really serious in my photo.

Such restrictive self-presentations sometimes felt odd to second-generation youth, but for their parents, the act of taking passport photos was an opportunity to begin to softly introduce them to the normative expectations of appropriate public behavior once they were in Iran.

Far more restrictive is the issue of age, which complicates boys' travel plans in a serious way. Those with Iranian citizenship via parentage, even if they have never lived in Iran, are technically eligible for mandatory military service. The minimum nonvoluntary age for young men to be drafted into the Iranian *sarbazi* is eighteen; thus, entering Iran as an "Iranian" with an Iranian passport activates this issue. As Farhad prepared to graduate from college soon and move out of the dormitories, he figured that a trip to Iran at this exact juncture of his life would be ideal, but the threat of military service constricted his choice:

> Right now, I am limited in my ability to go back. I would have to pay off my *sarbazi* somehow. It really sucks that I can't apply the knowledge

I have now, from taking classes in college to learn about Iranian history, to finally understand the political situation there . . . after everything I know about Iran and about myself now, this is when I would get the most from going. And I can't.

A few means of evasion have emerged in compulsory soldiering: Iranian-heritage men who have successfully dodged the draft by living abroad through age twenty-seven have an option to pay their way out of the mandatory service. Draft dodgers must pay two hundred million rials (between six thousand and seventy-five hundred dollars) to enter Iran from abroad and avoid military service. Before age twenty-seven, students at non-Iranian universities can use documentation of their active student status to gain an exemption stamp at the *daftar* (embassy office); or, in the case of those studying and living in the United States, where there is no Iranian embassy, men can obtain the stamp at the Embassy of Pakistan's Iranian Interests Section. The stamp then allows draft-aged men to visit Iran for up to three months twice a year while under active student status. Some young Iranian American men like Farhad do not learn about the student stamp until after their college or university graduation, at which point they are unable to take advantage of the exemption. Ambiguities aside, the issue of military service placed both physical and psychological limitations on the mobility of young Iranian American men. Not everyone possessed the commitment and resources necessary to make the journey. Recalling Pasha's insight that "going to Iran is not like going to Italy," the considerable level of preparation required to travel "home" added to the sense of hype and exceptionality.

Security Check: Boys Going to the Airport

When Mohamad, a recent Iranian American college graduate, got ready to leave his apartment in Philadelphia for the airport, he went through a ritual similar to the one all careful flyers go through: "It's my mental checklist . . . Do I have my ID? Do I need my passport? . . . Did I remember my cell phone charger? . . . I'm always sitting in traffic on the way to the airport like, "Damn, am I missing anything else?" Yet for Mohamad, there was also a mostly unspoken secondary checklist of which he is conscious, and it organized his preparation for flight. The items on this list were inexorably bound to his body: "Have I shaved close enough? Do I look too 'Middle Eastern'? Should I wear a baseball cap with, like, an American sports team logo on it? Or does wearing a hat make me look shady, make me scream 'terrorist'"? Hearing Mohamad express anxiety about doing good "body work" intrigued me: as a woman researcher who has been to Iran and dealt with a different repertoire of body work, I had not expected young male interlocutors to readily share information about the kind of self-management and disciplinary practices that guided their preparations for travel. But to stop at gender would be a problematic and reductive interpretation of Mohamad's concern—it reduces his strategic response to the disciplinary force of air travel solely to gender, but in fact his practices were animated by the interlocking nature of both the gendered and racialized body. Echoing Puar and Rai's "monster/terrorist/fag" complex, Mohamad organized his presentation of self around the intersectional specter of the "terrorist" and organized it so he could pass.[7]

The boys and young men with whom I spoke expressed far more body-related anxiety about the actual act of travel (going through security, interacting with TSA officials, and boarding aircraft) than did young women. This is somewhat counter to conventional understandings or treatments of gender and the body, which take as their starting point the assumption that the feminine body encounters a disproportionate amount of attention and surveillance. While this is certainly the case in a preponderance of social settings, it is instructive to turn attention to the spaces in which men's bodies are mined for meaning, such as "in-between" places like airplanes, transit carriages, and terminals.[8] Thus, terrorism was the organizing logic behind the gendered racialization of Iranian American boys and men as they attempted to fly to their destinations.

Like Mohamad, Khalil also favored athletic clothing that allowed freedom of movement for his broad frame. Both men kept their dark, jet-black hair in trim styles held together with gel. They both normally wore scruffy facial hair that they took care to shave completely and cleanly before travel. But Khalil, four years younger than Mohamad and a high schooler who attends Farsi classes in a New York–area suburb, revealed that packing his suitcase and carry-on bag also required significant management:

> I have to think really hard about what I'm packing. . . . I'm talking about all my flights, not just when I go to Iran but when I'm going somewhere within America too because of TSA and just imagining, like, I have this really full backpack and they ask me to open it up and my Farsi flash cards or workbook are in there. I'm labeled "terrorist" because I'm learning my language. So I have to think, "Do I need to study or do my homework on the plane?" and I'm always like, "Yeah . . . I'm just gonna leave this at home. It's too risky."

The risk to which Khalil referred is increased profiling, attention, and possible detention from security agents who are trained to interpret a grab bag of objects, signs, and gestures—coded as Islamic, foreign, violent—as indicative of a security threat. Far from being paranoid, Khalil understood how his body combines with his material possessions, such as Persian-language homework, to signal "terrorist." He knew, at a visceral level, how security personnel as well as fellow passengers interpreted him.

Evidence exists beyond the testimonies of the young men in my study, and well before the highly controversial 2017 "Muslim ban" on travel into the United States, to confirm the intense travel-related scrutiny under which Iranian American men are placed. In 2012, a young second-generation man named Kevin Iraniha (born to two US citizens: an Iranian-born father and white, European American mother) was barred from boarding a return flight to his hometown of San Diego, California. He had just graduated from the United Nations–affiliated University for Peace in Ciudad Colón, Costa Rica. Following extensive questioning at the local US embassy in San Juan about his previous trips to Iran, his Muslim faith and practice, and political affiliations, Iraniha was denied entrance via airplane and, instead, was forced to cross into the United States by foot after two flights through Mexico City and Tijuana.[9] One year prior to this no-fly incident, in 2011, after returning from a trip through Egypt, India, and Iran, Iraniha—who had no criminal record or evidence of any connection to terrorist organizations—was paid two unsubstantiated visits by the FBI at his home in San Diego. As a self-described "peace activist and beach boy" he came to believe that his inclusion on the no-fly list was likely related to the FBI's use of racial and religious profiling to target Muslim Americans and Iranian Americans with the intention of coercing them into becoming informants. Like the recent case of an Ivy League professor whose math equations were deemed "suspicious terrorist activity" on an airplane, this story is but one of many.[10] They are evidence of how "liminally raced" young men who are not necessarily perceived as racial threats in other spaces must pay special attention to their appearance, behavior, and travel plans in airports. By exercising caution about their bodily comportment and the contents of their bags, youth like Khalil and Mohamad exert whatever control is in their power to avoid becoming targets of gendered racial profiling.

The Layover: Girls Entering Iranian Airspace

Iranian American girls and young women faced a different set of challenges regarding their bodies and gendered and ethno-racial identities as they embarked on trips to Iran. Across town from Mohamad, who went through his mental checklist before every travel departure, Sahi, an Iranian American high school senior, did not worry about leaving from an American airport but rather, reminisced about a connecting flight to Tehran that she and her sister nearly missed in the Netherlands:

> To travel to Iran from America, it's really complicated. We flew to Amsterdam on an American plane, with an American passport, and then our connecting flight was on Iran Air, with an Iranian passport. We knew we had to have a separate outfit to wear, something modest. And my sister wasn't allowed [on the Iran Air flight] at first because her [bare] ankles were showing. I felt so guilty, like are we "bad" Iranians? Did we already mess up and show ourselves as "American" before we even got there?

As Sahi recalled, and as described earlier in this chapter, travel sanctions levied by the United States prohibit American carriers from operating in Iran, making direct flights to Iran impossible from American airports. In the case Sahi described involving her older sister, an employee of Iran Air intervened as the connecting flight was boarding to ensure that all women passengers were dressed in accordance with official standards. Unlike Sahi and her sister, however, the majority of diasporic travelers fly into Iran on non-Iranian carriers like Lufthansa or Emirates. In these cases, it is not interactions with gate agents or other airline employees at the layover airport that spur action but rather an official announcement over the airplane intercom that the plane is transferring into Iranian airspace. This is the "crossing point" during which women travelers change into clothes that they would wear in public while in Iran. As described by youth, a buzz permeates the cabin following the announcement, and women and girls reach for items (most often long-sleeved tunics called *roopoosh* or *manteau* and loose scarves, but inclusive of a range of acceptable items) that they have stashed in easily accessible places. This transitionary moment makes a lasting impression on youth of both sexes; Farhad recalls that passing though this somewhat invisible, suspended national border prompted him to ruminate on gender as a man who needs not change his appearance at that crossing point:

> We always had a connection in Frankfurt, always, always. And my mom would keep some stuff to the side for the layover in Frankfurt, her *manteau* and *roosari* (headscarf), and my sister too. And we'd be on the plane, and the announcement would come over the intercom, like, "You are now entering Iranian airspace; please respect the dress code according to the rules of the Islamic Republic of Iran," and in those moments I would just think to myself, "Thank God I am not a woman." But now I think I'm empathetic about the need to cover and change yourself and how hard or weird that might be.

The scrutiny that Iranian American women faced while in transit is crucially different from the kind of negative attention navigated by their brothers and sons. Farhad felt grateful that he did not have to adhere to

the level of enforced modesty to which his mother and sister were subjected. Yet Farhad and other young Iranian American men were already
scrutinized back in US airports through notions of terror and the perceptions of the masculine Middle Eastern body. Once their connecting
flights landed in Iran, second-generation boys and girls both faced new
forms of ethno-racial and gendered attention—this time due to their
class-privileged *Americanness*—attached to their bodies and identities.

Arrivals: Managing Family (Dis)Membership

Iranian American youth narrated feeling "difference" from the moment
they stepped onto the marble floors of Iran's major international airport,
about twenty miles south of the capital city, Tehran. As largely unsea-
soned travelers, they exercised great care in modifying their behavior and
comportment to avoid negative interactions with the *gashte ershad* (morality
police). Made up of officers of both genders, the *gashte ershad* is a branch
of law enforcement that patrols public spaces issuing warnings, and sometimes penalties, for improper dress and demeanor. Despite lack of experience with Iranian police, diasporic youth arrived with the knowledge that
their personal security and safety depended on their awareness of their
appearance. Keen to blend in with locals as much as possible, they showed
concern that any clue of their Americanness would pose a liability for
them and would be met with suspicion. For young men in particular, to be
viewed with suspicion for *being* Iranian while getting to Iran only to then
be possibly viewed with suspicion for not being Iranian *enough* once they
stepped foot on Iranian soil was particularly vexing.

Awareness of the impact of appearance and comportment was not
a new issue for youth. Growing up in the United States, they witnessed
how their own parents or grandparents managed unwanted attention
or social pressure that stemmed from locals' negative reactions to their
presence. Yet for second-generation youth, to travel to Iran was to have
the rules of appearance and belonging reversed. There, local notions
of phenotypical difference and cultural markers like American accents
worked in tandem to mark Iranian Americans as different from the majority. Thus, the dynamics at work for diasporic teens in Iran involved

a delicate balance between gaining recognition as Iranian without the negative associations of being Iranian American. Most painful for them were the moments when they were misidentified as lacking Iranian heritage at all. As described later, the literal and metaphorical masking tactics that underpinned these moments of social (mis)recognition hinged on their families' representations and misrepresentations of ethno-racial backgrounds of second-generation youth.

Asa, who described watching *Family Feud*, shared a particularly revealing story about these covering tactics. She had been to Iran twice, at age nine and seventeen, with her Iranian American family and among a large number of extended relatives. From behind her desk at the Cross Cultural Center on her local university campus, where she coordinates political action with students of color, she recounted her first trip in third grade. It was only memorable, she recalled, because of how little she wanted to be there at that age:

> I felt like I was being taken away from my American life, from all that I wanted to be doing in the summer with my friends. Swimming, birthday parties, wasting time in front of the TV. By the time I went back after senior year of high school, I'd been working really hard to not just make peace with my Iranian identity but to learn the history and to embrace all parts of being Iranian. To find a place for myself within that identity. And by the time I was about to go to college, I felt like I had gotten there, that I was different than the little kid who was eight years old and just . . . really assimilative and afraid and ashamed of her Iranian heritage. Like, I had worked hard to change those parts of myself by the time I went back. I was so excited to be in Iran, be part of a majority, to see people who looked like me.

When I asked Asa what it was like to go back the second time, she recounted what she called a "'so what am I?' emotional breakdown": "The whole thing was just . . . it really tested me. Here [in the United States], you end up feeling not *really* American and too Iranian. There [in Iran], you understand that 'whoa, I am not really Iranian; I'm actually so American.' It was actually a horrible experience." These kinds

of realizations ("I'm actually so American") were born out of real versus theoretical experiences in Iran. Consistent with scholarly findings
about other "return" migrations and heritage tourism, experiences on
the ground in Iran sometimes contradicted the hope of recognition and
ethno-racial acceptance that was anticipated in advance of their trips.[11]
I asked Asa to describe how she came to decide that a trip she had been
so excited for could actually be a "horrible experience":

> So my grandmother, a woman who loves us, who cares so much for us
> as her grandchildren, I remember being in the back of a taxi with my
> [Iranian American] cousins who are half black. And my grandma was
> so adamant that they keep quiet, that they not say a word, like speaking
> was going to draw more attention to them. She thought they already
> stood out, and so she said, "Okay, in this taxicab, you're not allowed to
> talk." It was stuff like that. And in Tehran, there's random people on the
> street telling me and my family to go back to India. Talking about us [in
> Persian] directly in front of us.

Here, Asa recounted how her family's diasporic identities were both
masked and misrecognized; she was pained by the memory of her loving
grandmother urging her mixed-race grandchildren to silence themselves
in order to not encourage unwanted attention in public. Locally bound
understandings of what Iranians looked like followed Asa throughout
the trip, as her family was also misidentified as Indian and assumed not
to understand the Persian language as most Iranians would. Rather than
find easy or comfortable acceptance while in Iran, Asa found that she
and her family were the subject of talk as racial others. Iranian American youth like Asa were somewhat used to misrecognition and prejudice
at home, and many were surprised and disappointed to find a similar
experience in their romanticized Iran.

For Asa, the "problem" was multiplied by the fact that her diasporic
family is multiracial, and according to the messages she received from
family and strangers, it was better to pose as not being there at all. In
other situations, described by Iranian American youth, an assumed or
invented mixed white racial identity could be deployed as a defense or

justification to explain a perceived lack of Iranianness. Seventeen-year-old Javad revealed to me something that happened between him and his father in Iran, which he had not been able to forget, years later:

> There was an experience I had in Iran when I was about thirteen or fourteen. I was in an electronics store in the *passage* [mall], and you know, I was looking at a game or something, and the shopkeeper asked [in Persian], "Why does he have an accent [when speaking Persian]?" And my dad, this has stayed with me, my dad, when he asks, "Why does he have an accent?," he hastily goes, "Oh, um, his mother's American."[12] And she's not! But he *said* that! And the guy was like, "Okay," and he accepted that, but my thoughts were like, ". . . but she's *not*. She's Iranian and so am I." And it's not a life or death situation, you know? It wouldn't be bad if he were to say, "My son has an accent because we are from America," like they're not going to call the police or anything. But it's the social reasons for why he said that. And I think about that to myself, and I kind of remember it whenever I think of going to Iran and I feel . . . I don't *want* to have an accent when I speak Farsi.

Javad remained vexed and upset by his father's choice to portray his Iranian mom, who wasn't there with them, as an American. After Javad relayed the story to me, I asked him what he meant about his father when he said, "It's the social reasons for why he said that." Javad said that he really didn't know, that he just had a "feeling" that his father felt it would be more expedient or easy to explain Javad's accent that way. This is a very valid possibility. Another might be that Javad's father felt a degree of shame that Javad's accent was noticeable; it had perhaps less to do with anything Javad did "wrong" but that his father felt that he had failed to protect Javad, his American-born son, from the critical and judgmental gaze of local Iranians. In both Asa and Javad's experiences, Iranian American diasporic identities were strategically muted while in Iran. In Asa's case, her black–Iranian American cousins were literally told to keep quiet, and in Javad's, his Iranian mother was whitewashed into hegemonic Americanness to explain away his second-generation accent.

Too Iranian for America, Too American for Iran

The US State Department considers dual-citizen Iranian Americans at special risk in their travels to Iran.[13] In recent years, a number of dual-citizen journalists, academics, and businesspeople have been arrested on contentious charges and held for years. Some remain imprisoned; others have been released and swapped as part of "prisoner deals."[14] Though youth in my sample were familiar with these situations and, in some cases, did much to circulate awareness about them, they did not personally describe fear of the "dual-citizen risk" in their own travels. Whether this was due to the casual tourism of their visits or their relative inexperience and youth, their Iranian families nonetheless advised them to mute their Americanness in public places. This involved conscientious choices around when to speak in public settings in order to remove the threat of being "found out" as an Iranian American. Like the revelation Javad described in the previous passage, Farhad's family urged him to recognize that, while in Iran, "Iranian American" was not socially synonymous with "Iranian." In this passage he recounted that his unwillingness to eschew shorts in the summertime, considered by the *gashte ershad* as un-Islamic for women and men, was particularly naïve, even for a diasporic teenager:

> I don't remember who told me this, but I distinctly remember being told by my family, "You're an American, so even though you might in some ways think that you blend in with the Iranians, you don't. They can tell you're an American from your clothes, by how you walk, by how you carry yourself." And I know that shorts was something that I was warned against packing, and I was just like, yeah whatever, it's the desert, you're not going to catch me in long pants. I am going to wear my damn shorts. And so I'm walking down the street in Tehran, and some workers, maybe they were Afghan, they yelled at me from the rooftop they were fixing. "Bah bah, in pesar-e Amrikaie bebin, lokhte-pati pahasho ovordeh be ma neshoon bedeh" [Wow, look at this American boy, stark naked and strutting his legs over to show us]. My family was like, "Keep walking; just ignore it and keep walking," but inside I was like, "Okay , I need to go to the nearest bazaar and buy some long pants and get these

shorts off of me." It was one of those moments where it's like . . . as an
American, you can understand these workers there who are the most
abused and looked down upon, and they had this moment where they
could throw dirt in my face to raise themselves up a bit, like at least they
know about customs, and the rules, and I'm just being a dumb American
in that moment.

In hindsight, Farhad understood the power dynamics behind this incident. On the most basic level, he had refused to conform to the compulsory ban on shorts and was thusly shamed. But as a privileged
dual-citizen teenager on vacation with his parents, the power differential
was stark between him and the noncitizen migrant construction workers
he described. The pool of labor for high-risk physical work in Iran draws
from the migrant labor of Afghan men, estimated at 1.4 million people;
there are an additional one million Afghan refugees in Iran.[15] Noncitizen
Afghan workers, who must pay off migration debts from a rapidly depre-
ciating Iranian rial, possess radically different lives from those of the ad-
vantaged diasporic Iranian American teenagers who visit during breaks
from school. Farhad's cultural breach offered an opportunity to upend
the conventional power dynamics that placed the "dumb American"
tourist—and the one in possession of American and Iranian citizenship—above the precariously employed, undocumented Afghan laborer.

These moments of interaction upended young Iranian American
men's romanticized hopes that they would find it easy to belong in Iran.
Interactions like these are also largely undertheorized or unreported in
writings on diasporic Iranian life. Instead, there has been considerably
more attention paid to diasporic young women's comportment, beauty
practices, wardrobe, and otherwise embodied identities in Iran. As opposed to the young men, the young women in my study were particularly
attuned to how overly rigid or unfashionable interpretations of cosmopolitan modesty revealed the Iranian American as "other." As Asa remarked,

We stood out just by walking around. Like, for example, at first, we
were not going to sacrifice being comfortable for being stylish. We were
on summer vacation, and who wanted to wear things that were tight

and constricting? So all of us, we were like in white muslin caftan-style clothes, flowing pants, things that no actual Iranians were wearing, right? They're in jeggings and tight *manteaux*. Honestly, we were sticking out. It was too much. So I started wearing my hair in a high bun underneath the *roosari* so that I could have my hair poking out fashionably like the other girls my age who live there. I took the one pair of tight jeans I'd brought with me and wore them constantly.

Following her trip, Asa came to recognize that "Iranian American is very different than Iranian," and for her, managing this meant sacrificing American comfort for Iranian fashion. To be sure, while traveling in Iran, issues of veiling and propriety were also of concern for Iranian American girls and women. In line with other accounts, some of the girls in my study recounted intimidating experiences with local morality police. In their ultimate recollections of these encounters, however, girls dwelled on their failure to pass as simply Iranian and not Iranian American rather than on their disciplinary repercussions. This was perhaps a condition and privilege of their diasporic identities: as holders of American passports, they felt that they could and would return to the United States and avoid further altercations with officials. Pardis, a sprightly and perpetually bronzed sixteen-year-old born and raised in the southeastern United States, remembered one specific encounter well:

> We were in Isfahan, and they had these women they hire who make sure that women are properly dressed [*gashte ershad*]. One of them caught my eye because my *roosari* had fallen back on my head, and, you know, the front of my hair was showing. She pointed at me to fix myself, and I felt so yucky. It didn't make me dislike Iran; it made me dislike my place in between these two worlds where I just don't fit. You know what they say: too Iranian in America and too American in Iran.

What Pardis described as "yucky" was not just her experience of having failed a routine modesty test in front of the *gashte ershad*. To her, it was almost worse to have failed to obscure her diasporic identity in favor of blending in as a local Iranian. Pardis took care to note that her negative feelings were not directed toward the morality officer, who warned Pardis to "fix" herself, or toward Iranian rules and social practices. Pardis's negative feelings were instead directed inward. The fairly routine admonition from the female officer instigated reflection about her Iranian American identity: messy, ungainly, and in-between.

Despite the intense attention that girls' and women's experiences typically receive in the West, both young women and men came away uncomfortable with feelings about their bodies and identities evoked during their homecomings. Negative attention about their looks, accents, and clothing from locals was compounded by what young people observed as strange or hurtful remarks from their more authentically Iranian parents and grandparents. As a result, youth returned to the United States with new insights. Rather than offer an easy panacea for matters of identity, visiting their ancestral homeland revealed a new layer of complexity.

Returning with More Questions Than Answers

As Iranian American young men and women returned to their American homes from visits to Iran, they were compelled to reflect on how their gendered and bodily practices had to shift again to accommodate local norms. Youth described internalizing the feeling that authorities and everyday people could accurately detect evidence of their Americanness. As a result, by the time their weeks or months in Iran wound to a close, their sartorial and physical transitions had begun to feel normal. Girls in particular described feeling a jolt of awareness that they needed to reorganize their bodies as they prepared for the return journey to America. As Tahmineh, a seventeen-year-old from Los Angeles put it, the transnational nuances of surveillance resulted in a residual paranoia she brought back:

> I felt naked when I came back, and I wasn't wearing *roosari* and everything. There's just something you have when you're there. It's very shocking at first. Same thing in Iran; you go there, and you're like, "Okay, well I guess I'm going to cover my head now." It's not a big deal, but it is different. It's this paranoia that's justified every time I get scolded when I'm out in public by the morality police. Then, it's weird to come back here and not even have to give that a second thought. In the US, you actually stick out for being observant, for wearing a scarf.

While Tahmineh expressed a clear difference between the clothes that felt comfortable on either side of her visit to Iran, her experience of feeling underdressed when back in the United States reflects the after-effects of travel on her identity. "Paranoid" about being "scolded" in Iran, Tahmineh—who identified as culturally Muslim but does not wear the hijab while in the United States—returned home highly cognizant of how her lack of hijab allowed her to avoid unwanted scrutiny or attention in her full-time American setting. For girls like Tahmineh, this felt like the simple reality of diaspora: one's Americanness was better muted in Iran, and Iranianness better muted in America. Their challenge, then, was to figure out how to navigate both homes and identities without sacrificing either.

For Iranian American boys and young men, however, the paranoia they felt about return was largely centered on the act of travel back to the United States rather than the United States as a destination. According to Pasha, whose testimony unfavorably compared the bureaucratic rigor of travel to Iran to the ease of a destination like Italy: "When I'm coming back to the US [from Iran], it's like, am I gonna get hemmed up at customs because I didn't shave close enough and I was just visiting my Iranian grandma? These are the thoughts that go through my head." Pasha described an awareness of how he would be read by law enforcement and border officials as an Iranian American traveler returning from a trip to Iran. Unlike Tahmineh, his internal dialogue was concerned with crossing borders at the airport, not with reintegrating into his everyday American setting. When I asked Pasha if he ever talked to friends or family about these concerns, he explained his decision to keep these "thoughts that go through [his] head" to himself:

> It's hard to articulate this to other people, because other people don't have a concept to get it. If you say, "Yeah, I got put in the corner again at the airport; they did that whole thing to me," your white friend might say, "Oh, that really sucks; yeah, that's really bad." But it's hard for them to really get what the hell is going on. And the other Iranian Americans I know, despite being smart, it's like none of us have a coherent philosophy of what's going on. So we're not talking about it.

Pasha's comments suggest that Iranian American youth each hold different pieces of a larger narrative of travel but that they lack the collective infrastructure and political access to do anything about it. He intuits that these stories do not reduce to a series of highly personalized microaggressions but encompass and reveal broader patterns. By juxtaposing their experiences, this chapter opens a door into how class-privileged young Iranian American men and women experience their trips from the United States to Iran and back again in racialized and gendered ways.

Conclusion

The body is subject to intrusive scrutiny, particularly in the course of transnational movement and mobility. Across a long history of geopolitical struggle—with renewed intensity in the past two decades—persons identified as Middle Eastern or Muslim face severe forms of racialization as threatening "outsiders" when they traverse the Global North as permanent immigrants, temporary workers, or casual travelers. In the context of travel in and out of the liminal homeland, it was Iranian American young men and boys who faced especially heavy policing at the moment of entry and exit across international borders.

Beginning with the hype that set the stage, to their disillusioning experiences within the idealized homeland itself, young Iranian American men and women came away with gendered ethno-racial experiences that rendered them liminal outsiders within.[16] For both sexes, attention to modesty, secular cosmopolitanism, and the body were an organizing principle for how Iranian and Iranian American family members could manage youth's unwieldy diasporic identities. While in Iran, speaking Persian with an American accent, navigating the nuances of modesty standards as *actually* practiced by locals, and other physical markers of difference (e.g., gait, general unsureness or unease) were the source of unwanted and hurtful attention.

When personal appearances and behaviors differ from a local norm, international travel—even to one's ancestral homeland—can provoke a racialized experience. Further, the practices or strategies exercised by Iranian American travelers within the constraints of such norms rendered them as "other" or different. Boys were highly aware of what they carried, wore, and said to security officials as they crossed borders. They did not want to be perceived as too Iranian. For girls, the enforced requirement to wear the hijab once in Iranian airspace made some nervous simply because they thought they would fail at it and be exposed in the moment as American. Their stories offer a slightly different angle to scholarship on Islamophobia, which is rightly critical of the overdeterministic and problematic academic obsession with hijab. While the rules of hijab are a relevant topic for secular diasporic travelers, second-generation youth were far less concerned with having to adhere to Islamic standards of dress than with their perceived inability to perform Iranianness (inclusive of hijab) correctly.

Upon their return to the United States, young men and women had to control and manage new forms of self-surveillance that resulted in paranoia about their bodies and identities. The valence of their behavior was shaped by two intertwined imperatives: navigating the deeply institutionalized belief systems of security agents who organized the spatial and temporal "in-between," while also navigating the implicit cultural norms on the ground in Iran of what "Iranians" and "Americans" looked like. As a result, official racial categories (as in the case of Iranians who are categorized as white in the United States) are reconfigured to match competing local realities. Iranian Americans are no longer "whitewashed" while in transit; this is predicated on both racial and gendered understandings of the Iranian body. While my young Iranian American interlocutors rarely if ever found the true sense of comfortable belonging in Iran they hoped for, through these travels they further refined their second-generation identities as real and meaningful in and of themselves. In the following chapter, I rely on participant-observational field research at one such site in which young Iranian Americans "finally" find themselves and one another: a summer camp created by and for second-generation youth.

CHAPTER 6

AT SUMMER CAMP

THE LIGHTS IN THE REC ROOM WERE DIM, and from the open windows a summer breeze gently swayed the crepe-paper streamers that crisscrossed the ceiling. A hundred thirteen- to eighteen-year-olds who just moments before were roughhousing and laughing now sat in rapt silence. Forty slightly older young people stood against the walls. They wore matching dark red T-shirts etched with vivid white Persian calligraphy, many with their arms draped around each other or head rested on a neighbor's shoulder. At the front stood Mana, the twenty-six-year-old executive director of the nonprofit that runs Camp Ayandeh (Camp Future). With wide, doleful eyes, Mana addressed the packed room:

> Here at camp, you are family. Here, we take care of each other. Here, you are *all* Iranian. No one is more Iranian than anyone else. I don't care if you are one-half, one-fourth, purple, or an alien. You are *Iranian*, and here you are *family*. Starting right now, every single thing that you do, you are doing to your family. Every single person wearing this red shirt is your relative [voice wavers]. And every single person sitting next to you is your cousin. So we are going to treat each other like that, okay? We are a family.

Mana paused to let the word "family" hang in the air, and the counselors and staff exchanged knowing smiles. Many had heard this speech, or a version of it, in previous summers as campers themselves. Others had waited for this moment, anticipating its rhetorical power based on what they had heard in counselor training or orientation. A few counselors—

the ones assigned to the youngest new campers—glanced over at their charges, curious to see their reactions to the speech. The campers' eyes remained locked on Mana, who now paced back and forth on the hardwood floor.

> You all came from different places in this country . . . different experiences, different communities. You came from a *great* one; you came from a little one. You came from one where you were the *only* Iranian and they messed up your name every single day.

> If you *want* that amazing, fantastic experience that you saw online, if you *want* that amazing, fantastic experience that your friends told you about, *this* is what's actually going to change that for you. This can be that life-changing experience you want.

> This is where all those things you heard in high school, all those things you *hate* about high school—but you still do just to get through those four years because you have to—this is where *none* of that applies. *This* is that place where you can have family. People who respect you, who appreciate you, and who love you for you. *This* is that utopian community that you all want.

Previous chapters of this book described how Iranian American youth live at the limits of whiteness. They are liminal racial subjects in their childhood homes, in schools, and during visits to the Iranian homeland. But for a couple hundred young people each summer, a fourth site of ethno-racial socialization also exists, and it is one that, in effect, was designed to address the limits and failures of belonging in the other three. Camp Ayandeh, an overnight summer camp for Iranian American youth, runs for just two weeks each year, but the relationships and ideas forged there are sustained through in-person and online "reunions" and deterritorialized from time and place to live on in participants' minds throughout the ensuing weeks, months, and years. To make sense of how and why Camp Ayandeh is a transformative experience for campers, counselors, and staff (all of whom are 1.5- and second-generation Iranian Americans), I draw from two major sources of data. First, I rely on two summers of ethnographic research on-site, inclusive of field recordings and observations and collected training materials, and one additional summer as a camp counselor. Second, I draw from formal and informal interviews with camp leadership, counselors, campers, and alumni, ranging from structured sixty-minute interviews to free-range conversations over the course of days. And though I did not intend to involve campers' parents as subjects in the research project, our communications regarding their legal consent offered the unanticipated opportunity for parents to share thoughts and observations about their children's experiences at camp as well.

About Camp

The idea for camp came out of late-night conversations between three politically active second-generation Iranian American women, who felicitously met around age twenty-one in London during their respective university study abroad programs. With fresh perspective afforded by distance, the young women thought critically about what their American childhoods had lacked. They realized that while they held a variety of ties to their parents' local Iranian American communities, a range of strong to weak ties in Iran, and a native understanding of the American political system, there was no bridging organization or institution in the United States to help them connect these strands of their lives and to connect to other Iranian American youth. They were especially interested in finding other young people who eschewed the "old country" politics of some elders in their parents' generation. With no background in how to form a nonprofit organization and no trust funds, two of the young women returned to the Boston area for their senior year of college and spent nights at Barnes & Noble scribbling notes from *Non-Profit Kit for Dummies* and *Fundraising for Dummies* into loose-leaf binders. By their graduation in 2004, they had won seed money from their universities, launched a biannual international scholarly conference on the Iranian diaspora, and incorporated as a 501(c)3 nonprofit, nongovernmental organization called Iranian Alliances across Borders (IAAB).

IAAB's signature program, Camp Ayandeh, began in 2006 with nineteen campers and counselors, who had to carry in potable water to a small island campsite off the Massachusetts coast. In the span of a decade it has grown into two annual sessions held in different sites around the country with around two hundred participants each year. Mana, the full-time executive director (herself one of the first counselors in 2006), and a handful of staff and unpaid volunteers in their twenties and thirties manage different facets of the organization and its year-round programming. IAAB's operating budget comes mostly from individual and philanthropic donations, which also fund need-based camp scholarships. Camp Ayandeh is explicitly open to all youth over age thirteen, regardless of demographic category or characteristic. In any given summer, it draws participants from up to forty different states, five countries, and three continents. IAAB, and by extension Camp Ayandeh, maintains a plainly nonpolitical and nonreligious stance in its promotional materials and correspondence with parents and the community. Concepts from US civil rights and global postcolonial political movements, however, suffuse the camp curriculum and dialogue. The campers participate in outdoor recreation along with anti-oppression workshops, leadership exercises, and arts/culture activities.

Camp participants typically self-identify as "Iranian" in some way, with one-quarter to one-third of the enrollment in any given year from mixed background (Iranian plus African American, Afro-Caribbean, Asian, European, and South American) households.[1] In her opening speech, Mana gestured to the inclusivity of the Ayandeh Iranian American "family" when asserting to campers on the first day that "no one is more Iranian than anyone else. I don't care if you are one-half, one-fourth, purple, or an alien." By leveling the racial distinctions and hierarchies by which these identities are typically organized in the world outside camp, Mana asserted a bold—if ultimately not entirely realistic—humanistic vision of ethno-racial equanimity inside the utopian campsite.[2]

At Camp Ayandeh, a new Iranian American subject is thus born out of a fictive family formed in utopian space. Shadows that haunt the second generation—the exceptional Aryan, the model minority child—fade as campers are initiated into an identity that decenters the gaze of white peers and authority figures from the other parts of their lives. Instead, at camp, other liminal groups (Arabs, Afghans) and racialized communities with more mature legacies of resistance in the United States (indigenous, Latina/Latino, Asian, and African Americans) are emphasized in the curriculum and discussed, in no uncertain terms, as allies to support in kind. At camp, youth practice race as a political identity and ask one another hard questions about Iranian American privilege, oppression, and accountability. Their liminal ethno-racial identities find new coherence as worthy of celebration and pride.

Like all good utopias, camp produces revelatory insights, flashes of brilliance, and the capacity to imagine and maybe even build a more fully realized Iranian community in America. But unlike all good utopias, Camp Ayandeh is legally accountable to a few hundred Iranian parents and guardians, and it's impossible for the real world not to occasionally creep in. For campers, the experience is still revelatory, and in some cases, transformative.

"If the Goal Is to Be Seen as Human, Then Let's Really Be Human"

The rec room, where campers had been initiated into the camp's utopian vision the night before, looked very different the next morning. Its location that year, in a Jesuit college in the foothills of a small Northern California city, had become newly conspicuous. In the harsh light of day, the eye was drawn to the Christian crosses on the walls and the etching of Colossians 3:12–17 ("And may the Peace of Christ reign in your hearts") across the wooden mantle of the fireplace; staff now rushed to drape leftover crepe-paper streamers across the biblical passage. Campers had begun to file into the room after their pale, unappetizing-looking breakfast of semi-toasted Eggo waffles and fruit salad. They scrambled to claim a place on the few couches and beanbag chairs, and the rest sat cross-legged on the floor. Counselors pulled curtains and lowered blinds to darken the room. A young staff member assembled a large tripod projector screen and earned a smattering of applause from the campers. Acknowledging their gesture, he bowed slightly and said, "Welcome to the anti-oppression workshop."

Mana and Narges, an original founder of IAAB, stood up. The most visible and senior people in the organization (twenty-five and twenty-seven years old, respectively, that summer), they commanded attention and respect from the group. Narges, the first to speak, described how membership in a loving community required understanding how words and images could not only hurt others but actively contribute to their miseries and struggles. To build a loving community required looking at things that one might really love—Hollywood films, pop music, and music videos—in a new, critical way. As Mana walked over to the laptop connected to the projector, Narges said, "What I want you all to think about as we screen these YouTube clips for you is how you find yourself reacting. Listen to each other; come to this conversation with a spirit to learn from each other. We want to hear from you." Mana projected a YouTube clip from the motion picture *300* (2006) on the screen. A few campers, perhaps knowing what was to come, sighed in emphatic, annoyed fashion.

The film, heavy with computer-generated imagery (CGI), an adaptation of Frank Miller's *300* (1998) comic book, dramatized the Battle of Thermopylae in the Greco-Persian Wars. The film takes the perspective of Leonidas, leader of the Spartan army, and recounts how over two weeks, three hundred Spartan soldiers were able to stave off the encroaching invasion into Greece of one hundred thousand Persians led by King Xerxes. In the YouTube clip, the Spartans, who fought different arms of the Persian Empire, were portrayed by white British actors and actresses with very little appearance-altering CGI. In contrast, a racially diverse cast played the Persians and were, through "movie magic," monstrously proportioned with CGI and prosthetics and had their voices deepened. They were also in two extreme states of dress throughout the film: naked, save for strategically placed chain jewelry, or fully covered in swirling robes and head wraps. The visual language used to set the Spartans and Persians apart from one another was, for dramatic purposes, immaculate.

Hadi, a sporty high school junior from the Northeast, was the first to raise his hand. At the time he was sixteen years old, outgoing and quick to make intentionally goofy jokes, and more prone to show interest in the physical and creative activities at camp than in bookish workshops. Clearing his throat, he said, "The film portrays us as uncivilized, as if *we* were the uncivilized ones. Whereas in reality, we were one of the greatest civilizations that had ever lived." Hadi's comment was met with an audible round of finger snaps from some campers. In the vernacular of camp, to offer snaps during a conversation or event meant that you appreciated what had just been said. Almost immediately Keyvan, a fifteen-year-old boy from the Northeast, raised his hand and spoke:

> When I saw that movie, I didn't like it because it wasn't historically accurate at all. My friends were like, "Yeah, you should chill; it's just a movie; it's entertainment value," but the *way* they portrayed Iranians, even if people look at it as just entertainment, it still puts things in their head psychologically that they associate Iranians with.

Keyvan, when identifying "the *way* they portrayed Iranians" was in part bringing attention to the film's binary aesthetic depiction of its Persian characters. There were the homogeneous hordes of Persian soldiers: dark, threatening, overwhelming. But there was also the detailed rendering of the main antagonist, King Xerxes. Monstrously large like the Persian soldiers, Xerxes was also portrayed as exotic and effeminate: completely hairless, with painted eyebrows and metallic maquillage across his body, and jewelry adorning his thighs, abs, shoulders, and face. In the film, Xerxes consorted with half-goat humanoids and maintained sexual slavery in his court through drugs and violence. On the battleground, too, Xerxes relied on cheap tricks and chicanery despite his army's size advantage. Played by a somewhat famous white Brazilian television actor, King Xerxes was presented as a monster in racial, sexual, and even human drag.

Interestingly, Keyvan's final comment of concern that the film could "put things in their head psychologically" was similar to how then-Iranian president Mahmoud Ahmadinejad had, three years earlier, described the film as American "psychological warfare" against

Iranians.[3] Until this point Keyvan and Hadi's comments had elicited some snaps from their same-aged peers in the audience, but camp counselors and staff had yet to join in. Yasmin, a longtime camper who was now a counselor and a freshman in college, was one of the most outwardly friendly people at camp. She intervened soon after Keyvan finished speaking:

> I have a comment and then a question. And my comment is in thinking about how do we respond to people, friends, people who don't really know a lot about Iran who might consume these images? I guess one thing that I feel is that sometimes, and I've done this too, our response is, "We're not bad, actually we are great, and we're the best civilization ever, and we're all actually educated." And that's one strategy, to enlighten people about our history. But if the goal is to be seen as human, then let's really be human. That means that we have our great things, but we have our problems too. So maybe the goal is to remind people of our humanity, our messy stuff and our great stuff [snaps]. And my question, we're talking about how these images portray us, but maybe we can think and talk about *why* they portray us this way. How do these connect to what's going on in Iran, Iraq, Afghanistan?

Yasmin's comment was met with affirmative snaps and a long pause after "Afghanistan." As the only college student to comment thus far in the conversation, Yasmin was the first to connect *300* to the War on Terror, the most prominent American military project to unfold over the childhoods of the camp participants. Over lunch later in the afternoon, I sat with a pair of counselors who mentioned that *300* director, Zack Snyder, a white European American, had cast his own white son as "young Leonidas," the Spartan hero/protagonist, in case there were any question about which nation or people the Spartans were supposed to represent. A sense began to build throughout the workshop that Sparta was not only meant to represent ancient "western civilization" but perhaps the present-day United States as well. The Persian army, dressed like the Taliban, on the one hand, and sexual slaves, on the other, who spoke an indecipherable language, were posed as a dark polyglot of Islamic terrorism—in a film set before the historical emergence of Islam no less.

The next to speak to the group was Zal, a seventeen-year-old from the southeastern United States whose mother is from the West Indies and father is from Iran. He offered an example from his own peer group of how the portrayal of Xerxes in *300* became the closest at-hand reference to Persianness. "Every time I met someone or I told them I was Persian on my dad's side, they're like, 'Oh, does your dad have a bunch of earrings, you know, down his cheeks like Xerxes?' Or [they ask] if he's super tall." Zal, unlike the majority of his Iranian American peers, personally encountered both anti-Iranian and antiblack racism and was keenly aware of when either or both of his parentages were negatively racialized. It is telling that Zal, who has a Persian first and last name, is mixed race and possesses a physical appearance that does not fit easily into dominant Iranian representations, yet he was the camper who described the most direct mocking from peers about the sexualized and racialized appearance of King Xerxes. But not all campers claimed to have thought about these issues in advance of camp. Following Zal's comment, Kamran admitted to the group:

> I remember watching [*300*] with my friend, and I didn't even feel anything, which I feel guilty about now because even though I'm Iranian and I know all the history, I came out of it and was just like, "Okay, that was a bad movie." But it wasn't until conversations like this where I was like, "Oh, this is a *horrible* movie," and how many images do we just ignore in our everyday lives that we just don't see? [snaps]

Narges stood up once more and gave Kamran a warm smile. "Kamran is posing the exact question that motivated us to do this workshop," she said, and walked over to the laptop. "If we can notice the images that target Iranians, that chip away at our humanity, our challenge then is to call out when we see this same othering happening to groups we may or may not belong to." After a round of snaps following Narges's statement, the group watched two additional clips, the song "Every Girl" (2009) by artists from the Young Money rap label and the final scene of Spike Lee's *Bamboozled* (2002). By posing questions and offering encouragement in the first part of the workshop, Narges and staff elicited campers' feedback about the portrayal of Iranians in order to help them then critically engage antifeminist and antiblack media. Before officially closing the workshop, Mana offered a few final thoughts:

> Every day here, we may be getting better at understanding *our* struggle. But we have to stand as witnesses for other people. And, trust, other people are standing as witnesses for us. We have power in this situation. We do play a role. As we walk away from this workshop, remember that we are part of this longer continuum, from films about Russians in the Cold War era to antiblack images before *and* after the Civil Rights Era. To understand the images produced about *us* and to do something about them, we have to understand and support how other communities have handled this and how we walk in their footsteps.

Narges and Mana had begun the session with very general guidelines for the campers. By the end of the session, however, they offered youth explicit direction to bring this spirit of critique and solidarity to other negatively stigmatized groups in the United States. The implicit message of the workshop (that, as non-white racial subjects in the United States, Iranian Americans must position themselves in solidarity with other non-white racial subjects) met second-generation Iranian American youth where they were. It took their experiences of being teased or mocked as a starting point of a conversation. For some of the youth, it was the first time they had engaged in a frank co-ethnic conversation that treated their non-white racial status in the United States, and the discrimination they faced from it, as obvious. At camp, youth did not have to defend the legitimacy of their racial feelings, nor did they have to uphold identities or divisions that made little sense in diasporic contexts. This became especially clear in matters of Iranian American and Arab American solidarity.

"People from Our Part of the World"

Part of the design of Camp Ayandeh was to invite outside speakers, including those from academia, the arts, industry, and media, who could speak knowingly to campers' experiences. During the sixth summer of camp one such speaker was Moustafa Bayoumi, an English professor whose scholarship extended Edward Said's *Orientalism* to the contemporary Arab American experience.[4] In advance of his arrival staff had photocopied and circulated to each camper two chapters of his book, *How Does It Feel to Be a Problem: Being Young and Arab in America*, which campers had been encouraged to read in free moments between other activities. Although not all campers had found time to read the text in full, those who did were quick to share that they were moved to goose bumps and tears by the stories of Arab American youth singled out for their ethnic, racial, and religious identities after 9/11. From the book, the teenage campers did not articulate an impossible difference between Iranians and Arabs as some had been taught to do as children (discussed in Chapter 3) but, instead, drew from it a description of Arab American racialization that resonated with their own.

In a light tweedy jacket and dark black jeans, looking the part of the hip professor, Bayoumi sat on a stool in an outdoor courtyard under a canopy of rustling leaves and chirping birds. He held a hardbound copy of the book and opened his talk with an anecdote about having attended "Muslim camp" as a young Egyptian Canadian growing up in Kingston, Ontario. Across an hour-long conversation, he paraphrased and read passages from his book that made campers gasp with emotion, and he shared personal stories of living and working in Brooklyn while serving as an advocate for Arab Americans in meetings with the FBI and counterterrorism organizations. Throughout his talk, Bayoumi used the phrase "people from our part of the world" when describing his Arab American research subjects and his Iranian American camper audience. A counselor asked him about the phrase during Q&A, and Bayoumi explained that "Middle Eastern," the most common term used to refer to Iranians and Arabs as a collectivity, was a geopolitical holdover from

British colonialism: "We are east of what, exactly? Europe? *Who* is to be at the center?" At this, camp participants broke out into applause and snaps. After the talk, as some campers approached Bayoumi to ask for hugs, photos, and "where are they now" updates on the young people profiled in his book, two fifteen-year-old campers, Hoda and Mojgan, came up to me. Both were flushed with emotion from the event and, I think, sought me out for encouragement:

> Hoda: I felt like I was going to cry when he said, "My book was my at-
> tempt to humanize a population being increasingly dehumanized."
> I have had this secret desire to write a book called *Getting by One*
> *Kabob at a Time*. About kids like us. He said, "No one but you can
> capture these moments." I have to do this.
>
> Mojgan: I want to be a director, and maybe I'll make a film at camp, I
> don't know. I am feeling really motivated right now. I want to grab
> my camera and *do* this.

Youth like Hoda and Mojgan drew significant inspiration from Bay-oumi's talk; his articulation of Arab American racialization resonated deeply with their observations as second-generation Iranian Americans. Campers, who before arriving were sometimes isolated and disempow-ered in their experiences of identity-based discrimination, took from Bayoumi's book and lecture that they were not alone and, more so, that they too could express resiliency through their own creative projects. The subtext of Bayoumi's presence at camp also had an impact—that there were solidarities and commonalities on which Arabs and Irani-ans might build in the United States, a running theme of both curricu-lum and casual discussion at camp. Questions of intergroup solidarity sparked new enthusiasm and passionate conversation among camp participants.

In the context of the camp, particularly for the benefit of campers, it went without question that Iranian Americans should work much harder on behalf of and among communities of color. Counselors spoke admir-ingly to campers of the grassroots advocacy groups and social move-ments they had joined or respected from afar, led by black, Latino, and

Asian elders and peers in their universities and neighborhoods. But in a meeting during counselor training before campers arrived, the topic of which groups Iranians were "most" racist against—and which racist ideologies needed to be addressed most urgently—was a matter of debate among counselors and staff:

> Newsha (a first-time counselor): I think if we want to get the Iranian American community to establish solidarity with Latinos or African Americans, we have significant racism that exists against Afghans and Arabs. Like, we are *bordered* by Afghans and Arabs, but we think we are so much better than them. Like, if someone asks, "Are you Arab," an Iranian won't just respond neutrally, like, "Oh no, sorry, I'm not." You're encouraged to be like, "Ugh, *no*, I'm *Iranian*," and you know, that needs to go away before we can even try to handle the other racisms our community holds.
>
> Yasmin (former camper, now counselor): I think racism within the Iranian American community is nothing short of disgusting. Personally, I'm offended when I hear comments people make at *mehmoonis* [parties and social gatherings with other Iranians] about Arabs, Afghans, also about religious people; that's I think one of our biggest problems. We hold ourselves back with these straight-up backwards comments. And we can't go anywhere unless that stops.
>
> Newsha: I agree, but I also have to say, I don't think this racism will be as strong as time goes on, because our generation isn't as racially secluded as our parents were. Our parents only saw Afghans and Arabs in the context of society in Iran. And since we don't have that, that stigma isn't there. And in terms of interracial relationships, a lot of our kids are probably not going to be "full Iranian." I don't know how many people this will be true for, but it *will* force us to be more accepting. Which makes it even more important that we don't have divisions . . . otherwise we'll just . . .

As Newsha trailed off, her peers in the counselor training session showed appreciation with a round of loud, emphatic snaps. In her second comment, Newsha drew from the liberal rhetoric of multiculturalism and the utopian belief that multiracial families would, by their very existence, diminish societal racism. But she had also identified and spoken out loud the particular racism of Iranians toward the other groups from "our part of the world" that, in the coming days, would be a unifying concern at camp.

For example, Yousef, another invited speaker and a graduate student in sociology, offered a social history that bridged these multiple conversations. Although his all-camp workshop was listed on the day's schedule as a talk about history, it was a deeply personal, interdisciplinary consideration of the Iraq-Iran border. He began his talk by describing his upbringing in a mixed Iraqi-Iranian household, playing at the feet of older family members, who would reminisce and discuss the war between the neighboring countries, long after the family's immigration to California. He projected maps and archival photos of the borderlands between Iraq and Iran, material that directly challenged the supposedly impregnable border that camp participants had known to exist between the two countries since their respective births in the 1980s and 1990s. He played an old midcentury recording of Zuhair Hussain, an Iraqi singer, and her large backing band.[5] Campers tilted and swayed their heads to the sounds of the fluted *ney*, a wind instrument common to the region, that followed Hussain's melodic Arabic singing note for note. As the chorus slid into a call-and-response verse at the 2:50 mark, Yousef asked the group: "Can you hear the Farsi after the Arabic here?"

"Oh shit, they're singing 'baleh' [yes] to her, aren't they?" I heard one counselor whisper to another. The call-and-response verse, executed in beautiful Arabic-tinged Persian, was the lyrics and melody of "Gol Pari Joon," a popular song from the same era in Iran. Yousef seized on this moment of recognition:

> So, you hear how she's going between Persian and Arabic, yeah? She's code-switching. This indicates to us, when we are listening to it today, her Arab audience was comfortable moving between the languages. She doesn't translate herself. Our people are transnational. They have been connected through time. The border between Iraq and Iran is porous; people and ideas have always moved through it and past it.

Across his multimedia presentation and in an hour's time, Yousef systematically deconstructed the boundaries between Arab and Iranian. By offering evidence of centuries of Arab-Iranian mutual affection, cohabitation, and amalgamation—juxtaposed alongside the realities of war and empire with which youth were familiar from the Iran-Iraq War of the 1980s—Yousef very consciously provided fellow 1.5- and second-generation youth an alternative to the dominant narrative about acrimonious relations between Iranians and Arabs. Without ever blatantly saying so, Yousef himself was living proof. With his powerful presentation in the forefront of their minds, how could campers resist shedding tears at Bayoumi's meticulous account of Arab American resilience in the face of racism? How could they resist asking Omar Offendum, a popular Syrian American rapper who led a spoken-word cipher and rap performance later that night, "What's Arabic for *Ayandeh* [future]?" "*Mustaqbal*," Offendum replied, grinning. The sound of more than a hundred Iranian American kids cheering in Arabic (*"Mustaqbal! Mustaqbal! Mustaqbal!"*) echoed through the warm night air.[6]

"We Are Lucky and Unlucky Though"

Among campers, Arash was a particularly beloved counselor. In his mid-twenties, he possessed an unforced cool and was known to be, as one camper put it, "the smartest dude here." A graduate student in politics and rhetoric, Arash possessed knowledge of the literatures about which campers thirsted to learn more, from classical and modern Persian through new- and old-school American hip-hop. He was tapped to lead writing workshops, and across two years of my field observations, I witnessed him expose Iranian American teens to a scholarly analysis of the collected lyrics of Jay-Z in *Decoded*, alongside the earlier works of Junot Díaz, the poems of Forough Farrokhzad (1935–67), and second-generation Iranian American poet Solmaz Sharif. Arash's focus on rap lyrics, genre-bending bilingual prose, and contemporary poetry was striking in its dissimilarity from the small canon of mainstream writing by diasporic Iranians with which campers were most likely familiar. On this day, Arash began the conversation by asking the campers how they, as

Iranian Americans, felt about poetry, and fourteen-year-old David was first to respond:

David: Poetry has always been part of Iranian culture. I mean, Iranians quote poetry all the time in conversation. As Iranian Americans, we can read and write poetry too.

Arash: Okay, so there's two points there; that's great. One of them is that there's been this tradition, this kind of history of poetry. So when you're in the act of writing, you're almost standing on the shoulders of Hafez. Or you're walking in the footsteps of Rumi, right? It's not just *you* in the room, but they're there with you as well. And the other one is that you could write *about* Iranian Americans or Iranians.

Gelareh (camper): Language is something too, like you could write in English and in Farsi as well.

Arash: That's a really good point. Farsi is an interesting language. Like, have you all ever noticed that when we say "he" or "she," we don't distinguish between genders [in pronouns] in Farsi? So if you look at somebody like Hafez, all of these moments in which he's just playing with your mind.[7] He's talking about love. You don't know if he's talking about a girl, you don't know if he's talking about his mom, you don't know if he's talking about God, and he's saying that he loves *Oo* [gender-neutral pronoun] right? But you don't know who *Oo* is, and he's using the language in order to make that happen. So Farsi allows you to do certain things with language that English may not.

Hengameh (camper): A lot of poetry expresses a lot of Iranian ideals. Like messages, a lot of Saadi's poems, they express really important messages, and that's how we can relate to them.

Arash: That's a great point. Saadi is the pragmatist.[8] He's the guy who's the world traveler; he's been all around the place. He's been in the bazaars; he knows how things work. So you want life lessons? You go to Saadi. He'll help you get through your day.

Kaveh (camper): There's different types of Iranian poems, with rhymes?

Arash: That's good. We have the old style, the *ghazal*. The *ghazal* is like thirteen lines, and its kind of got a structure. Right? And then we have the *Rubáiyát*, Omar Khayyam, and the four little lines.[9] And then, all of a sudden, here comes the twentieth century. You get Nima Yooshij, who breaks it all.[10] Everybody at that time was like, "This is crazy." He was broke, living day to day. He destroyed the forms; he destroyed the subject matter and made something new.

Starting the workshop by asking participants to reflect on their own knowledge and relationship to Iranian poetry allowed Arash to deliver an accessible mini-history that was catalyzed by what campers already knew. Without assuming that the youth had any specific knowledge of the poets or forms themselves, he established two concepts for campers to take forward with them: they are the inheritors of a rich poetic tradition, and they are empowered to situate themselves within or even break the tradition should they choose to do so. Up until this point, the conversation was celebratory while avoiding the ethnocentric traps that conversations about Iranian accomplishments sometimes encouraged. This precarious balance was threatened after a fellow counselor, male and the same age as Arash, joined the conversation:

Pouya (counselor): Poetry can save a language, because Ferdowsi's *Shahnameh* saved the Farsi language from dying away. Ferdowsi is the reason why we're not speaking Arabic right now [snaps and claps].[11]

Arash: History has its messy moments, let's be honest. There's wars, violence, people taking over other people's land, and destroying their lives, okay? We've done it too, as Iranians, if we're honest and you look back at Iranian history. And we've had it done *to* us. Yes, at one point in time, there was a conquest of Iran. It brought in a totally different style of script that wiped out writing for two hundred years. They call it the "Two Hundred Years of Silence."[12] But the language was preserved because somebody like Ferdowsi came along, and using the [Arabic] script that was available to him, he was able to preserve language itself. So he took a new thing that was forced upon him to maintain something that was old. So that we could still have it today. But the Iranian American experience isn't just being on the receiving end of things. It's not like "we just need to go back in the day and find Hafez or look at Saadi" and find what they can *give* us. We can give something too. What would it mean for you, as an Iranian American person, having had the specific experiences that bring you all together here, to write? What new thing would you offer? How would you look at the world? June Jordan, the poet, gives us a quote. She said to write is to "take control of the language of your life."[13] This is what we are asking you to do today.

In this interaction Arash did not reject Pouya's observation, but instead, knowing that it was the type of observation that had the potential to devolve into Persian exceptionalism or into Iranian and Arab tensions, Arash rerouted the observation back into historical context. He did so not by denying history but by pointing out that events are not historically one-sided and that experiences like these, be what they may, can produce unexpected innovations in culture. In the final turn, campers too, he argued, are empowered to have their experiences expressed through writing, to "take control of the language" of their lives, whether in Persian using Arabic script or in English. While the expressly stated goal of the workshop was to expose youth to a broad range of Iranian poetry, Arash, and Camp Ayandeh more generally, encouraged campers to integrate Iranian and American traditions into their own creative and intellectual visions. In so doing, Arash empowered the youth to see themselves as the inheritors of a sometimes inaccessible body of literature, due in some cases to barriers of language but most universally due to the absence of Iranian literature and history in the curricula of their American schools. He empowered them to innovate and write themselves into this history, to "give something too."

A bit later, Narges joined Arash for the second half of the day's writing workshop. Rather than discuss older Persian-language poetry as in the first part of the workshop, Narges and Arash asked campers to consider a piece of writing in English by a young diasporic writer roughly in the same generation as theirs, Solmaz Sharif. To analyze her poem "Thanksgiving," they used as a starting point a prompt given to Sharif herself by one of her professors at UC Berkeley's Poetry for the People: "What does it mean to write with the knowledge you're born into?" Michael, a seventeen-year-old returning camper was the first to connect the prompt directly to the poem:

> Michael: The question was "the knowledge you're *born* into." Throughout her poem there's constant references to death, and I just think that's interesting, the tension there. Like something you're born into as an Iranian American is just constantly other people's deaths and being confined into a nomadic lifestyle of . . . discomfort [snaps].
>
> Narges: Michael, I think you're offering a really close reading here. She's playing with the juxtaposition of being *born* with *dying*. My reading of it is that she's working through a lot of grief here. Because she's talking about women in prisons and her father . . . and seeing her uncle's ID coming out of the wash. And there's constant reference to death in her family and the struggles they had to go through and what happened to them that made it so they came to the United States. So what Michael is saying is right on.
>
> Vida (camper) [directed to Narges]: I have a question: Do you know what she's referring to when she says "coffins where the women were / made to crouch blindfolded for months?"
>
> Narges: Yeah. That's prison she is writing about. After the revolution and still today in prisons in Iran and prisons in Guantanamo and all over the world, they will blindfold you as a way to disorient you.
>
> Kurosh (camper): Also, one story I've heard is they make you sit down for months and months and won't let you get up.

In the passage above, campers seized the opportunity to ask the slightly older staff to contextualize the poem for them. From the loosely facilitated discussion of "Thanksgiving" followed questions about political repression and trauma, topics that youth do not typically explore in their other learning environments. The staff validated the existence of prison torture in Iran and America and other restricted topics that haunt some campers' family backgrounds. Vida, age fifteen, posed another question about the poem's title and a distinctly second-generation tension therein:

> Vida: Something else that seems important is the title; like you said, the poem is about grief, but the title is also "Thanksgiving." So it's almost like . . . what are we supposed to think about the title?
>
> Arash: Yeah, the title is two-sided, right? Like, what you hear when you grow up Iranian [in America is], "You're lucky," and that you need to take responsibility for the privilege you have and not waste it. But also, yeah, that realization of you *are* really lucky.
>
> Bahram (counselor): We are lucky and unlucky though. The line "You meet your family / not in hospital nurseries but around / luggage turnstiles." That line, it reminds me of, you know, going to Iran and meeting your grandparents for the first time there. It's like . . . we're so far away from our relatives on the other side of the world. What does this mean for us in a second generation . . . for a whole generation, to not know our own *families* [snaps]?

In this passage, participants drew from the poem to grapple with the privileges associated with their birthright as American citizens. They acknowledged the different life chances and opportunities that Iranian Americans possess by virtue of their citizenship status in the United States. At the same time, participants expressed a collective moment of longing and loss for that on which it is predicated: the US dissolution of relations with Iran and the breaking apart of their families. For second-generation youth, it sometimes felt as though their "luck" was based in no small part on the lack of luck for their kin in Iran. And this luck itself was bittersweet, given youth's own liminal and sometimes painful experiences in the homeland as "not Iranian enough."

The writing workshop achieved several unique goals for the development of a distinctly second-generation sensibility: It exposed youth to a poetic tradition they were rarely if ever formally taught, despite their general knowledge of its existence while growing up in diaspora. Second, the writing workshop validated that youth have an important contribution to make, and it did so by situating it in two traditions at the core of youth's developing identities: Iranian literature and also minority literature in America. A third, and perhaps most intriguing outcome, was the writing workshop as a general clearinghouse for youth to discuss difficult topics that are specific to their Iranian American experiences, creating a sense of group solidarity: they could enjoy their Americanness and Iranianness simultaneously while still feeling loss about their distance from extended family in Iran, while also re-creating a family of fictive kin with other second-generation youth who have shared their experiences.

"Cookie Mookie," Taarof, and Other Ways to Be Iranian

Not every conversation about identity at Camp Ayandeh was fraught with intense talk of trauma or estrangement. Camp was also a place to cultivate lighthearted, whimsical considerations of identity. In a conversation held during counselor training about identifying a vision for the future of the Iranian American community, first-time counselor Shiva put it this way: "I'd like to preserve cultural traits like—you know how our parents, they say things like 'cookie mookie' [huge laughs and claps]. What will happen to that stuff? The warmth, the hospitality, the jokes. I feel like I could never tell jokes the way my dad and his friends can. How can we maintain that lighthearted, warm hospitality?" In this quote, Shiva—who was, by all measures, a fluent Persian speaker—lamented something subtler but also a bit more essential than Persian itself. "Cookie mookie" was Shiva's example of a small quirk of the Persian language as practiced in ordinary life: heritage speakers sometimes repeating a word with an "m" replacing its first letter. In diaspora, Persian speakers often do this to English words, like "cookie." Thus, for second-generation Iranian American youth, the singsong reduplication of "cookie mookie" was just one example of an everyday type of speech they lovingly associated with their immigrant parents.[14] Additional examples, like "prom mrom" and "Coca[-Cola] moca" elicited more knowing laughter and appreciation. Observations like Shiva's gave youth a moment to pause and reflect on intergenerational cultural subtleties that were not always discussed or celebrated in their lives outside camp. Indeed, even at camp, it was wedged within a more ostensibly serious discussion of a utopian vision for the Iranian American community. Shiva brought it up to lament the ease with which she saw her parents having fun and loving and living in Persian.

Outside counselor training, however, there was a common emphasis on celebrating and rearticulating Iranian cultural norms and traditions at camp. Both for the campers and the staff this work served several purposes. First, certain customs and traditions cut across ethnic and religious differences among campers; they were shared cultural forms that fostered a sense of pan-ethnic Iranian commonality that could traverse both social divisions and national borders. Second, the enjoyment of cultural traditions flattened uneven language fluencies in Persian and instead drew on cultural knowledge that most campers already possessed. Finally, in creating common bonds out of cultural customs, Camp Ayandeh also allowed campers to engage in the creation of a uniquely second-generation Iranian American identity that celebrated the customs with which campers had been raised while also allowing them to remix them.

Nowhere was this more evident at camp than in the *Taarof* Tournament, a popular annual activity that literally made sport of a pervasive Iranian custom known in Persian as *taarof*.[15] Described as "the great national trait [of] exaggerated politesse, modesty, and self-deprecation that Iranians seem to be born with," *taarof* is a widespread ritual of verbal and nonverbal communication in which Iranian social actors perform mutual deference.[16] In practice *taarof* is the enactment of "hyper-politeness":

> [*Taarof*] involves both parties insisting they are not worthy of the other
> [and] is in constant play in Iranian society—people refuse to walk
> through a door first, cabdrivers refuse to accept payment as passengers
> beg them to, hosts must offer pastries even if guests don't want them,
> and guests must say they don't want them even if they do.[17]

I offer just one example of how campers' performances of *taarof*—that mirrored, played on, and sometimes parodied their shared experiences in diaspora—contributed to a new sense of group identity that reimagined their second-generation Iranian American identities as playful and worthy of celebration.

A fifteen year-old camper from California, Foroud was a first-time contestant in the *Taarof* Tournament. He was up against the counselor Yasmin, who had intervened diplomatically in the conversation about *300* during the anti-oppression workshop. A formidable opponent, Yasmin greeted Foroud enthusiastically at the imaginary front door of a home:

> Yasmin: How's it going? Come in, please come in.
>
> Foroud [slight bow of head]: No, *shoma aval* [you (formal) first].
>
> Yasmin: No, please, bro, I'm the dirt beneath your skateboard! Get inside!
>
> Foroud [deeply bowing from waist]: I mean, this is your house!
>
> Yasmin: Even the dirt is better than me! Get inside!
>
> Foroud: No, no, this is your house, I don't know where to go! I don't have a key.
>
> Yasmin: But this is the key to your heart! Get inside!
>
> Foroud [hands clasped in mock prayer]: Please go ahead, pleeeeease?
>
> Yasmin [deeply bowing]: Okay, I'll go [audience cheers wildly].

In this scene, Foroud made good use of culturally specific body movements and gestures. He initially invoked the formal pronoun *shoma* (you) while respectfully bowing his head. When this proved unsuccessful, Foroud bowed from the waist, literally lowering himself before Yasmin, otherwise of equal height. Finally, Foroud pled with hands clasped in mock prayer, signifying an increasing urgency that Yasmin enter the doorway first, before the indignity of the situation produced any further distress and anxiety for both of them.

Yasmin employed novel, hyperbolic *taarof*-style phrases to compel Foroud to enter the imaginary doorway. She began with a metaphor, verbally subordinating herself to the level of "dirt beneath [Foroud's] skateboard," and later insisted that "even the dirt is better than me!" She also seized on Foroud's manner of dress (shaggy haircut, oversized hooded sweatshirt) and referred to him as "bro" before employing the hyperbolic skateboard metaphor. Yasmin's creativity and quick wit was on further display when, upon Foroud's complaint that he didn't have a key to the door, she proclaimed, "But this is the key to your heart!" In this moment, she switched into a type of wordplay that explicitly recalled the Persian master poets Saadi and Hafez, whose romantic and self-referential *ghazals* were discussed earlier in the day during Arash's writing workshop. Her strategy here was not entirely comedic, however, as the recitation or imitation of Persian masterworks in ordinary conversation remained embedded as cultural reference point and mode of expression in everyday Iranian life. Accordingly, this practice was reflected in Yasmin's novel, hyperbolic contribution of a new *taarof*-style phrase into the tournament. The totality of her performance, which reflected the nature of these US-born young people's proximity to and distance from authentically Iranian modes of expression, is a creative, empirical example of the "empowering paradox of diaspora."[18] It is in the tender but ironic performance of *taarof*, a most "authentically" and uniquely Iranian social practice, that second-generation identity in diaspora was collectively and creatively forged.

Conclusion

Most nights at camp ended with a campfire. However, in recent years, there wasn't actually a real fire due to insurance and safety rules at different facilities. Nonetheless, the vibe of a campfire was simulated with the entire population of camp huddled together in a ring formation to sing and tell stories and experience closeness as a group. Campers, habitually underdressed in shorts and T-shirts, would good-naturedly gripe to their counselors about mosquitoes until a hush fell over the group. Staff usually pulled out a couple of instruments, always at least an acoustic guitar and *tombak*, a small Iranian drum to rest against the knees and tap with open palms and fingertips. Under the cover of night, shy campers revealed hidden talents like a beautiful singing voice or prodigious ukulele-playing skills. The unofficial camp songbook included sloweddown folk-acoustic versions of upbeat Top 40 music like "Hey Ya" by Outkast or jazz scat-singing versions of oldies like "Leyli Jan" by Ahmad Zarif, known as the Afghan Elvis, whose melodies campers recognized from home. Or, as in the following example, camp staff like Firouz would create original freestyle raps to the beat of the *tombak*:

Welcome to Ayandeh where the campers play

and learn deep things like every day

Intellectual and fun don't have to oppose

When this camp makes you grow like a tall glass of *shir moz*[19]

We welcome you with open arms, be free

Don't have to speak Farsi or recite Rumi

To help us explore our identities

and help us shape our community

This camp is not as seen on TV

Not a prepackaged deal from the grocery

Organically, we'll be who we want to be

Until we feel strong like *Maman joon*'s chai

Uh, Let me see

Diversity, check

Solidarity, check

You got one hundred role models here, just pick

I'll say it loud to resound in your eardrum

Khosh amadid be Camp Ayandeh: welcome!

Firouz's rap was, in many ways, a distillation of what youth claimed were the most impactful and unique characteristics of camp: unabashedly hybrid in its Iranian and American cultural references, at once cool and nerdy, and above all else, the invitation to join a new, inclusive Iranian American family. It was, in effect, utopia around the campfire.

Firouz's rap was on my mind many months later when fifteen-year-old Yara and I were eating potato chips in an exurban strip mall, as described in Chapter 3. Yara had attended Camp Ayandeh for one summer, and, although according to her she had a good time, she was unlikely to return because "camps aren't really my thing, but I got what I needed from it." In the middle of our conversation about her father's claim that potato chips were an Iranian invention, her cell phone rang. Yara picked it up, turned to me, and said, "My mom wants to talk to you." I was surprised and also nervous; in the course of my research, I had never experienced a parent interrupting an interview via telephone. Holding the phone up to my ear, I could hear Yara's mother calling us from the car. Over the sound of traffic in the background, I had barely exchanged the necessary pleasantries in Persian before her mother's voice became urgent: "Are you asking Yara about camp? Camp did for her in *one week* what her father and I couldn't do in fifteen years!" she said. I replied that yes, I'd asked Yara some questions about camp but that I was curious to hear her observations, too, if she wanted to share them over the phone. As she began talking, I demonstratively placed my hand over the phone and mouthed to Yara, "Is this okay?!" She laughed and nodded her assent.

According to her mother, Yara had come home from camp with a changed relationship to her Iranian American identity. Whereas her mother and father used to worry that Yara avoided or seemed outright embarrassed about her Iranian heritage, they were now shocked that she spent nights Skyping with a new network of Iranian American friends from around the country. As a family, they had recently attended an Iranian winter solstice event (*Shabe Yalda*) with other local Iranian Americans, a dramatic change from earlier holidays, when Yara would beg her parents to let her stay home. According to her mom, Yara was newly interested in strengthening her Persian skills, and maybe even adding Arabic too.

I gave the phone back to Yara after much back and forth with her mom and disclosed to her what we had talked about. Yara rolled her eyes and laughed: "Typical mom! Don't get me wrong though because I did like [camp]. It for sure made me feel more comfortable with myself." Now six years later, Yara has studied abroad in the Middle East and is finishing credits for her Arabic and international relations double major while working at a peace and security studies organization. It's impossible to know if this career path would not have happened anyway as a result of Yara growing up and finding her way, eventually, to a strong academic interest in the region. But, at least to her own family, camp seems to have played a large role.

From sunrise to sundown and for the many months in between, participants described Camp Ayandeh as a "utopia." Utopias can be as troublesome and difficult as they are radical and inspiring. Anthropologist Cati Coe writes that "it is through . . . images of community and consensus that utopian thinking undercuts itself, for the images and metaphors themselves, often vague but full of emotional force, reinforce the exclusion of difference for the sake of harmony."[20] In some ways, because camp leveled its participants' relationship to Iranian identity for the sake of equity (recalling Mana's speech: "I don't care if you are one-half, one-fourth . . . alien") it accepted the risk of excluding difference for the reward of consensus and community. Vectors of class, gender, religion, and mixed racedness were conscientiously muted in the controlled setting of camp, but they never went away. In this way, Camp Ayandeh is not by definition a perfect utopia.

What respondents gestured to, I think, when they used the term "utopia" is a place apart. Camp is not the childhood home, made up of exceptional Aryan immigrants, nor is it the white-majority neighborhood school where Iranians are constructed as foreigners and racial outsiders. It is not the romanticized homeland, where diasporic youth stick out as too American, nor is it the contemporary university, where diversity is rationalized and Iranian Americans remain mostly illegible. Through the bonds of fictive kin at camp, group and individual esteem builds; through interactive workshops and dialogue, creative and potentially transformative critiques of the United States and of Iranian Americans' place within it are emboldened. At camp, a place by and for second-generation youth, to be Iranian and American was finally a complex but ultimately affirmative identity.

CHAPTER 7

BEING BROWN

JULY 4, 2002, was a particularly humid Independence Day in Boston. That year, my family and I were among the thousands of revelers who descended in undulating waves down to the banks of the Charles River to see the fireworks. My mom and little sister scrambled onto the first available patch of grass while I unrolled a blanket I had snatched off my twin-size dorm room bed hours earlier. My aunt unpacked almonds, cantaloupe, and soda from a plastic shopping bag; my dad, ambling slowly, as he does, brought up the rear. It was the summer between my sophomore and junior years of college, and I had stayed on campus to work. For the first time my family had come to visit me in New England.

As we fanned ourselves on the blanket, my parents discussed how twenty years earlier to the day they had boarded a Fourth of July flight to Portland, Oregon, with me, at nine months old, in tow. We were striking out on our own, away from New York City, where I was born and where, as new immigrants, my parents worked in a Persian rug store owned by my dad's extended family. Within a year of arriving in Portland, my parents had opened a Persian rug store on Skid Row, in Portland's Old Town–Chinatown. By the time my sister was born and my aunt had come from Iran to live with us during the vicious and protracted Iran-Iraq War, our family's store had relocated a half mile west to a historic building called the Pittock Block. In 1914, when it was first built, among the Block's many tenants were the city's major daily newspaper, the *Oregonian*, and the local electric company. By the late 1980s, the building remained stately, though dilapidated, and the utility company, the paper, and many of the other businesses had long since moved out. Our rug store was on the southeastern corner of the building along with a needle-sharing program, and in the wake of the first dot-com boom and bust when I left for college, my parents' store was struggling. I didn't know that by the time I would graduate, they would be forced to close it.

That morning in Boston I was the last to notice the white woman on the next blanket over who was staring at us in disgust. She stared at my dad in particular, who in a bit of confusion politely smiled back at her between his bites of cantaloupe. She whispered something in her companion's ear; they rolled up their blanket and left, flip-flop sandals smacking up and down against the ground. We didn't see or think about the women for a few minutes until two men in sunglasses and cargo shorts began to walk in wide circles around our blanket. "Oh my God," my mom whispered to me in Persian. "The cops are watching us." The July humidity was already intense, but it began to feel suffocating. Within seconds, a uniformed police officer and his K-9 approached us.

"What brings you folks down here today?" the officer asked my dad.

"Fourth of July, the fireworks," my dad replied.

The K-9 sniffed the plastic bag that held our snacks as the officer probed further: "Okay, where are you from?"

"We're visiting our daughter; she goes to college here. We are from Portland, Oregon," my dad said softly.

Like the two women before him, who now stood smirking at a safe distance away from us, the officer seemed unconvinced. He scrutinized our blanket and what sat on it: four women, one man, all of them sweaty, with dark hair, skin between white and brown, speaking to each other in English and something else. The uniformed officer made a slight gesture and, before the plainclothes officers he'd signaled swooped in for backup, he clarified the question: "I didn't ask where you *live*. I said where are you *from*?"

· · ·

For a long time, where an immigrant was "from" defined his or her ability to become an American, or to even enter America in the first place.

And where an immigrant was "from" functioned, in some ways, as an immigrant's race. Whiteness was an imprecise business with incredibly high stakes. Being white or from a white place meant eligibility for citizenship, home and business ownership, and intermarriage with other whites. Immigrants from Asia and the broad Middle East put the boundaries of whiteness to the legal test in the early twentieth century. Their racial prerequisite cases etched into law exactly which immigrants from which countries were white and, in the process, even pushed groups not yet present in the United States back and forth across the color line. A half century before their arrival en masse, "Persians" were a racial hinge for competing claims to whiteness and strategically portrayed as white or not white to help determine the radically different fates of Armenian, Arab, and South Asian Americans.

Although Portland, Oregon, is not typically known for its place in the racial history of the United States, two of the most famous racial prerequisite cases, *United States v. Bhagat Singh Thind* (1923) and *United States v. Tatos Cartozian* (1925), began there at the courthouse near my family's rug store. At the mercy of V. W. Tomlinson, a particularly unforgiving naturalization examiner at the US District Court, Thind, a Punjabi Sikh from India, and Cartozian, a Christian Armenian, faced intense racial scrutiny. Thind was an honorably discharged US Army soldier who identified himself as "Caucasian" and claimed that he was white. Over the course of eighteen years, the courts repeatedly granted and then revoked Thind's whiteness. By 1923, his case went from Portland to the US Supreme Court, which ruled that despite ambiguities of caste, geography, language, ethnicity, and religion, Thind and, by extension, all South Asians were definitively "not white" and therefore ineligible for US citizenship.

That same year, as a new federal Bureau of Immigration and Naturalization was established, Tatos Cartozian also applied for US citizenship, also in Portland, Oregon. When Cartozian was ordered to present himself to the court for visual scrutiny, he brought his wife, Helen, and three of their four children. Following Judge Robert Bean's inspection of their "trifle olive-complexioned" skin and Tatos's adequate ability to read and speak English, Cartozian's citizenship and whiteness were provisionally approved, with the caveat that, if the government saw fit, it could initiate cancellation proceedings immediately.[1]

Inspector Tomlinson, who had already received guidance from the new chief of naturalization to hold applications from "Hindus, Turks, peoples of the Barbary states [Algeria, Morocco, and Tunisia] and Egypt, Persians, Syrians, and other Asiatics" for extra scrutiny, wrote to his supervisor in Seattle to object to the approval of Cartozian's application. To Tomlinson, Armenians like Cartozian were "so closely related to the Persians, the Kurds, the Afghans, and the Beluchis that it is difficult to distinguish them . . . as white persons." In short order, the attorney general's office initiated a suit, *United States v. Cartozian*, to cancel Cartozian's citizenship based on racial ineligibility.[2] Across the country, a different US District Court ruled that, pending *Cartozian*, four Chicago-area applicants (Armenian, Syrian, Turk, and Persian) also did not qualify for naturalization as "free white persons." In every corner of the United States, naturalization applications for these racially in-between immigrants were suspended, with all eyes on the Portland court to settle the matter.

.   .   .

Just as it was for my own family, Portland, Oregon, was not the original port of entry for the Cartozians. My parents arrived in New York City after leaving Iran; Tatos and Hazel Cartozian arrived in New York City from Armenia, escaping the Armenian-Tatar massacres of 1905–7. Tatos, like my father, was put to work in the family business: Cartozian Brothers Inc., a Persian rug store. Within a year the Cartozian business expanded, and Tatos and Helen, like my parents, headed west to open a store in Portland. With them they brought their children, Hazel (age six), Vahan (age four), and Orie (age two), and had another child, Ardash, after their move. And just like my sister and me, the littlest Cartozian kids were raised on the rug store floor until they reached school age.

By all accounts, the Cartozians thrived in Portland. In short order the family opened two other store locations in the Pacific Northwest, transporting rugs in a distinctive "Cartozian Bros." truck to remote communities across Idaho, Oregon, and Washington. They also established a busy rug export office in Hamadan, Iran, to support their retail operations. By 1925, when the government took Tatos Cartozian to court to test the whiteness of Armenians, his Portland store was celebrating its tenth anniversary at Tenth and Washington in the Pittock Block, the same storefront where my parents would open a store, and I would grow up, seventy-five years later.

.   .   .

Cartozian and the other racial prerequisite cases described in Chapter 2 anticipate the present-day treatment of Iranians and other Middle Easterners in the United States by revealing the "court-determined dramaturgy of whiteness."[3] In other words, they lay bare how American immigration, citizenship, and race-based laws and policies demanded a performance of white identity from liminal, in-between people for the judgment of powerful, majority-group European Americans. For a claimant like Cartozian to effectively perform whiteness meant that he had to organize and deploy a full suite of characteristics, alliances, affiliations, behaviors, and appearances to the court. To win his suit— and to carry Armenian Americans along with him—Cartozian and his legal team not only presented sworn testimony supporting Armenian whiteness from expert witnesses like anthropologist Franz Boas but also called to the stand "ordinary" Armenians who had married especially well (meaning, they had "out-married" with white European Americans) or were Protestant rather than Apostolic. During a time of supposedly scientific racial knowledge, Cartozian was required to stage a social construction of Armenian whiteness.

One feature that has not been analyzed in these types of racial prerequisite cases are the roles played on- and offstage by liminal claimants' American-born or -raised children, even though the most famous image from *Cartozian* prominently featured Tatos with his young adult daughters, Hazel and Orie. Originally published by the *Oregonian* on April 8, 1924, under the headline "Racial Questions Involved in Trial," the photo captured the patriarch from the waist up, a handsome middle-aged man in a fitted three-piece wool suit, watch chain draped prominently off the top buttonhole of his waistcoat. Cartozian's daughters flanked him on either side: young women with slightly bobbed hair, the most conservative of the fashionable hairstyles of the mid-1920s. Orie (age twenty-two) wore a mink stole, its head turned prominently to face the camera. Hazel (age twenty-six) was tucked under her father's outstretched arm and wore a modest overcoat, dress, and delicate necklace. It's not hard to imagine that the image, conveying the family's not-too-prosperous prosperity, was carefully staged.

At the trial, it was Orie and Hazel—not their brothers—who took the stand in defense of their father's naturalization application. The lawyers for the defense presented the daughters as strong evidence of their father's whiteness: upstanding, well-groomed, and confident young women with perfect attendance as pupils in local Portland public schools. They were, it was argued, proof incarnate of Armenian assimilability and Christian grace. With the fate of their citizenship on the line, the Cartozian family and their legal counsel strategically deployed or muted every possible piece of social evidence at hand to make Armenians legibly white to the court. Presenting the Cartozian daughters as having sloughed off their Armenianness in favor of a mainstream American identity was essential, to prove not only the whiteness of their father but the whiteness of their ethno-national community in its entirety.

Outside the *Cartozian* ruling, however, the evidence left behind about the everyday lives of the Cartozian daughters tells a slightly different story. Hazel, in particular, radically self-identified as Armenian and was strongly affiliated with her heritage in Portland. As a teenager at Franklin High School she appeared in the pages of the local newspaper with fascinating regularity: she was an outspoken leader of her girls' debate team on which she orated about Armenian history during tournaments; she sang patriotic songs about Armenian liberty in her native Armenian tongue at a niece's elementary school recital; she demonstrated Persian rug-weaving techniques for customers in the corner of her father's rug store. Even as a teenager, and into her twenties, Hazel was an outspoken critic of war crimes against Armenia and raised thousands of dollars for the Armenian victims of massacre and genocide, delivering well-received public lectures to both secular and religious audiences around town. Before the court, however, Hazel's—and her father's—race was debatable and contested. Through the prism of the *Cartozian* ruling, the racial fate of Armenian Americans was the subject of public curiosity and of grave legal consequence. In punishingly assimilative times, Hazel nonetheless practiced a hybrid identity as a second-generation youth. Evidence of her love, commitment, and affiliation with where she was from, not just where she lived, cannot not be denied.

In July 1925, the US District Court in Portland ruled on *Cartozian*: Armenians were found to be white, and the government's cancellation suit was dismissed. Cartozian could retain his American citizenship. In July 2002, on the banks of the Charles River, my family—with our similar quasi-threatening, semilegible race—warranted extra scrutiny too. To the Boston police and the concerned citizens on the next blanket over, the important thing wasn't figuring out where we lived but pinning down the dark, elusive place where we, and the people who look like us, are from. Our white legal classification and American citizenship, granted by proxy since *Cartozian*, couldn't shield us that day.

Racial Hinges, Racial Loopholes

Iranians, not yet physically present in large numbers in the United States, were a flexible illusion in racial prerequisite cases like *Cartozian*. Across a variety of cases involving Arab, Armenian, and South Asian claimants, Iranians or "Persians" functioned largely as racial hinges. Geographically set in between the Middle East and South Asia, their liminal in-between racial status found theoretical clarity in the legal fights waged by earlier immigrant groups. The Zoroastrian and Muslim faiths practiced by Iranians became a legal fact harnessed to "whiten" and Europeanize Christian Arabs and Armenians; the same Zoroastrians and the shared presence of Indo-European languages and "Aryan" heritage in Iran and India were evidence that could whiten and Europeanize South Asians in turn. The specter of Iran was a racial hinge between white Europe and non-white Asia: a face, a body, a culture, and a race that could open or close the door to whiteness as needed.

Historically and theoretically, the limits of whiteness are no longer for American courts to prescribe. And in the intervening years, some things have changed. In the United States Iranians are no longer an imagined specter in the margins of other groups' immigration stories. They have since arrived as immigrants and refugees themselves. Given their relatively late migration from Iran, Iranian Americans were not, as a class, privy to the historically punishing racial prerequisites for US immigration and citizenship or legally barred from homeownership or employment on the basis of their race. In addition, Iranians continue to arrive to the United States in possession of, if not an agreement with or adherence to, distinct nationalist ideologies about their own Aryan roots as well. As Iranian Americans arrived white and remained legally white, the outcome of their racial identification should be uncomplicated.

Were their *ex ante* and *ex post* whiteness not enough to predict a seamless white Iranian American identity, classical and updated theories of assimilation would suggest that, barring significant racial discrimination, immigrants' social integration or whitening into a mainstream American identity is possible based on socioeconomic achievement. In this way, Iranian Americans also strongly conform to the successful outcomes predicted by this literature. A majority of Iranian Americans hold bachelor's degrees or higher, own their homes, and work in white-collar professions; they also possess significantly greater levels of income and education than the average American.[4] Most live in majority-white neighborhoods and attend, or send their children to, majority-white schools.

Despite possessing these common markers of status achievement, in the everyday politics of race, Iranian Americans are not exactly socially white. Although their legal whiteness in the United States has been more or less consistent since the end of the racial prerequisite era, their social whiteness, or, whiteness on the ground, has remained consistently elusive. As a class, Iranian Americans experience patterns of discrimination, interpersonal harassment and violence, and stigmatization in media and politics akin to those navigated by communities of color. Iranians and other Middle Easterners in the United States have to navigate what I call racial loopholes, which are the everyday inconsistencies produced in the gap between their legal white category and their acute racialization. Racial loopholes occur because Iranians and other Middle Easterners are denied formal recognition and recourse as a group apart from whites, and their experiences are assimilated into the social fabric of the United States as anything but race. The loophole is even indicated by the tentative, in-between historical moment in which the largest wave of Iranians migrated to the United States: a moment of social hypervisiblity—the 1979 Iranian Revolution—paradoxically paired with new legal invisibility—the 1978 federal classification of all Middle Easterners as white.

Racial loopholes are made especially clear in a growing area of research on Arab and Muslim Americans, Islamophobia, and the racialization of Islam in the United States.[5] This cross-disciplinary body of scholarship has extended Omi and Winant's racial formation theory to show how racial categories involving liminal groups expand, contract, and transform through social, economic, and political force. Although racial formation theory envisions racialization as a process that is at once top down and bottom up, a focus on the state has particularly flourished through a top-down approach. Research on the racial status of Iranians and other Middle Easterners, which calls attention to paradoxical everyday interactions that sometimes contradict legal racial assignations, demands the integration of bottom-up everyday struggles over the meaning and content of racial categories.

By taking note of large- and small-scale phenomena, new critical research on Middle Easterners in America breaks ground by taking very seriously that what has been previously compartmentalized as ethnic bigotry, religious intolerance, or anti-immigrant nativism flows from and attaches itself to bodies that are racialized, no matter the legal racial category of their subjects. Thus, in an era shaped by the War on Terror, a racialized master category governs and links Arab, Middle Eastern, Muslim, and South Asian Americans, despite the seeming incompatibility of their ethno-racial labels and their internal diversity. In this climate, race is no longer but one of many variables to help understand the integration of immigrants and their children in the United States; rather, race has been and still remains the master category. It is impossible to understand two generations of Iranian American life, or multiple generations of Arab American and other Middle Eastern communities in the United States, without taking race and the limits of whiteness seriously.

Becoming Brown

As the American-born second generation comes of age, there is evidence that Iranian Americans have begun to chafe against their social position at the limits of whiteness and to defy researcher expectations by eschewing the "white" category altogether. The second-generation youth whose stories make up this book grapple with an on-the-ground white racial category that seems to tighten and shrink to exclude Iranians everywhere except the census. As discussed in Chapter 2, Iranian Americans are positioned outside the limits of whiteness when their "hybrid" homemaking practices and aesthetic choices are targeted for exclusion by neighborhood and local-level architectural codes built on "purity." Iranian Americans are pushed outside its limits when they are forcibly recused as immigration judges or when they are detained and arrested as hostile threats while waiting to use the bathroom at a truck stop. As discussed in Chapters 3 and 4, second-generation youth are pushed outside the limits of whiteness when the unpalatable, pseudo-scientific Aryan history of Iran fails them, and they are bullied for their non-whiteness by European American peers, and sometimes their teachers as well. Iranians fall well outside the bounds of whiteness when, as discussed in Chapter 5, they prepare for hyper-scrutiny in international airports and security lines or forge new strategically inclusive Iranian identities, as discussed in Chapter 6. Iranians, who have from their arrival in the United States been legally situated inside whiteness, have been simultaneously escorted, framed, and deported out of its everyday social limits.

Like Cartozian and the millions of liminal racial subjects in the annals of American immigration before them, Iranian Americans face intense social pressure to pledge fealty, sincerely or performatively, to the United States. Like many other groups in American society, they face strong internal and external pressure to disavow their roots, change their names, and disassociate with one another to conform, to the extent that they are able, to the racial category to which they have been assigned—no matter how futile the task. They are asked to do so, often at the cost of their heritage and identities and at the cost of meaningful connections with other minority communities.

But precisely because of their position at the limits of whiteness, second-generation Iranian Americans do not behave in predicted assimilative ways and, even as young teenagers, are mostly wise to the racial loophole in which they find themselves. They understand that despite their legal whiteness and the claims of some first-generation parents, in the United States they are seen as ethno-racial outsiders and that American whiteness is not really for them. Throughout this book, second-generation youth actively struggle to forge new racial identities: by finding common cause and friendship with communities of color and similarly in-between groups; by successfully and unsuccessfully agitating to change official racial categories to better reflect their lived experiences; and by contesting Aryan ideologies that continue to circulate within their own families and communities. Like Hazel Cartozian, who was radically Armenian in the face of the homogenizing forces of assimilation and whiteness that both law and society compelled of her a century earlier, Iranian American youth do not shirk their Iranian identities despite the many ways in which they are incentivized to do so. Instead, they intuitively live as racial hinges, crafting political identities as racial outsiders, banding together with other youth to promote more racially inclusive schools and universities, and practicing an antiracist and strategically inclusive Iranianness in co-ethnic spaces like Camp Ayandeh. They are becoming brown by choice and by force.

Iranian American youth are perceptive to the everyday reminders—via micro-interactions, state surveillance, and media representation—that their off-white racial status is not just subordinate and conditional to normative whiteness but only partially legitimate and mostly in name. By virtue of their proximity to whiteness at its limits, they can articulate in detail the catchall racialized markers used to cast particular bodies and identities outside its borders, even though by all sociological accounts,

Iranian Americans should be among the newest entrants into the "racial contract" between whites.[6]

In this way the stories of second-generation Iranian American youth expose not only the limits of whiteness as they relate to Iranians specifically but also the fragility of whiteness more broadly and the aggressive policing of its borders. As it stands, identities and bodies—and the fine-grade differences between them beyond skin tone—are irreducibly part of the racial lingua franca of race in America. As populations in the United States can either be folded into or cast out of whiteness, the experiences of Iranian American youth expose the constantly shifting ground on which it sits. The power of whiteness in the United States comes not only through force and strength but also from its flexibility: its contractions and expansions, its ability to bend over time, and to define itself simply by defining what it is not.

ACKNOWLEDGMENTS

The experiences of eighty-four young people form the basis of this book. I treasure each of you and give thanks for the circumstances that brought you to this project and into my life. As I drafted the analysis in libraries, coffee shops, and in my office, I felt your expressive voices with me. As I fussed over the book, I benefited from your gentle pressure to finish up already so you could finally hold it in your hands.

Now that I am a parent myself, I newly comprehend what a gift your families gave to me when they consented to your participation. They asked me inside for chai, hosted me overnight as I schlepped around the country to meet you, and included me in your birthday parties and high school graduations. My gratitude for your families' trust is difficult to describe with words and better demonstrated by how Clayton and I strive to open our home as warmly to friends and strangers as yours did.

Stephanie Adams, Olivia Bartz, Jenny Gavacs, Frances Malcolm, Marcela Cristina Maxfield, Emily Smith, and the editorial board at Stanford University Press shepherded this book from idea to reality with great care. The manuscript reviews solicited by SUP strengthened the book; I am grateful to the anonymous readers for their time and feedback. Cynthia Lindlof copyedited with skill and a graceful touch. For everything we could anticipate and everything we couldn't, Kate Wahl is simply the very, very best editor in chief in academic publishing.

I have had the fortune of learning from mentors whose intellectual rigor is underpinned by their commitment to a more peaceful world. At Smith, Ginetta Candelario and Jennifer Guglielmo were my advisers, and I studied their exemplary feminist practice as scholars, activists, and whole people. Rick Fantasia, Nancy Whittier, and Marc Steinberg were instrumental to getting a couple generations of Smith sociologists through the academic pipeline. At UC Santa Barbara (UCSB), Reg Daniel and George Lipsitz were creative, rigorous iconoclasts and mentors. Howie Winant, Kum-Kum Bhavnani, Jon Cruz, Simonetta Falasca-Zamponi, Carolyn Pinedo-Turnovsky, Cedric Robinson (*rooheshoon shad*), Denise Segura, and Verta Taylor were generous advocates. I thank the funding bodies behind the grants and fellowships that helped me through graduate school: the National Science Foundation, Steck Family Endowment at UCSB, the UC Center for New Racial Studies, the Flacks Fund for the Study of Democratic Possibilities, and the Mendell Fellowship in Cultural Literacy at the Walter Capps Center for the Study of Religion, Ethics, and Public Life. Thank you to the Consortium for Faculty Diversity in Liberal Arts for matching me with Muhlenberg College and Janine Chi for an important postdoctoral year.

This book was written in my first few years in the Department of Sociology at the University of Toronto, in an exciting intellectual environment. I thank Shyon Baumann, Anna Korteweg, Patricia Landolt, Melissa Milkie, and Scott Schieman for their leadership. For their mentorship and example, I also thank Zaheer Baber, Monica Boyd, Bob Brym, Hae Yeon Choo, Jennifer Chun, Randol Contreras, Cynthia Cranford, Ronit Dinovitzer, Bonnie Erickson, Phil Goodman, Ping-Chun Hsiung, Josée Johnston, Jooyoung Lee, Vanina Leschziner, Ron Levi, Paula Maurutto, Ann Mullen, Michelle Pannor, Ito Peng, Jeff Reitz, Erik Schneiderhan, Luisa Schwartzman, Dan Silver, and Judy Taylor. Warm thanks to Jayne Baker, Ellen Berrey, Fidan Elcioglu, Alex Hanna, Steve Hoffman, Rachel LaTouche, A. W. Lee, Sida Liu, Andrew Miles, Akwasi Owusu-Bempeh, Kim Pernell, David Pettiniccio, Ashley Rubin, Rania Salem, and Geoff Wodtke. For her transformational friendship and effect on my work, I thank Jennifer Carlson. Sincere thanks to the awesome Sherri Klassen, Pamela Armah, Tina Colomvakos, Joanna Mackie, John Manalo, Jeremy Nichols, and Lorna Taylor. I am grateful for the robust Iranian studies community at University of Toronto, especially Mohamad Tavakoli-Targhi, Victoria Tahmasebi-Birgani, Farzaneh Hemmasi, Nasim Niknafs, and Sara Saljoughi. Minelle Mahtani sent me an e-mail in 2012, before we moved to Canada, that set the tone for everything to come since: thank you for that and everything else, Minelle *joon*.

For producing unique work that has influenced me and, in some cases, offering comments on written chapters or public presentations, I thank my Whats App *doreh* (Beeta Baghoolizadeh, Narges Bajoghli, Sarah Khanghahi, and Amy Malek), Donya Alinejad, Arash Azzizada, Yousef Baker, Mehdi Bozorgmehr, Umayyah Cable, Samira Damavandi, Arash Davari, Nina Farnia, Ali Ferdowsi, René Flores, Sarah Gualtieri, Arian Jadbabaie, Amira Jamarkani, Persis Karim, Hani Khafipour and USC Iranian Studies, Sheefteh Khalili, Mana Kharazzi, Sunaina Maira, Michael Musheno, Arian Nakhaie, Anthony Ocampo, Sahar Sadeghi, Ariela Schachter, Saher Selod, Nazanin Shahrokni, Mana Tahaie, John Tehranian, Stan Thangaraj, the University of Manitoba workshop on Middle East Diasporas in December 2015 (especially Louise Cainkar, Sally Howell, Akram Khater, and Hamid Naficy), Shirin Vossoughi, Hanif Yazdi, Reza Zia-Ebrahimi, and Beth Zilberman. Saumi Shokraee's enthusiasm pushed me across the finish line.

Conversations with University of Toronto grad students in my fall 2016 seminar on race, Shervin Etemad and the Iranian Student Group at University of Connecticut, Smith undergrads in my spring 2012 course on "Middle Eastern Americans," and University of Toronto undergraduates such as Jamilah Dei-Sharpe, Mitra Fakhrashrafi, and Maleeha Iqbal influenced this book. Research assistance from Salina Abji, Roksana Borzouei, and especially the amazing Mishana Garschi moved the writing forward. The editors of Ajam Media Collective (Beeta Baghoolizadeh, Alex Shams, Rustin Zarkar; Shima Houshyar, Kamyar Jarahzadeh, Asher Kohn, and Behzad Sarmadi) embraced this project in multiple ways.

I am grateful to friends outside academia for their kinship: in Toronto, Hanna Faghfoury, Mark Bolumsjak, and Zoia; Kathy Kim; Mercedes Lee and Ian Doty; Chris Nuttall-Smith, Carol Toller, and Cormac; Effie Tassiopoulous and Greg Ko, little Ignatius, and Effie's mom; Cyn Wang, Eva Larson, and Sloane. Because of Janeny Emmanuel, Erin Graham, and the teachers at Downtown Montessori and N'sheemaehn Child Care Centre, I was able to write knowing that Neelu was thriving in their care. Since Smith, Lillian Carrasquillo, Elizabeth Kim, Ian Lovett, Angela Serratore, Jacqui Shine, and Leigh Weisenburger Albert have been inspiring, wonderful friends. The Brown/Hutchison, Dutton/Mattern, and Gaffney/Winkler families, the Schetkys, Lauren Hunter, and the Zilberman/Benederets, Wyles/Roses, and Small/Spragues deserve special thanks for adopting us into their clans.

I love my friends in the UCSB sociology diaspora so much, which includes Carlos Alamo, Tanya Smallwood, and Eggi; Melissa Guzman and Patrick Lopez-Aguado; Maryam Griffin; Rolondo Longoria; Erik Love, Helene Lee, and Aurora; Emily Tumpson Molina, Devin Molina, and Tali; Bob Ngo; Rachel Parker and James Walsh; and Greg Prieto. Befriending sociologists like Alison Gerber, Jennifer Huck, and Adam Slez while we were away from UCSB was a blessing.

Our families have been a soft place to land in the hardest times. To my in-laws in Berkeley, Nashville, Philadelphia, and Santa Cruz; my maternal and paternal families in Iran, Canada, France, Portugal, and the United States; and most of all, to my father, mother, aunt, sister, brother-in-law, and niece: thank you for your sacrifices and your unconditional love. I am only here because of the rebellious streak that threads through the history of our family's survival. My parents are a love story that would take an entire, other book to explain.

I have been in love with Clayton Childress since the first moment I met him. For eleven years now, he has been my 50/50 partner, moral compass, and strength. Our daughter is every dream I had for our future, made real. Neelu, you are a singular miracle and the greatest joy of my life.

.   .   .

I am grateful to the following journals for allowing me to use portions of published articles for this book. Parts of Chapters 4 and 6 originally appeared in small scale in the following journals, but this book offers new analysis and different ethnographic supplements:

"The War at Home: Militarized & Racialized Identities in the University Critical Language Classroom," *Critical Sociology* 41 no. 7–8 (2015): 1137–55.

"The *Ta'arof* Tournament: Cultural Performances of Ethno-national Identity at a Diasporic Summer Camp," *Ethnic and Racial Studies* 36, no. 5 (2013): 818–37.

"'Inherited Nostalgia' among Second-Generation Iranian Americans: A Case Study at a Southern California University," *Journal of Intercultural Studies* 31, no. 2 (2010): 199–218.

REFLECTIONS
ON THE RESEARCH

Researchers aiming to study Iranian Americans must grapple with fundamental challenges for sampling and case selection. Due to their federal classification as "white," there are no reliable population-level data on how many Iranian Americans reside in the United States, where they live, and so on.[1] It is a subject of great consternation for Iranian Americans who have advocated for new census classifications and "write it in" campaigns to better document the locations and contours of Iranian American lives. No matter the methodological approach, the predicament of studying a "visibly invisible" group makes it challenging for both qualitative and quantitative researchers to identify a comprehensive population from which to sample. To be able to collect original data on Iranian American experiences, I had to devise a sampling frame by other means.

Researching a "Visibly Invisible" Group

The data for this book draw on a variety of qualitative methods commonly used by sociologists: structured and open-ended life history interviews, conventional observation and (more often) fluid "observant participation," and textual and historical analysis. By giving up the pretense of representativeness in favor of sampling for range, it was clear that I would need to conduct interviews and ethnographic observations of young Iranian Americans across the country.[2] Though I knew many Iranian Americans personally, I decided to recruit only interlocutors with whom I had no previous relationship or acquaintance before starting the project. I began by conducting interviews and observations through chain-referral sampling with second-generation youth in and around "Tehrangeles" in Southern California. An L.A. subset of the overall Iranian American population, however, is not illustrative of the whole: as others have shown, significant class and ethno-religious stratification shapes Tehrangeles.[3] Were the experiences of second-generation youth in West L.A. indicative of Iranian Americans like Yara (Chapter 3), who commuted to an arts-based public school in Washington, D.C., from the exurbs of Northern Virginia? Or Shahram and Amir (Chapter 4), who went to high school in the rural Midwest? I was not sure. To get a wider sense of what life was like, I would need to meet youth raised in different faiths (Muslim, Zoroastrian,

Jewish, Baha'i, Christian, atheistic, and agnostic); those with one Iranian parent or two; and those from urban, suburban and rural communities. With an eye toward diversifying my sample, I connected with potential interlocutors through a variety of means: via extended personal networks, through campus organizations, and through Camp Ayandeh, which itself drew a wide swath of Iranian Americans from around the country and heterogeneous family backgrounds.

Inspired by inductive research on immigrant youth cultures, my research design involved sleeping on the floor in college students' dorm rooms in Maryland; sitting beside them in mega-sized classrooms in New Jersey; watching TV in living rooms with their families in suburban communities like Braintree, Massachusetts; and spending evenings with youth around the campfire at summer camp in the wooded hills of Northern California. Taking stock of the photos, collages, ticket stubs, and doodles that decorate bedrooms across the new American ethno-burbs, I enrolled in introductory Persian classes alongside heritage learners at the University of California, hung out as respondents joined in Asian American hip-hop dance groups in rural Connecticut, and watched as they forged bonds with Arab American peers in Washington, D.C.–based Students for Justice in Palestine meetings.

In total, across two years of sustained fieldwork and three additional years of follow-up communication, I conducted ninety-six interviews with eighty-four 1.5- and second-generation Iranian American youth, who ranged from ages thirteen to twenty-eight during the period of research. I visited their schools and childhood homes and went on tours around their neighborhoods, which brought back evocative memories for them. Some I met in favorite coffee shops or restaurants; others, in their first apartments, shared with roommates. Handwritten field notes and audio of our conversations were recorded with permission. Out of this sample, the voices of fifty-one participants are quoted in the book and form the empirical basis for the original data presented throughout.

It was from this cross-country fieldwork that one universal theme emerged: Across disparate neighborhoods and schools, youth consistently encountered messages from their respective social environments that Iranians are not white, regardless of what their parents or the US government claimed. These messages were sometimes articulated as bullying or harassment for perceived physical and cultural difference from a European American norm. From this anecdotal observation, a secondary pattern emerged: the "whiter" the neighborhood, the more acutely negative stigma and bullying Iranian American youth seemed to face. This was not a regionally limited experience or a purely faith-based experience of Islamophobia. In this way, the limits of whiteness began to show themselves to me through these travels: Legal, socioeconomic, and geographic proximity to white Americans did not seem to make Iranian Americans white. Their everyday experiences actually suggested the opposite. Young people described acute racialization, especially in majority-white spaces.

The most concentrated, immersive ethnographic research for this project happened over two summers (2010 and 2011) of participant observation in a co-ethnic setting, Camp Ayandeh, which forms the empirical foundation for Chapter 6. With permission of IAAB, consent was collected at the time of camp registration (70 percent positive response rate from parents/guardians for under-eighteen participants; 98 percent positive response rate for over-eighteen participants). It was clarifying to observe how race and identity were discussed by Iranian American youth in the atypical, exclusive presence of co-ethnics. From their collective actions at camp, I was beginning to understand that the fine-grained experiences of race of second-generation youth were not entirely captured in quantitative or anecdotal data about their first-generation parents' occupational status or educational attainment. Rather than integrate seamlessly into a variety of majority-white places, as their families' socioeconomic status and official racial designation suggested, Iranian Americans seemed to sit somewhere at the social boundary of whiteness. After two years of fieldwork, I had identified this core paradox.

The challenge of studying a visibly invisible group became significant again once I turned to the historical record to better contextualize, or in some cases, challenge my interpretations of the qualitative data I had collected. The lack of reliable, comprehensive demographic data on Iranian Americans is compounded by their newness as an immigrant group. There simply doesn't exist the same rich archive of historical documents and accounts of the Iranian American experience as for other groups. Even tracking down the identity of the "first" Iranian immigrant to America is murky due to issues of racial categorization and national identity.[4] By virtue of these limitations, I had to make an epistemological shift: to reimagine the recent past and present as a developing Iranian American archive that could offer insights into the social futures of the young people whose stories form the bulk of my original data.

In 2014, I began to keep records of recent discrimination lawsuits, news reports, and other public documents in which Iranian Americans are legible as variably raced and racialized subjects, which forms the basis of Chapter 2. I also assembled a small corpus of court transcripts and early twentieth-century racial prerequisite cases involving non-Iranian South Asian and Middle Eastern claimants. From here I was led to American anthropologist Henry Field's pre-war "discovery" of the "Iranian Plateau race," discussed in Chapter 3. I found that across documents old and new, Iranians had been variably positioned at the conceptual limits of American whiteness. Collectively these qualitative methods represent only one feasible approach to the study of the racialization of a "visibly invisible" group like Iranian Americans. The integration of quantitative and experimental methods in future research would only strengthen and clarify any official/legal versus social distinctions that can be made about Iranians' racial status in diaspora.

The Identities We Share

Apart from epistemic challenges of research design, there were more general methodological issues related to shared group identities and affinities. As an American-born child of parents who emigrated from Iran, I share at least one fundamental characteristic with my study respondents, who each have at least one first-generation immigrant parent of Iranian descent. A good deal of ethnographic ink has been spilled over insider/outsider dynamics in research and, in particular, "racial matching" between interviewers and interviewees.[5] Scholars have yet to come to a consensus on how racial matching may enhance or hinder the quality of data collected.

Given the rich heterogeneity across my research sample (inclusive of participants' mixed-race backgrounds, gender, sexuality, religiosity, and socioeconomic status), it would be inaccurate to assert that, even across these differences, I shared a sense of cultural currency and heritage with all of the respondents included in this project. But my ability to move between casual Persian and fluent English, along with my familial-based knowledge of Iranian customs, folkways, and history, presented each interaction with a degree of rapport and, in most cases, goodwill before the formal interviews even began. In these ways, I was read as an "insider" by some of the research participants.

In other significant ways, research participants also positioned me as an "outsider." First, I was not a member of organizations through which I met some interlocutors. Though I would, in some cases, eventually join as an observant participant, interviewees often recounted events or memories from these organizations' histories prior to my having joined them. This initial outsiderness, I think, made the interviews fuller: previous events, a variety of personalities, and other social dynamics had to be explained to me in rich detail by respondents.

Without ever formally soliciting feedback about my own physical appearance or race, roughly a quarter of the research participants with whom I spoke made unprovoked references to my appearance as one of a typically "Iranian woman" or "Persian/Iranian" (irrespective of gender). This was done usually as a basis for comparison in which, for example, the participant would compare my appearance with others they were describing or with the research participant herself or himself. They nearly universally positioned me as the standard-bearer of a typical Iranian appearance or look. This book does not systematically analyze such interactions between myself and the respondents, or researchers and research participants more generally. Using an inductive approach, I have included my ascribed description of a respondent's physical appearance (body/facial hair, skin color, and/or other visible features) in cases where the respondent himself or herself made reference to it in the interview data. A more systematic approach, like Roth's "photo elicitation" technique for everyday racial schemas, could be productive for future research on Iranian Americans and other Middle Easterners.[6] Outside the vignette set on July 4, 2002, in the book's Conclusion, this book does not venture into auto-ethnographic accounts of how ethno-racial taxonomies are created "on the fly" in such interactions. This is, however, a potentially fruitful avenue for investigation that would add depth to the "racial matching" and insider/outsider discussions that continue in qualitative research.

Conducting Research with Youth in Practical and Ethical Ways

The last major area of methodological challenge had to do with conducting research with underage youth. I now see that these age-related challenges co-here around three different themes: institutional oversight, digital/social media, and an ethics of care. On a strictly bureaucratic level, conducting research with underage youth meant that the project was subject to significant oversight by research ethics boards. Close attention had to be paid to protecting sensitive information about participants' identities; formal consent had to be gained from parents and guardians. Pseudonyms are used for all but four interlocutors; in most cases, the names of small towns and suburbs have been anonymized. Beyond these straightforward safeguards, I built a small degree of reciprocity into the research design when possible: volunteering time, effort, and a very modest amount of financial subvention to the organizations that hosted my presence as a researcher. I drew from my work experience in college admissions and financial aid to offer advice, general or specific, to research participants who asked; for one nonprofit group and several university student groups, I organized and delivered academic workshops, and in one case applied for and received a grant on the behalf of the co-ethnic Iranian student organization at my home university.

On a practical level, conducting research with youth meant that I utilized social media as a technique for arranging, managing, and conducting research in a way that I could not have anticipated when I initially began this project in 2009 as a graduate student. Social media as a way of life and phenomenon unto itself developed dramatically throughout the course of my research. Across the five years of this project, Instagram, Twitter, and Facebook, in particular, were indispensable to ongoing communications with interlocutors. Social media posts and interactions were also sometimes the very artifacts of racialized experience to which youth referred in our conversations and interviews (see, for example, the opening anecdotes in Chapters 4 and 5). "Best practices" for the incorporation of digital/social media as technique and as data in qualitative academic research are still in development and subject of debate.[7] Thus, for the purposes of this study, I did not collect or systematically analyze interlocutors' social media posts and interactions. In the few cases where I felt that reproducing a post was essential to the presentation of data from fieldwork, I did so with explicit permission.

Beyond bureaucratic and practical matters related to conducting research with underage youth, my experience in this project has left me with more questions than answers about how to conduct rigorous research while practicing an ethics of care for the communities one attempts to represent. Even when I was protecting sensitive information and gaining parental consent, what does it mean to solicit painful memories from young people, no matter how voluntarily? Is it empowering or humiliating to have stories about your childhood and teen years analyzed and discussed by a sociologist? Studying the Iranian American case from within the first two generations of the community's formation means that this text, inclusive of its methodological limitations, is at best, an early and incomplete analysis.

IRANIAN AMERICAN DEMOGRAPHICS AND THE "RACE QUESTION"

Due in large part to the kinds of racial loopholes described in this book, the US government is potentially transforming how it counts Iranian Americans, Arab Americans, and others from the Middle East and North Africa. As part of its 2015 National Content Test (NCT), the Census Bureau conducted a formal test of a MENA category, offering to respondents "Iranian" as one of six "example" ancestry groups listed under MENA. When no MENA category was offered, respondents with ancestry from the Middle East, including Iranians, predominantly self-identified as "white" or "some other race." But when offered the MENA category as a racial option, an overwhelming majority of respondents with ancestry in Iran and the Arab world shifted their self-identification to MENA.[1] Though the bureau has not gone as far as to officially recommend the inclusion of a MENA category for the 2020 census, as of October 2016, it has solicited public feedback on the formal inclusion of a new "MENA" racial category for the 2020 US census.[2] Though the bureau has long acknowledged a need for further research on how to improve federal data on MENA communities, previous efforts to break Middle Easterners out of the white box have been unsuccessful except in key local settings.

As the categories currently stand, it is very difficult to measure or understand Iranian American demographic trends because of the way the Census Bureau aggregates data. For decades, individuals who chose the "some other race" box and wrote in "Iranian" or "Middle Eastern," for example, were treated as having mislabeled their racial classification and recoded by the Census Bureau as "white." According to the Census Bureau 2015 American Community Survey (ACS), which asks a question about ancestry, 486,994 (+/− 20,370) individuals in the United States reported their first- or second-generation ancestry as Iranian. Scholars argue, however, that the ACS and census, by design, underreport the number of Middle Easterners in the United States, making it difficult to estimate how many individuals are actually of Iranian descent.[3]

While the Census Bureau currently recodes as "white" those Iranians who mark "some other race," alternative estimates provided by the Iranian Interest Section (a part of the Embassy of Pakistan in Washington, D.C.) are similarly questionable. By using passport information, there is no way to account for persons who left Iran without passports or to account for second-generation children born to Iranians in the United States, unless those children themselves have applied for Iranian passports. Major Iranian American lobbying organizations like the National Iranian American Council (NIAC) have also lamented that "many in our community don't submit their census information out of fear for their privacy."[4]

In 2009 a coalition between at least fifteen major Iranian American advocacy groups, professional organizations, and service providers titled "Stand Up and Be Counted" resulted in television and radio public service announcements, e-mail and YouTube viral marketing campaigns, and traditional community organizing around the issue of the community's illegibility in the census.[5] The coalition's most widely disseminated "Frequently Asked Questions" handout tackled the question of racial liminality, and by all accounts, was the first time any Iranian American advocacy group had been so explicit:

> 10. What "race" should I put on the census? It is very important that on Question 9 of the Census that you check the box for "Some other race" and write in "Iranian" or "Iranian American." Otherwise, Iranian Americans will not be counted as a distinct cultural group in the U.S. and will not wield the power that comes with numbers. In other words, unless you specifically designate that you are "Iranian" or "Iranian American" when answering Question 9, you will not be counted as an Iranian American. For this reason, almost every Iranian American organization is encouraging Iranian Americans to designate their race as "Iranian or "Iranian American." Without being counted as "Iranians," we risk being disenfranchised both politically and economically for another 10 years.[6]

The previous passage provided direct advice to Iranian Americans on how they should answer the race question on the census form. It's important to recognize that it did so through the vocabulary of identifying Iranians as a "distinct cultural group." To what extent this language was used to assuage the Iranian American community's beliefs or anxieties about its whiteness is unclear. Though the preliminary results from the 2015 NCT of the MENA category may reflect a tipping point in the Iranian American community's paradoxical relationship with whiteness and assimilation, it is unclear what effects may or may not occur as a result of this possible categorical shift. Nonetheless, the 2010 campaign was, according to insiders, a failure due to Iranian Americans' "post-9/11 fears of [census] data being used against people."[7]

In spite of these significant methodological and categorical limitations to collecting an accurate count of Iranian Americans, news sources and scholarly articles sometimes cite the number as between one million and two million persons.[8] The most frequently quoted estimate is outdated and likely conservative: 690,000 Iranians living in the United States as of 2004.[9] At the county level, the ACS offers a sense of where Iranian American enclaves are located. Though Iranians are dispersed throughout every US state, they live predominantly in the same greater metropolitan areas to which they migrated immediately after the revolution: San Francisco/San Jose, Houston, Washington, D.C., and Los Angeles.[10] Good studies exist on the social and economic integration of Iranian Americans in enclaves like Los Angeles and in the "digital diaspora."

At this point, it is impossible to predict what the current Republican-led federal government will do with the Census Bureau's recent recommendation that a MENA response category be further tested and considered for inclusion in the official 2020 census. This book nonetheless represents a first attempt to document and theorize Iranians' everyday experiences of race as a visible and established presence in the United States.[11]

NOTES

Chapter 1

1. Coombes 2011.

2. Casiano 2011.

3. Ibid.

4. For more on American cowboys and the Middle East, see Jamarkani 2015; Kollin 2015.

5. I borrow the concept of "rank-and-file" ethnic and racial distinctions from Brubaker, Loveman, and Stamatov 2004. For more on how racial boundaries are drawn, see Lamont 2001.

6. Tehranian 2010, p. 74.

7. *Chola*, a feminine term used to describe both mixed Mestizo and indigenous American identities and a cultural and aesthetic style, is used in this instance as a colloquial marker of similarity and a term of endearment and belonging.

8. Mills 1997.

9. The white de facto versus white de jure statuses of Middle Eastern Americans is discussed in Tehranian 2010.

10. Whether the scholarship in question has theorized whiteness as hegemonic norm, hierarchy, or system of supremacy and terror, the consequences of an academic and political project centered on whiteness remains uncertain. See S. Ahmed 2004; Garner 2007. For an example of foundational research in whiteness studies, see Jacobson 1998.

11. Roediger 1991; Brodkin 1998; Guglielmo 2003.

12. Notable works include Roth 2012; Willoughby-Herard 2015; Molina 2014; Foley 1999; Twinam 2015.

13. Gans 2016.

14. Eduardo Bonilla-Silva 2006; Feagin 2013; Omi and Winant (1986) 2014. For studies of Middle Eastern Americans that incorporate a racial formation framework, see Love 2017; Zarrugh 2016; Marvasti and McKinney 2004. For an incorporation of Muslim identities into the sociology of race, see Selod and Embrick 2013.

15. Haney López (1996) 2006; Spickard 1992; Delgado and Stefancic 2012.

16. For recent exemplars, see Ocampo 2016; Roth 2012, pp. 176–201; Roth and Kim 2013; Zamora 2016.

17. For the original formulation of their underutilized concept of "racial rearticulation," see Omi and Winant (1986) 2014, p. 89.

18. Definitive studies of the post-1965 immigrant second generation and its assimilation include Alba and Nee 2003; Kasinitz et al. 2008; and Portes and Rumbaut 2001. On how theories of immigrant assimilation fail to adequately address race and racism, see Bashi Treitler 1998. For an analysis of the racial identification of South Asian Americans and its implications for theory, see Morning 2001.

19. For more on implicit and explicit bias in assimilation theory, see Bashi Treitler 2015; Jung 2009.

20. For an elucidation and critique of "honorary whiteness," see Kim 2016.

21. Bozorgmehr 1997, 1998; Chaichian 1997; Daha 2011; Ghaffarian 1998; Mobasher 2006, 2012; Mostofi 2003; Sabagh and Bozorgmehr 1986.

22. Portes and Zhou 1993: Bozorgmehr and Douglas 2011.

23. For more on covert racism in majority-white spaces, see Brunsma 2011.

24. An emerging body of research demonstrates an analytic shift from studying Arab American experiences of "ethnicity" to "racialization." See Cainkar 2009; Howell 2014; Shryock and Lin 2009. For further sociological elaboration of "racialization," see Lamont, Beljean, and Clair 2014.

25. On connecting the top down and with the bottom up in the sociology of race, see Brubaker, Loveman, and Stamatov 2004; Omi and Winant (1986) 2014. For an exception to historical research on Iranians in the US, see Farnia 2011.

26. As of October 2016, the White House has proposed adding the "MENA" category to federal racial definitions used by the Office of Management and Budget. The proposal is currently in a thirty-day public comment period, and if approved, "MENA" could appear as early as 2020 on the US census.

27. Gualtieri 2001, 2009.

28. Gualtieri 2001; Munshi 2015.

29. Lipsitz 2011, p. 29.

30. Tuan 1998.

31. For the most comprehensive, interethnic accounts, see Bakalian and Bozorgmehr 2009; Bozorgmehr, Ong, and Tosh 2016; Jamal and Naber 2008.

32. For an explanation of "hegemonic whiteness" as a synthesis of Feagin and Omi and Winant's formulations of white power and privilege, see Hughey and Byrd 2013.

33. For more on the War on Terror and the racial profiling of Muslims via "appearance and visual cues," see Daulatzai 2007; Rana 2007, 2011.

34. Roth 2012; Ocampo 2016; Dhingra 2012; Vasquez 2011; Kibria 2011.

Chapter 2

1. Gualtieri 2009; Tehranian 2010.

2. An exception is Bozorgmehr (1998), which outlines the very small pre-1950 Iranian American population before describing two critical waves of migration, 1950–79 and 1979–present.

3. The Fourteenth Amendment (1868) extended rights of citizenship to African Americans, but, in effect, the execution of the law was to create a formal pipeline into "second-class citizenship." See Karst 1977.

4. Ferdowsi (2002) describes the discovery of Hajj Sayyah's 1875 US naturalization as documented in the US National Archives Records of the Department of State, Dispatches from US Ministers to Persia 1883–1906, and Diplomatic Instructions, 1801–1906, Persia; see also Lorentz and Wertime 1980.

5. By no means do I offer a comprehensive review of all racial prerequisite cases for all racially liminal groups here. There are approximately fifty major racial prerequisite cases adjudicated in federal courts and involving non-European claimants. For foundational research on these cases, see Haney López (1996) 2006, specifically the tables in appendix A.

6. See Farnia 2011.

7. "Parsee" initially appears in quotes in this chapter to reflect how it is spelled in early twentieth-century primary documents related to South Asian racial prerequisite cases; the dominant spelling today is "Parsi." I use Parsee to signal how and when the term is used in the earlier historical and geographic context of the United States.

8. Gualtieri (2009) offers the most complete historical analysis of *In re Najour* and other cases involving Syrian claimants. For more on racial prerequisite cases involving the Muslim world, see Moore 1995. For extensions into contemporary Muslim American life, see Beydoun 2013; Bayoumi 2006.

9. *In re* Halladjian, F. 174, 841 (Cir. Ct. D. Mass.1909).

10. *Ex parte* Dow, F. 211, 487 (1914).

11. Ibid.

12. *In re* Dow, F. 213, 357 (1914).

13. Ibid., 365.

14. Dow v. United States, F. 226, 148 (1915) (emphasis added).

15. Ibid. (emphasis added).

16. The literacy rate in 2001 was 97.9 percent. See "Parsis Tops Literacy" 2004.

17. Luhrmann 1996.

18. *In re* Balsara, 171 F. 294, 294 (S.D.N.Y. 1909).

19. See Motadel 2013; Zia-Ebrahimi 2011, 2016.

20. United States v. Thind, 261 U.S. 204 (1923).

21. Thind's briefing as quoted and described in Coulson 2013, p. 129. I borrow the evocative term "dislocated" from Zia-Ebrahimi 2016, p. 5.

22. United States v. Thind, 261 U.S. 204, 207 (1923).

23. Wadia v. United States, 101 F.2d 7, 9 (C.C.A. 2d Cir. 1939).

24. Bryne 2013.

25. Tavakoli-Targhi 2001; Boroujerdi 1996.

26. See Mobasher 2012, introductory chapter; 2013.

27. Maryam Kashani's documentary film *Best in the West* (2006) provides a rare glimpse into the lives of Iranian student visa holders in 1960s and 1970s California. See also Torbat 2002.

28. During the twenty-five-year period from 1925 to 1950, the Immigration and Naturalization Service (INS) documented fewer than 2,000 Iranians admitted as "immigrants." Between 1952 and 1961, however, 3,148 Iranians were admitted, roughly the same number as from India and Lebanon in that same period. As Bozorgmehr and Douglas (2011) have pointed out, the significant population of Iranians on student visas residing in the United States from 1952 through 1961 is not counted in the INS "immigrant" data because of their nonimmigrant student visa statuses.

29. Bozorgmehr and Sabagh 1998.

30. Said 1981; Chan-Malik 2011a.

31. Mahdavi (2005, p. 212) offers a comprehensive account of discrimination against Iranian Americans from 1979 through the post-9/11 era.

32. See, for example, Karim 2006; Naficy 1993; Malek 2011, 2015.

33. Mobasher 2012.

34. Bozorgmehr and Douglas 2011; Bozorgmehr 1997, 1998.

35. See Hanassab 1991; Ghaffarian 1998.

36. See Nasrabadi 2014; Sadeghi 2016.

37. Kelley, Friedlander, and Colby 1993, pp. 299–320.

38. Bozorgmehr 2007.

39. Mobasher, 2013, p. 1002.

40. Mobasher, 2012, pp. 4–5.

41. Taken from promotion taglines for the film *Not without My Daughter*, archived at the Internet Movie Database, http://www.imdb.com.

42. Ebert 1991.

43. Pew Research Center 2016.

44. Twenty-four of twenty-five countries included are Muslim majority; more than eighty-two thousand men complied with the registration, and almost fourteen thousand (17 percent) were deported. See Mobasher 2013, p. 1002.

45. Garner and Selod 2015.

46. In the case of Latinos, Wendy Roth (2010) has outlined the incompatibility of racial self-identification with legal mechanisms for addressing racial discrimination and suggests measures to additionally account for externally ascribed markers of race.

47. Pourghoraishi v. Flying J, Inc., 449 F.3d 751, 758 (7th Cir. 2006).

48. Morris v. Office Max, Inc., 89 F.3d 411, 413 (7th Cir. 1996).

49. Pourghoraishi v. Flying J Inc., R. at 36, Ex. A, 130–32.

50. Ibid., 45.

51. Ibid.

52. Ibid., 1.

53. Ibid., 130–32.

54. Ibid.

55. Abdullahi v. Prada USA Corp.,520 F.3d 710, 712 (N.D. Ill. 2007; 7th Cir. 2008).

56. Abdullahi and Prada dispute the timeline of events; in his ruling, Judge Der-Yeghiayan determined that the allegations of harassment would have taken place after Abdullahi no longer worked at Prada; therefore, her allegation could not count as "workplace discrimination."

57. According to the latest available EEOC reports, individuals of "Middle Eastern or Muslim" national origin filed 13 percent of all national-origin-based discrimination charges in 2012.

58. Abdullahi v. Prada, 728.

59. Ibid., 728. For more on discrimination suits brought by Middle Eastern American complainants, see Khanghahi 2017.

60. As of October 2016, the EEOC has prioritized policing bias against Middle Easterners and Muslims because "tragic events in the United States and abroad have increased the likelihood of discrimination against these communities." See Iafolla 2016. For legal-theoretical work, see Volpp 2003; Tehranian 2010.

61. Tuan 1998.

62. Abdi 2012.

63. Viteri 2012.

64. The Tabaddor case has been a "top story" watched and blogged closely by attorneys across the entire legal profession. Pers. comm., attorney Jamey Borell, November 4, 2015. For more on the DOJ settlement, see Gonzalez 2015.

65. See Fessenden et al. 2017.

66. At time of writing, a federal judge in Washington State temporarily blocked enforcement of the travel ban. For data on the demographics of affected travelers, workers, and permanent residents, see Vitkovskaya et al. 2017.

67. Miguel Sarzosa (@MSarzosaEcon), "Physically attacked in @wmata metro yellow line because I 'looked Iranian.' I am OK, but I think that the beard needs to go," May 8, 2015, 2:27 p.m. [Tweet].

68. See Hamad 2001.

69. Levenson 2017.

70. For more on the incorporation, or lack thereof, of Jewish Iranians into wealthy enclaves in Los Angeles, see Amanat 2013; Soomekh 2012.

71. Smith 2009.

72. Moaveni 2004.

73. Goldin 2006.

74. Talinn Grigor generously shared her conference paper that puts the "Persian palace" phenomenon into art-historical perspective; she argues for recognition of an inclusive style called "Californian Persian Revival." See Grigor 2016, p. 2.

75. Trousdale Estates Homeowners Association, 2017.

76. McKenzie 1994.

77. Alexander 2004.

78. Anderson 2012.

79. Anti–Persian palace sentiments and subsequent actions climaxed during the tenure of Beverly Hills' first and only Iranian American mayor, Jimmy Delshad.

80. Planner Nicole Farnoush's online article (2009) on the Persian palace controversy helpfully pulls together a time line of the events referenced here.

81. Goldin 2006.

82. Ibid.

83. Pepp, quoted in Anderson 2012.

84. West 2009.

85. Goldin 2006.

86. Alexander 2004.

87. Said 1978; Puar 2007.

88. Address changed to provide confidentiality.

Chapter 3

1. Persepolis is the historical and cultural capital of the Achaemenid Empire (550–330 BC), also known as the Persian Empire, the largest empire of ancient history. It lies in the center of present-day Iran near the major city of Shiraz.

2. I very occasionally use Persian words like *soghati* throughout this book; Persian words also appear in quoted passages from interviews, when interlocutors themselves have spoken in hybrid Persian-English. In order to privilege ease of reading, I use a very simplified system of transliteration that draws on the most conventional spellings of Persian words as they appear in the English-speaking US diaspora, in effect privileging English-language readers. All Persian-to-English translations are my own.

3. Khakpour 2014.

4. Sociologist Ruben Rumbaut coined the term "1.5 generation" to "describe the situation of immigrant children who are socialized and begin their primary schooling abroad but immigrate before puberty" (1997, p. 950).

5. Roth and Kim (2013) present a comparative account of how racial ideologies and hierarchies are transferred and transformed by migrants. See also Zamora 2016.

6. See Boroujerdi 1996; Schayegh 2009.

7. Zia Ebrahimi 2016, p. 4.

8. Bailey 1987.

9. The French aristocrat and white supremacist Arthur de Gobineau (1915) developed this branch of racial science.

10. An interview with historian Beeta Baghoolizadeh sheds light on the historical presence of black Iranians, particularly during the Qajar era. See Grillot, Hardinski, and Dyson 2015. See Khosrownejad 2016 for visual historical materials on Afro-Iranians.

11. The Indian subcontinent and its peoples are conveniently and entirely expunged from the version of the Aryan myth circulated among Iranians. As blisteringly put by Hamid Dabashi, "Orientalists have instructed [Iranians] that they are 'Aryan' and as such of the same superior stock as Europeans; only by some unfortunate accident of geography do they find themselves somewhere between the Arab lands and India. The Orientalists' tales—about Cyrus the Great, Darius the First and Xerxes the Conqueror—continue to haunt them, generation after generation. The racism of Iranians runs viciously deep; they have a horror of being taken for Arab (though they would be delighted to be taken for Italian)." See Dabashi 2011, p. 28.

12. Zia Ebrahimi 2016; Shams 2012.

13. Ruben Rumbaut offers the designation "1.75 generation" to highlight the "different development stages and social contexts of children who immigrate at ages 0-5" (1997, p. 950). Nonetheless, in the literature on immigrant generations, children like Javad, who were born in their respective countries of origin but moved to the United States as very young children, are more often collapsed into the "second generation" alongside American-born children of immigrants. I maintain this categorical convention throughout the book.

14. Malek 2011; Najmabadi 2005.

15. Ashraf 2006.

16. Zia Ebrahimi 2011.

17. See Zia Ebrahimi 2016, in particular, his analysis of Akhundzadeh and Kermani on pp. 41–72.

18. See Elling 2013 for a definitive analysis of Iranian/Persian nationalism and minority ethnicities in Iran.

19. Winegar and Deeb 2015.

20. Field 1939, p. 506.

21. W. W. Howells, a fellow physical anthropologist, was unmoved by Field's discovery of a new race: "Now it is not quite clear just what kind of a 'race' is meant. . . . I would question the naming of a new race on the basis of a nose which is not really peculiar to the Persian plateau" (1941, p. 462).

22. Field 1939, p. 507.

23. Howells 1941, p. 464.

24. Each claim has been problematized with subsequent scholarship. See, for example, Bajoghli 2015.

25. For more on Google Maps and related controversies concerning the "Persian" versus "Arabic Gulf" in diaspora, see Slaughter 2014.

26. For more on sanguine nationalistic aphorisms like "the Arts belong to Iranians, period [*honar nazde Iranian asto bas*]," see Gholami 2016; Amanat and Vejdani 2012.

27. The "Persian vs. Iranian" self-identification among Iranian Americans is described most memorably by stand-up comedian Maz Jobrani: "It's not a great time to be from the Middle East. Iranians have learned how to deal with it. We've learned how to trick Americans. 'No no, I'm not Iranian, no no, I am Persian, like the cat, meow! I am not Axis of Evil, no no, I am Persian like the rug, hello!'" See Jobrani 2012.

28. Sima is from the Washington, D.C., area and describes "Persian" as a relatively nonstigmatized identity there. Respondents in California, particularly Los Angeles and Orange Country, described "Persian" as a stigmatized "spoiled" identity due to the visible presence of a large pro-shah Iranian community and media such as the TV series *Shahs of Sunset* that draws from classed and raced stereotypes. See Maghbouleh 2012.

29. *Inheritance*, a 2011 short by filmmaker and media studies scholar Aggie Ebrahimi-Bazaz, is an affecting documentary on intergenerational Iranian American domestic interiors like the ones described in this chapter.

30. Amitis 2015.

31. For more about Tehran Ghasri and his activism and art, see " Imperfect Gentleman Says Being Persian Is Hip" 2013.

32. Eldeib 2014.

33. Antiblack discourse and symbols in Iranian culture and history, along with ethnocentric beliefs about the primacy of Iranian family values over those found in *sefid* (white) America, are just two of many other interrelated internal Iranian American racial narratives this book does not analyze. For the latter, an emerging field in Iranian studies, see interview with Baghoolizadeh in Grillot, Hardinski, and Dyson 2015.

34. Zia-Ebrahimi 2010.

Chapter 4

1. For more on "racialized ethnicity," see Vasquez 2011; Dhingra 2007.

2. With regard to the racial referents embedded in the "terrorist" label, a renewed debate in the sociology of race and ethnic studies concerns the emergence of a new "brown/Muslim" racial category in academic and policy research influenced by racial formation theory. Though some scholars have used this terminology to describe and analyze racial profiling and the War on Terror, others argue that such "brownness" rests on antiblackness, which elides a history of racist

association of blacks with terrorism since early American slavery. This elision in turn props up the racialization of "Muslim" as "not-black," effectively excluding the experiences of blacks and black Muslims out of analyses of post- 9/11 racial profiling and antiterrorism. For background, see Chan-Malik 2011b. For a recent example of the debate in action, see Tamara Nopper (@tnopper), "What Role Did Progressive South Asian Ams Play in Silencing Black Critique of Kal Penn's Stop and Frisk Commentary?," September 30, 2013, 12:19 p.m. [Tweet].

3. Like Asian American students, who face a much higher proportion of bullying in school than do other racial groups, my respondents said that school was where they were most often bullied. Recent data on the bullying of Asian youth, however, reflect a significant increase in attacks against those perceived to be Muslim following September 11. In qualitative interviews from a 2009 study, and from follow-up studies done by the New York City Department of Education, the racial nature of this bullying becomes quite clear. Issues like hair color, skin tone, religious/cultural dress, and other physical traits are used by majority-white bullies as evidence of youth's "terroristic" identity. As is the case with Iranian Americans, matters of the body and physical appearance are part of the lingua franca of this bullying. What is quite bewildering about this already overwhelming data, however, is that these studies account for only those Asian American youth who are harassed for their perceived Muslim identities; by all accounts, South Asian youth (Indian, Pakistani, Bangladeshi, and in some ethno-racial configurations, Afghan) bear much of the weight of this type of bullying. Important and impactful research like this underreports, or entirely overlooks, the persistent bullying experienced by Middle Eastern and North African youth. Outside the bounds of conventional racial minority status, these everyday "racial others" are known to endure bullying, yet their experiences are not incorporated into such widely shared reports. In short, both the character and frequency of the bullying reported by interlocutors mirror what has been widely reported for Asian American youth. This lends empirical heft to the chapter's finding that Iranian youth tend to form associations and friendships with other minority youth in their respective local contexts. See Sikh Coalition, CACF, and AALDEF 2009.

4. The concept of "racialized ethnicity" also appears in Purkayastha 2005; Kibria 2003; Tuan 1998.

5. "Pinglish" is a hybrid code-switching language that freely mixes Persian and English idioms, phrases, and words. See Rahimi 2008.

6. On "intimidation gap," see Carriera 2004, p. 18.

7. On "laissez-faire racism," see Bonilla-Silva 2006; Bobo, Kluegel, and Smith 1997.

8. For more on the formation of ethnic studies departments in the United States, see Biondi 2012; Rojas 2012; Chang 1999.

9. Daneman 2011.

10. Especially notable here for their foci on Middle Eastern diasporas are the Program in Arab American Studies within the Department of American Culture at the University of Michigan–Ann Arbor, the University of Michigan–Dearborn, and the Middle East and Middle Eastern American Center at the Graduate Center of the City University of New York.

11. This particular Middle Eastern Resource Center, located at a midsize public university in the southwestern United States, is shared by several student organizations, including the Armenian Students Association, Iranian Student Group, Lebanese Club, Muslim Students Association, and Students for Justice in Palestine.

12. For more on second-generation "cultural nostalgia," see Maira 2002.

13. On the framing of most space on college campuses as "racially neutral," see Barajas and Ronnkvist 2007, pp. 1517–18.

14. See Yoder 2013.

15. Importantly, "SWANA" and "Asian" students are not classified as "underrepresented minorities" (URMs) at the University of California. The URM designation redresses systemic imbalances and discrimination especially faced by African American, Chicanos/ Latinos, and Native Americans by according additional resources and support to students from those backgrounds.

16. See Griffin 2011, p. 1.

17. The thirty-two subcategories follow broad national or ethnic categories: Algerian, Afghan, Armenian, Assyrian/Chaldean, Azerbaijani, Bahraini, Berber, Circassian, Djiboutian, Egyptian, Emirati, Georgian, Iranian, Iraqi, Jordanian, Kurdish, Kuwaiti, Lebanese, Libyan, Mauritanian, Omani, Palestinian, Qatari, Saudi Arabian, Somali, Sudanese, Syrian, Tunisian, Turkish, Yemeni, Other North African, and Other Southwest Asian.

18. See Associated Students of the University of California Bill #170 2012, pp. 8–14.

19. Ibid.

20. See Shirinian and Mehranbod 2013.

Chapter 5

1. Gallup Poll 2016.

2. The data and resultant analyses I offer in this chapter are limited to "nonspecialist" Iranian American travelers to Iran: young people whose preparation for such recreational travel is on the whole casual and everyday. They are traveling largely under the guardianship of their parents and grandparents, and their elders' facility with customs and codes in Iran mediates their travel in significant ways. Apart from the nonspecialist travelers who are the focus of this chapter, there is a subset of the Iranian American second generation whom I would term "specialist" travelers. These are typically young adults working as journalists, academics, and/or researchers. Specialist travelers are a case apart,

as their frequent travels to (or regular, part-time residence in) Iran, scholarly engagement, and professional identities exclude them from the experiences analyzed here.

3. Simone Browne (2015) has argued that surveillance is a deeply racial and racist practice. She offers the terms "racialized surveillance" (p. 10) and "racial baggage" (p. 132) to understand racialization as practice and effect on black women and men in airports.

4. For a discussion of "inherited nostalgia," see Maghbouleh 2010; for "migrant nostalgias," see Bonnett 2012, p. 97.

5. Before needing to obtain their own passports as young adults, second-generation children can travel on a parent's Iranian passport.

6. New legislation in 2012 by the Iranian Parliament made inroads for second-generation youth born abroad to Iranian mothers: they remain ineligible for full Iranian citizenship but qualify for permanent residency, which represents an improvement from the lack of rights previously offered.

7. Puar and Rai 2002, p. 117.

8. An evocative essay by actor and musician Riz Ahmed (2016) describes how South Asian and Middle Eastern men's bodies are specifically mined for meaning in "in-between" places like airports.

9. McGlone and Shroder 2012.

10. Rampell 2016.

11. Kelner 2012.

12. Iranian Americans, like Asian and white Americans, typically associate the identity category "American" as synonymous with "white." African Americans, notably, depart from the "American = white" association. See Devos and Banaji 2005.

13. US Department of State 2016.

14. Gladstone 2016.

15. Wickramasekare et al. 2006.

16. The data I have presented in this chapter, highlighting the racial profiling of second-generation Iranian-heritaged youth in spite of their American citizenship and white "legal" categorization, reflect how pervasive and well established these racist security practices were long before the "Muslim" travel and immigration ban of 2017.

Chapter 6

1. Though all campers identify in some way as "Iranian," over time, camp staff has grown to include a small number of non-Iranians from racialized backgrounds such as West Indian, South Asian, or Afghan who are partners or significant others of Iranian American staff.

2. Mana's utopian/humanistic use of "purple" as a hyperbolic racial category recalls, in some ways, Ruth Frankenberg's respondents in *White Women,*

Race Matters and her analysis that referring to races like "green, yellow, pink" is "euphemism or strategy for avoiding race: it shifts attention away from color differences that make a political difference by embedding meaningful differences among non-meaningful ones." See Frankenberg 1993, p. 38.

3. Oliver 2007.

4. Bayoumi 2008.

5. See Hussain 2011 for the difficult-to-find song "You Are Beloved."

6. I vetted my own field notes against Yousef's moving account of his experience at camp. See Baker 2011.

7. Hafez (1326–90), known around the world for his aphorisms, is arguably the famous Iranian poet.

8. Arash expanded on Hengameh's reference to the medieval Iranian poet and philosopher Saadi Shirazi, whose most familiar poem "Bani Adam" (written 1259) is inscribed on the United Nations building in New York.

9. Arash referred to the quatrains of Tajik-Iranian poet and scientist Omar Khayyam (1048–1131) in his *Rubáiyát*. See FitzGerald 2009.

10. "Yooshij" refers to Nima Yooshij (1895–1960), the father of "new" Iranian poetry.

11. Iranians regard Abolqasem Ferdowsi's eleventh-century masterpiece *Shahnameh* (Book of Kings) as the definitive retelling of ancient Iranian history and folklore, written in "pure" Persian against the backdrop of an Arab "conquest" of Iran. For the most popular English translation, see Davis 2006.

12. Arash refers to Zarrinkoub ([1957] 1996), a nationalist historical text that has defined Iranian history.

13. Jordan 1995, p. 3.

14. "Cookie mookie" is an example of what in linguistics is called "reduplication" (*Do gān sāzī* in Persian). In diaspora, reduplication is especially prominent when Persian speakers use English words. In and out of diaspora, reduplication is often used when a speaker describes a sundry collection of things ("chert o pert" = this and that; "kar mar" = busywork). For more on reduplication in Persian, see Ghaniabadi 2009.

15. For a more complete analysis of the tournament, see Maghbouleh 2013, pp. 818–37.

16. Majd 2008.

17. Bahrampour 2007.

18. Clifford 1995, p. 322.

19. *Shir moz* is a popular banana-flavor milkshake in Iran.

20. Coe 1998, p. 410.

Chapter 7

1. This categorical hodgepodge reflects the diversity of immigrants arriving on US shores at the time. It also reflects a concretization of naturalization

boundaries and racial designations that today map neatly onto the categories of "South Asia," the "Middle East," and "North Africa."

2. For a more detailed and deeply researched account, see Craver 2009, pp. 34, 37.

3. Tehranian 2010, p. 52.

4. US Census Bureau 2015.

5. See Bakalian and Bozorgmehr 2009; Cable 2013; Cainkar 2009; Garner and Selod 2015; Gualtieri 2009; Jamal and Naber 2008; Karem Albrecht 2015; Love 2017; Maira 2009; Malek 2009, 2011; Naber 2012; Read 2008; Selod 2017; Stifler 2012; Thangaraj 2015.

6. Mills 1997.

Appendix A

1. Common estimates are based on numbers derived from answers to the "ancestry" question in the American Community Survey. For more on the methodological challenges to measuring the shape and size of the Iranian American community, see Appendix B; see also Fata and Rafii 2003.

2. Small 2009.

3. See Modarres 1998; Tsubakihara 2013.

4. Pers. comm., Ali Ferdowsi, June 1, 2015.

5. See Twine and Warren 2000; Merton 1972; Baca Zinn 1979.

6. Roth 2015.

7. Daniels and Feagin 2011; Gregory, McMillan-Cottom, and Daniels 2016; Hargittai and Sandvig 2016; Wynn 2009.

Appendix B

1. See Jones and Bentley 2016.

2. A special Census Bureau forum on ethnic groups from the Middle East and North Africa was held in May 2015 and solicited expert testimony from academics and advocacy organizations, including Iranian American sociologist Mehdi Bozorgmehr and law professor John Tehranian. The forum's overwhelming support for the "MENA" category was also affirmed in 2016 by the Census Bureau's National Advisory Committee on Racial, Ethnic, and Other Populations, on which Morad Ghorban of PAAIA (Public Affairs Alliance of Iranian Americans) sits. For the OMB's public notice posting, see Office of Management and Budget 2016.

3. Fata and Rafii 2003, p. 4.

3. National Iranian American Council 2010.

4. Abdulrahim 2009.

5. See National Iranian American Council 2017.

6. Jamal Abdi, policy director for the National Iranian American Council, quoted in Bahrampour 2016.

7. See Public Affairs Alliance of Iranian Americans 2011.
8. Fata and Rafii 2003.
9. Foad 2013, p. 13.
10. See Alinejad 2017.

REFERENCES

Abdi, Jamal. 2012. "Sanctions at the Genius Bar." *New York Times*, July 12, p. A23.

Abdulrahim, Raja. 2009. "Iranian Americans Are Urged to Stand and Be Counted." *Los Angeles Times*, December 29. http://articles.latimes.com/2009/dec/29/local/la-me-iranian-census29-2009dec29.

Ahmed, Riz. 2016. "Typecast as a Terrorist." *The Guardian*, September 16. https://www.theguardian.com/world/2016/sep/15/riz-ahmed-typecast-as-a-terrorist.

Ahmed, Sara. 2004. "Declarations of Whiteness: The Non-performativity of Anti-racism." *Borderlands e-Journal* 3 (2). http://www.borderlands.net.au/vol3no2_2004/ahmed_declarations.htm.

Alba, Richard and Victor Nee. 2003. *Remaking the American Mainstream: Assimilation and Contemporary Immigration.* Cambridge, MA: Harvard University Press.

Alexander, Karen. 2004. "The Big-Box Battle of Beverly Hills." *Los Angeles Times*, June 13. http://articles.latimes.com/2004/jun/13/magazine/tm-bev hills24/3.

Alinejad, Donya. 2017. *The Web and Formations of Iranian American-ness: Next Generation Diaspora.* London: Palgrave Macmillan.

Amanat, Abbas, and Farzin Vejdani, eds. 2012. *Iran Facing Others: Identity Boundaries in a Historical Perspective.* New York: Springer.

Amanat, Mehrdad. 2013. *Jewish Identities in Iran.* London: I. B. Taurus.

Amitis. 2015. "King." *Avangmusic.* YouTube video (3:37), June 1. https://www.youtube.com/watch?v=TzlXohvphN4.

Anderson, Melanie. 2012. "Building Character: The Weekly's Exclusive Interview with Design Review Commission Chair Arline Pepp." *Beverly Hills Weekly*, April 12. http://bvh.stparchive.com/Archive/BVH/BVH04122012p08.php.

Ashraf, Ahmad. 2006. "Iranian Identity, 19th and 20th Centuries." *Encyclopaedia Iranica* 13 (5): 522–30.

Associated Students of the University of California Bill #170. 2012. https://www.usac.ucla.edu/documents/minutes/USAC%20MINUTES%2003-12-13.pdf.

Baca Zinn, Maxine. 1979. "Field Research in Minority Communities: Ethical,

Methodological and Political Observations by an Insider." *Social Problems* 27:209–19.

Bahrampour, Tara. 2007. "Courtesy around the Campfire." *Washington Post*, July 7. http://www.washingtonpost.com/wp-dyn/content/article/2007/07/06/AR2007070601974.html.

———. 2016. "A U.S. Census Proposal to Add Category for People of Middle Eastern Descent Makes Some Uneasy." *Washington Post*, October 21. https://www.washingtonpost.com/local/social-issues/a-proposal-to-add-a-us-census-category-for-people-of-middle-eastern-descent-makes-some-uneasy/2016/10/20/8e9847a0–960e-11e6–bb29–bf2701dbe0a3_story.html.

Bailey, H. W. 1987. "Arya." *Encyclopaedia Iranica* 2 (7): 681–83.

Bajoghli, Narges. 2015. *Perpetuating a Legend? Washington DC.* Documentary film in *7 Sides of a Cylinder*, produced by Haleh Anvari. https://www.youtube.com/watch?v=FEaluhDAo90.

Bakalian, Anny, and Mehdi Bozorgmehr. 2009. *Backlash 9/11: Middle Eastern and Muslim Americans Respond.* Berkeley: University of California Press.

Baker, Yousef K. 2011. "Camp Ayandeh Teaches Community and Solidarity While Celebrating Difference." *Payvand Iran News*, July 11. http://www.payvand.com/news/11/jul/1126.html.

Barajas, Heidi, and A. Ronnkvist. 2007. "Racialized Space: Framing Latino and Latina Experience in Public Schools." *Teachers College Record* 9:1517–38.

Bashi Treitler, Vilna. 1998. "Racial Categories Matter Because Racial Hierarchies Matter: A Commentary." *Ethnic and Racial Studies* 21:959–68.

———. 2015. "Social Agency and White Supremacy in Immigration Scholarship." *Sociology of Race and Ethnicity* 1:153–65.

Bayoumi, Moustafa. 2006. "Raceing Religion." *CR: The New Centennial Review* 2:267–93.

———. 2008. *How Does It Feel to Be a Problem? Being Young and Arab in America.* New York: Penguin.

Beydoun, Khaled. 2013. "Between Muslim and White: The Legal Construction of Arab American Identity." *NYU Annual Survey of American Law* 69:1–35.

Biondi, Martha. 2012. *The Black Revolution on Campus.* Berkeley: University of California Press.

Bobo, Lawrence, James R. Kluegel, and Ryan A. Smith. 1997. "Laissez-Faire Racism: The Crystallization of a Kinder, Gentler, Antiblack Ideology." In *Racial Attitudes in the 1990s: Continuity and Change*, edited by Steven Tuch and Jack Martin, 5–42. Westport, CT: Praeger.

Bonilla-Silva, Eduardo. 2006. *Racism without Racists: Color-Blind Racism and the Persistence of Racial Inequality in the United States.* Lanham, MD: Rowman & Littlefield.

Bonnett, Alastair. 2012. *The Geography of Nostalgia: Global and Local Perspectives on Modernity and Loss.* London: Routledge.

Boroujerdi, Mehrzad. 1996. *Iranian Intellectuals and the West: The Tormented Triumph of Nativism.* Syracuse, NY: Syracuse University Press.

Bozorgmehr, Mehdi. 1997. "Internal Ethnicity: Iranians in Los Angeles." *Sociological Perspectives* 40:387–408.

———. 1998. "From Iranian Studies to Studies of Iranians in the United States." *Iranian Studies* 31:5–30.

———. 2007. "Iran." In *The New Americans*, edited by Mary Waters, Reed Ueda, and Helen Marrow, 469–78. Cambridge, MA: Harvard University Press.

Bozorgmehr, Mehdi, and Daniel Douglas. 2011. "Success(ion): Second-Generation Iranian Americans." *Iranian Studies* 44:3–24.

Bozorgmehr, Mehdi, Paul Ong, and Sarah Tosh. 2016. "Panethnicity Revisited: Contested Group Boundaries in the Post-9/11 Era." *Ethnic & Racial Studies* 39:727–45.

Bozorgmehr, Mehdi, and Georges Sabagh. 1998. "High Status Immigrants: A Statistical Profile of Iranians in the United States." *Iranian Studies* 21:5–36.

Brodkin, Karen. 1998. *How Jews Became White Folks and What That Says about Race in America.* New Brunswick, NJ: Rutgers University Press.

Browne, Simone. 2015. *Dark Matters: On the Surveillance of Blackness.* Durham, NC: Duke University Press.

Brubaker, Rogers, Mara Loveman, and Peter Stamatov. 2004. "Ethnicity as Cognition." *Theory and Society* 33:31–64.

Brunsma, David. 2011. "Now You Don't See It, Now You Don't': White Lives as Covert Racism." In *Covert Racism*, edited by Rodney Coates, 321–32. London: Oxford University Press.

Bryne, Malcolm. 2013. "CIA Confirms Role in 1953 Coup." National Security Archive, August 19. http://nsarchive.gwu.edu/NSAEBB/NSAEBB435/.

Cable, Umayyah. 2013. "New Wave Arab American Studies: Ethnic Studies and the Critical Turn." *American Quarterly* 65:231–43.

Cainkar, Louise A. 2009. *Homeland Insecurity: The Arab American and Muslim American Experience after 9/11.* New York: Russell Sage Foundation.

Carriera, Maria. 2004. "Seeking Explanatory Adequacy: A Dual Approach to Understanding the Term 'Heritage Language Learner.'" *Heritage Language Journal* 2:1–10.

Casiano, Louis. 2011. "BBQ Joint with 'Iranian' Poster Draws Fans and Foes." *Houston Chronicle*, November 6. http://www.chron.com/news/houston-texas/article/Protesters-target-restaurant-with-Iranian-poster-2254303.php#photo-1730837.

Chaichian, Mohammad A. 1997. "First Generation Iranian Immigrants and the Question of Cultural Identity: The Case of Iowa." *International Migration Review* 31 (3): 612–27.

Chang, Michael. 1999. "Expansion and Its Discontents: The Formation of Asian American Studies Programs in the 1990s." *Journal of Asian American Studies* 2:181–206.

Chan-Malik, Sylvia. 2011a. "Chadors, Feminists, Terror: The Racial Politics of

U.S. Media Representations of the 1979 Iranian Women's Movement." *Annals of the American Academy of Political and Social Science* 637:112–40.

———. 2011b. "Common Cause: On the Black-Immigrant Debate and Constructing the Muslim American." *Journal of Race, Ethnicity, and Religion* 2:1–39.

Clifford, James. 1995. "Diasporas." *Cultural Anthropology* 9 (3): 302–38.

Coe, Cati. 1998. "Defending Community: Difference and Utopia Online." *International Journal of Cultural Studies* 1:391–414.

Coombes, Tony. 2011. "Controversial Poster Hangs in Texas Restaurant: Is It Offensive?" *ABC 7 Amarillo*, November 13. http://abc7amarillo.com/news/local/controversial-poster-hangs-in-texas-restaurant-is-it-offensive?id=682942.

Coulson, Douglas. 2013. "The Rhetoric of Common Enemies in the Racial Prerequisites to Naturalized Citizenship before 1952." PhD diss., University of Texas at Austin.

Craver, Earlene. 2009. "On the Boundary of White: The *Cartozian* Naturalization Case and the Armenians, 1923–1925." *Journal of American Ethnic History* 28:30–56.

Dabashi, Hamid. 2011. *Brown Skin, White Masks*. London: Pluto Press.

Daha, Maryam. 2011. "Contextual Factors Contributing to Ethnic Identity Development of Second-Generation Iranian American Adolescents." *Journal of Adolescent Research* 26:543–69.

Daneman, Matthew. 2011. "More US Colleges Adding Muslim Chaplains." *USA Today*, March 24. http://usatoday30.usatoday.com/news/education/2011-03-24-muslimchaplains24_ST_N.htm [site discontinued].

Daniels, Jessie, and Joe Feagin. 2011. "The (Coming) Social Media Revolution in the Academy." *Fast Capitalism* 8. http://www.uta.edu/huma/agger/fastcapitalism/8_2/Daniels8_2.html.

Daulatzai, Sohail. 2007. "Protect Ya Neck: Muslims and the Carceral Imagination in the Age of Guantánamo." *Souls* 9:132–47.

Davis, Dick. 2006. Translation of Ferdowsi's *Shahnameh*. New York: Penguin.

De Gobineau, Arthur. 1915. *Inequality of the Human Races*. New York: G. P. Putnam's Sons.

Delgado, Richard, and Jean Stefancic. 2012. *Critical Race Theory*. New York: NYU Press.

Devos, Thierry, and Mahzarin R. Banaji. 2005. "American = White?" *Journal of Personality and Social Psychology* 88:447–66.

Dhingra, Pawan. 2012. *Life behind the Lobby: Indian American Motel Owners and the American Dream*. Stanford, CA: Stanford University Press.

Ebert, Roger. 1991. "Review: *Not without My Daughter*." RogerEbert.com, January 11. http://www.rogerebert.com/reviews/not-without-my-daughter-1991.

Ebrahimi-Bazaz, Aggie. 2011. *Inheritance*. Center for Asian American Media. Short film. http://caamedia.org/films/inheritance/.

Eldeib, Duaa. 2014. "Teen Pleads Guilty in Attack, Hate Crime Charge Dropped." *Chicago Tribune*, April 29. http://articles.chicagotribune.com/2014

-04-29/news/chi-teen-pleads-guilty-in-hate-crime-attack-20140429_1_
hate-crime-charge-omid-babakhani-melissa-babakhani.

Farnia, Nina. 2011. "Law's Inhumanities: Peripheral Racialization and the Early Development of an Iranian Race." *Comparative Studies of South Asia, Africa, and the Middle East* 31:455–74.

Farnoush, Nicole. 2009. "Persian Palaces: The Levittowns of Beverly Hills." *Four Story: Fact and Fiction for a Fair Future* (blog), 2012. http://fourstory.org/features/story/persian-palaces-the-levittowns-of-beverly-hills.html.

Fata, Soraya, and Raha Rafii. 2003. *Strength in Numbers: The Relative Concentration of Iranian Americans across the United States: Iran Census Report*. Washington, DC: National Iranian American Council. https://www.niacouncil.org/docs/iran census.pdf.

Feagin, Joe. 2013. *Systemic Racism: A Theory of Oppression*. London: Routledge.

Ferdowsi, Ali. 2002. "Hajj Sayyah." *Encyclopaedia Iranica* 11 (5): 556–60.

Fessenden, Ford, Jasmine Lee, Sergio Pecanha, and Anjali Singhvi. 2017. "Immigrants from Banned Nations: Educated, Mostly Citizens, and Found in Every State." New York Times, January 30. https://www.nytimes.com/inter active/2017/01/30/us/politics/trump-immigration-ban-demographics .html?_r=0.

Field, Henry. 1939. *Contributions to the Anthropology of Iran*. Chicago: Field Museum of Natural History.

FitzGerald, Edward. 2009. *The Rubáiyát of Omar Khayyam*. Oxford: Oxford University Press.

Foad, Hisham S. 2013. "Waves of Immigration from the Middle East to the United States." Working paper, SSRN, December 20. http://dx.doi.org /10.2139/ssrn.2383505.

Foley, Neil. 1999. *The White Scourge: Mexicans, Blacks, and Poor Whites in Texas Cotton Culture*. Berkeley: University of California Press.

Frankenberg, Ruth. 1993. *White Women, Race Matters: The Social Construction of Whiteness*. Minneapolis: University of Minnesota Press.

Gallup, Inc. 2016. "What Is Your Overall Opinion of Iran?" Gallup, February 3–7. http://www.gallup.com/poll/116236/iran.aspx.

Gans, Herbert. 2016. "Racialization and Racialization Research." *Ethnic and Racial Studies* 40 (3). http://dx.doi.org/10.1080/01419870.2017.1238497.

Garner, Steve. 2007. *Whiteness*. London: Routledge.

Garner, Steve, and Saher Selod. 2015. "The Racialization of Muslims: Empirical Studies of Islamophobia." *Critical Sociology* 411:9–19.

Ghaffarian, Shireen. 1998. "The Acculturation of Iranian Immigrants in the United States and the Implications for Mental Health." *Journal of Social Psychology* 138:645–54.

Ghaniabadi, Saeed. 2009. "Optionality and Variation: A Stochastic OT Analysis of M/p-Echo Reduplication in Colloquial Persian." In *Aspects of Iranian*

Linguistics, edited by Simin Karimi, Vida Samiian, and Donald Stilo, 57–84. Newcastle upon Tyne, UK: Cambridge Scholars Publishing.

Gholami, Reza. 2016. *Secularism and Identity: Non-Islamiosity in the Iranian Diaspora.* London: Routledge.

Gladstone, Rick. 2016. "Consultant's Continued Detention Chills Iranian-Americans." *New York Times*, February 8. http://www.nytimes.com/2016/02/09/world/middleeast/consultants-arrest-chills-iranian-americans.html.

Goldin, Greg. 2006. "In Defense of the Persian Palace." *Los Angeles Times*, December 17. http://articles.latimes.com/2006/dec/17/magazine/tm-palaces51.

Gonzalez, Richard. 2015. "U.S. Government Settles Lawsuit Filed by Iranian-American Judge." National Public Radio, November 3. http://www.npr.org/sections/thetwo-way/2015/11/03/454394225/government-settles-lawsuit-filed-by-iranian-american-judge.

Gregory, Karen, Tressie McMillan-Cottom, and Jessie Daniels. 2016. *Digital Sociologies*. Bristol, UK: Policy Press.

Griffin, Maryam S. 2011. "We Ain't White: Forged and Forging Terrains of Racial Identity for SWANA Students at the University of California." Paper presented at the annual meeting of the Law and Society Association, San Francisco, CA, May 30.

Grigor, Talinn. 2016. "Recycling the Glory of Ancient Persia in California." Paper presented to Society of Architectural Historians, Pasadena/Los Angeles, CA, April 6–10.

Grillot, Suzette, Brian Hardinski, and Ivey Dyson. 2015. "Historian Beeta Baghoolizadeh Sheds Light on Iran's Unique, but Forgotten, History of Slavery." KGOU, November 6. http://kgou.org/post/historian-beeta-baghoolizadeh-sheds-light-iran-s-unique-forgotten-history-slavery#stream/0.

Gualtieri, Sarah. 2001. "Becoming White: Race, Religion and the Foundations of Syrian/Lebanese Ethnicity in the United States." *Journal of American Ethnic History* 4:29–58.

———. 2009. *Between Arab and White: Race and Ethnicity in the Early Syrian American Diaspora*. Berkeley: University of California Press, 2009.

Guglielmo, Thomas. 2003. *White on Arrival: Italians, Race, Color, and Power in Chicago, 1890–1945*. London: Oxford University Press.

Hamad, Claudette Shwiry, ed. 2001. "Appendix: Hate-Based Incidents September 11–October 10, 2001." Arab American Institute Foundation Report prepared for the United States Commission on Civil Rights, October 11. http://b.3cdn.net/aai/08676be5849ccd51ef_rjm6bh2z1.pdf.

Hanassab, Shideh. 1991. "Acculturation and Young Iranian Women: Attitudes toward Sex Roles and Intimate Relationships." *Journal of Multicultural Counseling and Development* 19:11–21.

Haney, López, Ian. (1996) 2006. *White by Law: The Legal Construction of Race*. Reprint, New York: NYU Press.

Hargittai, Eszter, and Christian Sandvig. 2016. *Digital Research Confidential: The Secrets of Studying Online Behavior*. Cambridge, MA: MIT Press.

Howell, Sally. 2014. *Old Islam in Detroit: Rediscovering the Muslim American Past*. London: Oxford University Press.

Howells, W. W. 1941. "Europe and Asia: Review of *Contributions to the Anthropology of Iran* by Henry Field." *American Anthropologist* 43:462–64.

Hughey, Matthew W., and W. Carson Byrd. 2013. "The Souls of White Folk beyond Formation and Structure: Bound to Identity." *Ethnic and Racial Studies* 36:974–81.

Hussain, Zuhair. 2011. "You Are Beloved." YouTube video (5:02), uploaded January 27. https://www.youtube.com/watch?v=uwmWuCBH1bs.

Iafolla, Robert. 2016. "EEOC to Focus on Complex Employment Structures, Anti-Muslim bias." Reuters Legal, October 18. http://www.reuters.com/article/usa-employment-eeoc-idUSL1N1CO0C0.

"Imperfect Gentleman Says Being Persian Is Hip." 2013. NPR. *Tell Me More*, March 20. http://www.npr.org/2013/03/20/174839320/imperfect-gentle men-says-being-persian-is-hip.

Jacobson, Matthew Frye. 1998. *Whiteness of a Different Color: European Immigration and the Alchemy of Race*. Cambridge, MA: Harvard University Press.

Jamal, Amaney A., and Nadine Christine Naber. 2008. *Race and Arab Americans before and after 9/11: From Invisible Citizens to Visible Subjects*. Syracuse, NY: Syracuse University Press.

Jamarkani, Amira. 2015. *An Imperialist Love Story: Desert Romances and the War on Terror*. New York: NYU Press.

Jobrani, Maz. 2012. "Persian vs. Iranian." Comedy Time, YouTube video (2:15), December 26. https://www.youtube.com/watch?v=cHkNNjs4F1U.

Jones, Nicholas, and Michael Bentley. 2016. "2015 National Content Test Preliminary Results on Race and Ethnicity." Presentation for the Census Scientific Advisory Committee, October 6. https://www2.census.gov/cac/sac/meetings/2016-10/2016-csac-jones.pdf.

Jordan, June. 1995. *Poetry for the People: A Revolutionary Blueprint*. London: Routledge.

Jung, Moon-Kie. 2009. "The Racial Unconscious of Assimilation Theory." *Du Bois Review: Social Science Research on Race* 6:375–95.

Karem Albrecht, Charlotte. 2015. "Narrating Arab American History: The Peddling Thesis. *Arab Studies Quarterly* 37:100–117.

Karim, Persis M. 2006. *Let Me Tell You Where I've Been: New Writing by Women of the Iranian Diaspora*. Fayetteville: University of Arkansas Press.

Karst, Kenneth L. 1977. "The Supreme Court 1976 Term: Equal Citizenship under the Fourteenth Amendment." *Harvard Law Review* 91:1.

Kashani, Maryam. 2006. *Best in the West*. Documentary film. http://www.mary amkashani.com/2011/best-in-the-west.

Kasinitz, Phil, John H. Mollenkopf, Mary C. Waters, and Jennifer Holdaway.

2008. *Inheriting the City: The Children of Immigrants Come of Age*. New York: Russell Sage Foundation.

Kelley, Ron, Jonathan Friedlander, and Anita Colby. 1993. *Irangeles*. Berkeley: University of California Press.

Kelner, Shaul. 2012. *Tours That Bind: Diaspora, Pilgrimage, and Israeli Birthright Tourism*. New York: NYU Press.

Khakpour, Porochista. 2014. "Inspiration Information: 'The Last Illusion.'" *New Yorker*, June 17. http://www.newyorker.com/books/page-turner/inspiration-information-the-last-illusion.

Khanghahi, Sarah. 2017. "Thirty Years after Al-Khazraji: Revisiting Employment Discrimination under Section 1981." *UCLA Law Review* 64: 4–61.

Khosrownejad, Pedram. 2016. "The Face of African Slavery in Qajar, Iran." Edited by Denise Hassanzade Ajiri. *The Guardian*, January 14. https://www.theguardian.com/world/iran-blog/2016/jan/14/african-slavery-in-qajar-iran-in-photos.

Kibria, Nazli. 2003. *Becoming Asian American: Second-Generation Chinese and Korean American Identities*. Baltimore: Johns Hopkins University Press.

———. 2011. *Muslims in Motion: Islam and National Identity in the Bangladeshi Diaspora*. New Brunswick, NJ: Rutgers University Press.

Kim, Nadia Y. 2016. "Critical Thoughts on Asian American Assimilation in the Whitening Literature." In *Contemporary Asian America: A Multidisciplinary Reader*, 3rd ed., edited by Min Zhou and Anthony Ocampo, 554–75. New York: NYU Press.

Kollin, Susan. 2015. *Captivating Westerns: The Middle East in the American West*. Lincoln: University of Nebraska Press.

Lamont, Michele. 2001. *The Dignity of Working Men: Morality and the Boundaries of Race, Class, and Immigration*. Cambridge, MA: Harvard University Press.

Lamont, Michele, Stefan Beljean, and Matthew Clair. 2014. "What Is Missing? Cultural Processes and Causal Pathways to Inequality." *Socio-Economic Review* 12:573–608.

Levenson, Eric. 2017. "911 Calls Reveal the Kansas Shooter Thought He'd Shot 'Two Iranians.'" CNN, February 28. http://www.cnn.com/2017/02/27/us/kansas-olathe-bar-shooting-indian-court/.

Lipsitz, George. 2011. *How Racism Takes Place*. Philadelphia: Temple University Press.

Lorentz, John, and John Wertime. 1980. "Iranians." In *Harvard Encyclopedia of American Ethnic Groups*, edited by Stephen Thernstrom, 521–24. Cambridge, MA: Harvard University Press.

Love, Erik. 2017. *Islamophobia & Racism in America*. New York: NYU Press.

Luhrmann, Tanya M. 1996. *The Good Parsi: The Fate of a Colonial Elite in a Postcolonial Society*. Cambridge, MA: Harvard University Press.

Maghbouleh, Neda. 2010. "'Inherited Nostalgia' among Second-Generation Iranian Americans: A Case Study at a Southern California University." *Journal of Intercultural Studies* 31:199–218.

————. 2012. "'Shahs of Sunset': The Real Iranians of Los Angeles?" Salon. com, December 1. http://www.salon.com/2012/12/01/shahs_of_sunset_ the_real_iranians_of_los_angeles.

————. 2013. "The *Ta'arof* Tournament: Cultural Performances of Ethno-national Identity at a Diasporic Summer Camp." *Ethnic and Racial Studies* 36:818–37.

Mahdavi, Sara. 2005. "Held Hostage: Identity Citizenship of Iranian Americans." *Texas Journal on Civil Liberties and Civil Rights* 11:211.

Maira, Sunaina. 2002. *Desis in the House: Indian American Youth Culture in New York City*. Philadelphia: Temple University Press.

————. 2009. *Missing: Youth, Citizenship and Empire after 9/11*. Durham, NC: Duke University Press.

Majd, Hooman. 2008. *The Ayatollah Begs to Differ*. New York: Knopf Doubleday.

Malek, Alia. 2009. *A Country Called Amreeka: U.S. History Retold through Arab-American Lives*. New York: Simon & Schuster.

————. 2011. *Patriot Acts: Narratives of Post-9/11 Injustice*. San Francisco: McSweeneys.

Malek, Amy. 2011. "Public Performances of Identity Negotiation in the Iranian Diaspora: The New York Persian Day Parade." *Comparative Studies of South Asia, Africa and the Middle East* 31:388–410.

————. 2015. "Claiming Space: Documenting Second-Generation Iranian Americans in Los Angeles." *Anthropology of the Middle East* 10:16–45.

Marvasti, Amir, and Karyn McKinney. 2004. *Middle Eastern Lives in America*. Lanham, MD: Rowman & Littlefield.

McGlone, Ashly, and Susan Shroder. 2012. "San Diego Man on No-Fly List Returns Home." *San Diego Union-Tribune*, June 7. http://www.sandiegounion tribune.com/news/2012/jun/06/no-fly-list-keeps-sdsu-grad-grounded-in -costa-rica/.

McKenzie, Evan. 1994. *Privatopia: Homeowner Associations and the Rise of Residential Private Government*. New Haven, CT: Yale University Press.

Merton, Robert. 1972. "Insiders and Outsiders: A Chapter in the Sociology of Knowledge." *American Journal of Sociology* 78:9–47.

Mills, Charles W. 1997. *The Racial Contract*. Ithaca, NY: Cornell University Press.

Moaveni, Azadeh. 2004. "Councilman Plays Role of Cultural Mediator." *Los Angeles Times*, April 19. http://articles.latimes.com/2004/apr/19/local/ me-iranian19.

Mobasher, Mohsen M. 2006. "Cultural Trauma and Ethnic Identity Formation among Iranian Immigrants in the United States." *American Behavioral Scientist* 50:100–117.

————. 2012. *Iranians in Texas: Migration, Politics, and Ethnic Identity*. Austin: University of Texas Press.

————. 2013. "Iranians and Iranian Americans, 1940–Present." In *Immigrants in American History: Arrival, Adaptation, and Integration*, edited by Elliot Barkan, 999–1010. Santa Barbara, CA: ABC-CLIO.

Modarres, Ali. 1998. "Settlement Patterns of Iranians in the United States." *Iranian Studies* 31:31–49.

Molina, Natalia. 2014. *How Race Is Made in America: Immigration, Citizenship, and the Power of Racial Scripts*. Berkeley: University of California Press.

Moore, Kathleen. 1995. *Al-Mughtaribun: American Law and the Transformation of Muslim Life in the United States*. Albany: SUNY Press.

Morning, Ann. 2001. "The Racial Self-Identification of South Asians in the United States." *Journal of Ethnic and Migration Studies* 27:61–79.

Mostofi, Nilou. 2003. "Who We Are: The Perplexity of Iranian-American Identity." *Sociological Quarterly* 44:681–703.

Motadel, David. 2013. "Iran and the Aryan Myth." In *History, Myths, and Nationalism from Medieval Persia to the Islamic Republic*, edited by Ali Ansari, 119–47. London: I. B. Taurus.

Munshi, Sherally. 2015. "'You Will See My Family Became So American': Toward a Minor Comparativism." *American Journal of Comparative Law* 63:655–718.

Naber, Nadine. 2012. *Arab America: Gender, Cultural Politics, and Activism*. New York: NYU Press.

Naficy, Hamid. 1993. *The Making of Exile Cultures: Iranian Television in Los Angeles*. Minneapolis: University of Minnesota Press.

Najmabadi, Afsaneh. 2005. *Women with Mustaches and Men without Beards: Gender and Sexual Anxieties of Iranian Modernity*. Berkeley: University of California Press.

Nasrabadi, Manijeh. 2014. "'Women Can Do Anything Men Can Do': Gender and the Affects of Solidarity in the US Iranian Student Movement, 1961–1979." *WSQ: Women's Studies Quarterly* 42:127–45.

National Iranian American Council. 2009. "NIAC Partnering with U.S. Dept. of Commerce for 2010 Census." April 9. http://www.niacouncil.org/niac-partnering-with-u-s-dept-of-commerce-for-2010–census/.

———. 2017. *Iranian American 2010 Census Project*. Accessed February 17. http://www.niacouncil.org/images/PDF_files/census%202010%20brochure%20english..pdf.

Ocampo, Anthony C. 2016. *The Latinos of Asia: How Filipino Americans Break the Rules of Race*. Stanford, CA: Stanford University Press.

Office of Management and Budget. 2016. "Review and Possible Limited Revision of OMB's Statistical Policy Directive on Standards for Maintaining, Collecting, and Presenting Federal Data on Race and Ethnicity." *Federal Register* 81, September 30. https://www.federalregister.gov/documents/2016/09/30/2016-23672/standards-for-maintaining-collecting-and-presenting-federal-data-on-race-and-ethnicity.

Oliver, Mark. 2007. "Ahmadinejad Weighs into Row over U.S. Film." *The Guardian*, March 21. http://www.theguardian.com/world/2007/mar/21/iran.film.

Omi, Michael, and Howard Winant. (1986) 2014. *Racial Formation in the United States*. Reprint, London: Routledge.

"Parsis Top Literacy, Sex Ratio Charts in City." 2004. *Times of India*, September 8. http://timesofindia.indiatimes.com/city/mumbai/Parsis-top-literacy-sex-ratio-charts-in-city/articleshow/843036.cms.

Pew Research Center. 2016. "Half Say at Least Some Muslims in the U.S. Are Anti-American." Pew Research Center, Religion and Public Life, February 3. http://www.pewforum.org/2016/02/03/republicans-prefer-blunt-talk-about-islamic-extremism-democrats-favor-caution/.

Portes, Alejandro, and Ruben Rumbaut. 2001. *Legacies: The Story of the Immigrant Second Generation*. Berkeley: University of California Press.

Portes, Alejandro, and Min Zhou. 1993. "The New Second Generation: Segmented Assimilation and Its Variants." *Annals of the American Academy of Political and Social Science* 530:74–96.

Puar, Jasbir. 2007. *Terrorist Assemblages: Homonationalism in Queer Times*. Durham, NC: Duke University Press.

Puar, Jasbir K., and Amit Rai. 2002. "Monster, Terrorist, Fag: The War on Terrorism and the Production of Docile Patriots." *Social Text* 20:117–48.

Public Affairs Alliance of Iranian Americans. 2011. "Demographics & Statistics." http://www.paaia.org/CMS/demographics—statistics.aspx.

Purkayastha, Bandana. 2005. *Negotiating Ethnicity: Second-Generation South Asian Americans Traverse a Transnational World*. New Brunswick, NJ: Rutgers University Press.

Rahimi, Babak. 2008. "The Politics of the Internet in Iran." In *Media, Culture, and Society in Iran*, edited by M. Semati, 37–51. East Sussex, UK: Psychology Press.

Rampell, Catherine. 2016. "Ivy League Economist Ethnically Profiled, Interrogated for Doing Math on American Airlines Flight." *Washington Post*, May 7. https://www.washingtonpost.com/news/rampage/wp/2016/05/07/ivy-league-economist-interrogated-for-doing-math-on-american-airlines-flight/?utm_term=.8466e658da6d.

Rana, Junaid. 2007. "The Story of Islamophobia." *Souls* 9:148–61.

———. 2011. *Terrifying Muslims: Race and Labor in the South Asian Diaspora*. Durham, NC: Duke University Press.

Read, Jen'nan Ghazal. 2008. "The Effects of Post-9/11 Discrimination on Arab-American Racial Identity." In *From Invisibility to Visibility: The Racialization of Arab Americans before and after September 11th*, edited by Nadine Naber and Amaney Jamal, 305–17. Syracuse, NY: Syracuse University Press.

Roediger, David. 1991. *The Wages of Whiteness: Race and the Making of the American Working Class*. New York: Verso Books.

Rojas, Fabio. 2012. *From Black Power to Black Studies: How a Radical Social Movement Became an Academic Discipline*. Baltimore: Johns Hopkins University Press.

Roth, Wendy D. 2010. "Racial Mismatch: The Divergence between Form and Function in Data for Monitoring Racial Discrimination of Hispanics." *Social Science Quarterly* 91:1288–1311.

————. 2012. *Race Migrations: Latinos and the Cultural Transformation of Race*. Stanford, CA: Stanford University Press.

————. 2015. "Studying Ethnic Schemas: Integrating Cognitive Schemas into Ethnicity Research through Photo Elicitation." In *Studying Ethnic Identity: Methodological Advances and Consideration for Future Research*, edited by Carlos E. Santos and Adriana Umaña Taylor, 111–51. Washington, DC: American Psychological Association.

Roth, Wendy D., and Nadia Y. Kim. 2013. "Relocating Prejudice: A Transnational Approach to Understanding Immigrants' Racial Attitudes." *International Migration Review* 47:330–73.

Rumbaut, Ruben. 1997. "Assimilation and Its Discontents: Between Rhetoric and Reality." *International Migration Review* 34 (1): 923–60.

Sabagh, Georges, and Mehdi Bozorgmehr. 1986. "Are the Characteristics of Exiles Different from Immigrants? The Case of Iranians in Los Angeles." *Institute for Social Science Research* 71:77–84.

Sadeghi, Sahar. 2016. "The Burden of Geopolitical Stigma: Iranian Immigrants and Their Adult Children in the USA." *Journal of International Migration and Integration*: 17:1109–24.

Said, Edward. 1978. *Orientalism*. New York: Pantheon.

————. 1981. *Covering Islam*. New York: Vintage.

Schayegh, Cyrus. 2009. *Who Is Knowledgeable Is Strong: Science, Class, and the Formation of Modern Iranian Society, 1900–1950*. Berkeley: University of California Press.

Selod, Saher. 2017. *Forever Suspect: Muslim Americans and Racialized Surveillance in the War on Terror*. New Brunswick, NJ: Rutgers University Press.

Selod, Saher, and David Embrick. 2013. "Racialization and Muslims: Situating the Muslim Experience in Race Scholarship." *Sociology Compass* 7:644–55.

Shams, Alex. 2012. "A Persian Iran? Challenging the Aryan Myth and Persian Ethnocentrism." *Ajam Media Collective*, May 18. https://ajammc.com/2012/05/18/a -persian-iran-challenging-the-aryan-myth-and-persian-eth nocentrism/.

Shirinian, Nairi, and Christina Mehranbod. 2013. "Students Fight the Imposing of Identities." *Daily Californian*, June 2. http://www.dailycal.org/2013/06/03/invisible-no-more/.

Shryock, Andrew, and Ann Chih Lin. 2009. "Arab American Identities in Question." In *Citizenship and Crisis: Arab Detroit after 9/11*, edited by Wayne Baker, Sally Howell, Amaney Jamal, Ann Lin, Andrew Shryock, Ronald Stockton, and Mark Tessler, 35–68. Detroit, MI: Detroit Arab American Study Group.

Sikh Coalition, the Coalition for Asian American Children and Families (CACF), and the Asian American Legal Defense and Education Fund (AALDEF). 2009. "Bias-Based Harassment in New York City Public Schools." http://www.aaldef.org/Bias-based-Harassment-in-NYC-Public-Schools.pdf.

Slaughter, Graham. 2014. "Is It the 'Persian' or 'Arabian' Gulf? Toronto Protest Sets Record Straight." *Toronto Star*, January 27. https://www.thestar.com/

news/gta/2014/01/27/is_it_the_persian_or_arabian_gulf_toronto_protest_
sets_record_straight.html.

Small, Mario. 2009. "'How Many Cases Do I Need?': On Science and the Logic
of Case Selection in Field-Based Research." *Ethnography* 10:5–38.

Smith, Dakota. 2009. "Explaining Beverly Hills' Persian Palaces." *Curbed: Los Angeles*, June 17. http://la.curbed.com/archives/2009/06/in_defense_of_bev
erly_hills_persian_palaces.php.

Soomekh, Saba. 2012. *From the Shahs to Los Angeles: Three Generations of Iranian Jewish Women between Religion and Culture*. Albany: SUNY Press.

Spickard, Paul R. 1992. "The Illogic of American Racial Categories." In *Racially
Mixed People in America*, edited by Maria P. Root, 12–23. Thousand Oaks, CA:
Sage Publications.

Stifler, Matthew Jaber. 2012. "Race and Arab Americans in Michigan." In *Struggles and Triumphs of People of Color in Michigan*, edited by Matt Hoerauf, 11–13.
Battle Creek, MI: W. K. Kellogg Foundation.

Tavakoli-Targhi, Mohamad. 2001. *Refashioning Iran: Orientalism, Occidentalism, and
Historiography*. London: Palgrave Macmillan.

Tehranian, John. 2010. *Whitewashed: America's Invisible Middle Eastern Minority*. New
York: NYU Press.

Thangaraj, Stanley I. 2015. "Kurdish America: Challenging, Negotiating, Managing, and Disrupting Arab America." Paper delivered at the annual conference of the American Studies Association, Toronto, ON, November 4.

Torbat, Akbar. 2002. "The Brain Drain from Iran to the United States." *Middle
East Journal* 56:272–95.

Trousdale Estates Homeowners Association. 2017. Accessed January 19. http://
www.trousdaleestateshomeownersassociation.com/Trousdaleestateshome
ownerassociation/Home_Page.html.

Tsubakihara, Atsuko. 2013. "Putting Tehrangeles on the Map: A Consideration
of Space and Place for Migrants." *Bulletin of the National Museum of Ethnology*
37:331–57.

Tuan, Mia. 1998. *Forever Foreigners or Honorary Whites? The Asian Ethnic Experience
Today*. New Brunswick, NJ: Rutgers University Press.

Twinam, Ann. 2015. *Purchasing Whiteness: Pardos, Mulattos, and the Quest for Social
Mobility in the Spanish Indies*. Stanford, CA: Stanford University Press.

Twine, France Winddance, and Jonathan Warren. 2000. *Racing Research, Researching Race: Methodological Dilemmas in Critical Race Studies*. New York: NYU Press.

US Census Bureau. 2015. "Selected Population Profile in the United States:
Iran: 2015 American Community Survey 1-Year Estimates." American Fact-
Finder. https://factfinder.census.gov/faces/tableservices/jsf/pages/product
view.xhtml?src=CF.

US Department of State. 2016. "Iran Travel Warning." US Passports & International Travel, March 14. https://travel.state.gov/content/passports/en/
alertswarnings/iran-travel-warning.html.

Vasquez, Jessica. 2011. *Mexican Americans across Generations: Immigrant Families, Racial Realities*. New York: NYU Press.

Viteri, Amy. 2012. "Customer: Apple Store Denied Me iPad for Speaking Farsi." WSB-TV Atlanta, June 18. http://www.wsbtv.com/news/local/customer -apple-store-denied-me-ipad-speaking-farsi/242878717.

Vitkovskaya, Julie, Kayla Epstein, Kevin Uhrmacher, and Samuel Granados. 2017. "Previously Barred Refugees, Immigrants Can Continue Entering the U.S." *Washington Post*, February 9. https://www.washingtonpost.com/ graphics/national/immigration-order-explainer/.

Volpp, Leti. 2003. "The Citizen and the Terrorist." *Immigration and Nationality Law Review* 23:561–88.

West, Kevin. 2009. "The Persian Conquest." *W Magazine* 38 (1): 80.

Wickramasekare, P., Jag Sehgal, Farhad Mehran, Ladan Noroozi, and Saeid Eisazadeh. 2006. "Afghan Households in Iran: Profile and Impact." ILO/ UNHCR, October. http://www.unhcr.org/455835d92.pdf.

Willoughby-Herard, Tiffany. 2015. *Waste of a White Skin: The Carnegie Corporation and the Racial Logic of White Vulnerability*. Berkeley: University of California Press.

Winegar, Jessica, and Laura Deeb. 2015. *Anthropology's Politics: Disciplining the Middle East*. Stanford, CA: Stanford University Press.

Wynn, Jonathan. 2009. "Digital Sociology: Emergent Technologies in the Field and the Classroom." *Sociological Forum* 24:448–56.

Yoder, Chris. 2013. "UC to include Southwest Asian, North African Category on Next Year's Undergraduate Application." *Daily Californian*, May 27. http:// www.dailycal.org/2013/05/27/uc-to-introduce-new-category-for-southwest -asian-and-north-african-students-in-2013-2014-undergraduate-application/.

Zamora, Sylvia. 2016. "Racial Remittances: The Effects of Migration on Racial Ideologies in Mexico and the United States." *Sociology of Race & Ethnicity* 2:466–81.

Zarrinkoub, Abdolhossain. (1957) 1996. *Two Centuries of Silence*. Reprint, Santa Ana, CA: Mazda Publishers.

Zarrugh, Amina. 2016. "Racialized Political Shock: Arab American Racial Formation and the Impact of Political Events." *Ethnic and Racial Studies* 39:2722–39.

Zia-Ebrahimi, Reza. 2010. "Iranian Identity, the 'Aryan Race' and Jake Gyllenhaal." PBS Frontline Tehran Bureau, August 6. http://www.pbs.org/wgbh/ pages/frontline/tehranbureau/2010/08/post-2.html.

———. 2011. "Self-Orientalisation and Dislocation: The Uses and Abuses of the 'Aryan' Discourse in Iran." *Iranian Studies* 44:445–72.

———. 2016. *The Emergence of Iranian Nationalism: Race and the Politics of Dislocation*. New York: Columbia University Press.

INDEX

Note: page numbers in italics refer to tables or figures; those followed by n refer to notes, with note number.

racial learning, family as site of, 53
racial loopholes: definition of, 5;
Middle Eastern Americans and,
169–70
racial loopholes for Iranian Americans, 169–70; Iranian identity and,
76; Iranian navigation of, 16; legal
protections against racial discrimination and, 10, 30–36, 45–46,
170; second-generation Iranian
Americans' awareness of, 172
racial misrecognition, violence
against Iranians and, 38–39
racial prerequisite cases, 9–10; adjudication of Iranian legal whiteness in, 16, 17–24, *18*, 45, 164;
adjudication of Parsi whiteness in,
20–24; author's research on, 181;
"commonsense" racial categories
in, 19–20, 23; and geographical
racial criteria, 23–24; Iranians
as racial hinges in, 9, 10, 16, 45,
162–63, 164, 168; linguistic theories of race in, 18, 19, 20; and performance of white identity, 166;
in Portland, Oregon, 164. See also
Dow v. United States (1915); *Ex parte
Dow* (1914); *In re Balsara* (1909);
In re Dow (1914); *In re Halladjian*
(1909); *In re Najour* (1909); *United
States v. Bhagat Singh Thind* (1923);
United States v. Tatos Cartozian (1925);
United States v. Wadia (1939)
racial science: and development of
Aryan myth, 54–55, 62–64; and
Iranian Plateau race, discovery of,
64–66, *65*, 181
Rai, Amit, 120
religion, as racialized immigration
category, 30
research on Iranian Americans:
future directions for, 181, 182–83;
limitations of demographic data

and, 179, 181. *See also* methodol-
ogy of this study
residential codes restricting home
ownership to whites, 80
Reza (study participant): on bullying
of Iranian American students, 87;
maintenance of Persian language
skills by, 86–87; on Persian pride
of parents' generation, 68
Rock Creek (DC suburb): bullying of
Iranian students in, 81–82; chang-
ing demographics of, 80–81; as
conservative town, 80
Roosevelt, Franklin D., 64
ROTC (Reserve Officers' Training
Corps), and critical language
courses, 97–101
Roth, Wendy, 192n46
Roya (study participant): assimilation
of, 7; college application racial self-
identification, 1, 3; exclusion from
whiteness, 8; racialization experienced by, 4; rejection of identification as white, 1, 2, 3, 4, 94
Rumi (Iranian poet), 150

Saadi. *See* Shirazi, Saadi (Iranian
poet)
Sabet, Sahar, 37
Sahi (study participant), on travel to
Iran, 122–23
Said, Edward, 145
Sarzosa, Miguel, 38
schools: changed attitude toward Iranian American students after 9/11
attacks, 81, 84–85, 87, 197n3;
Iranian American students'
friendships with other non-white
students, 4, 94–97, 197; majority-
white, greater opportunities in,
81. *See also* bullying of Iranian
American students; colleges and
universities

The authorized representative in the EU for product safety and compliance is:
Mare Nostrum Group
B.V Doelen 72
4831 GR Breda
The Netherlands

www.ingramcontent.com/pod-product-compliance
Lightning Source LLC
Chambersburg PA
CBHW031556060326
40783CB00026B/4099